To the
American Indian

Reminiscences of a Yurok Woman

by Lucy Thompson

Foreword by Peter E. Palmquist
Introduction by Julian Lang

Heyday Books, Berkeley
In Conjunction with Peter E. Palmquist

Acknowledgements

The publishers wish to express their gratitude to:
Dennis Dutton for hours of hard work;
Ray Moisa, also for hours of hard work;
Eric Schimps, special collection librarian at Humboldt
State University, Arcata, for his interest and cooperation;
Arlene Hartin, past-president of the Humboldt County
Historical Society, for her sustained and kind involvement.

Library of Congress Card Catalog Number: 91-070671

Original edition copyright © 1916 by Lucy Thompson

Text amendments and other new material copyright © 1991
by Heyday Books

Interior design and production: Peter E. Palmquist

Cover design: Sarah Levin

Typesetting: Mary Louise Rowe, Eureka Printing Co., Inc.

Published by: Heyday Books
P.O. Box 9145
Berkeley, CA 94709

Published in conjunction with Peter E. Palmquist

ISBN: 0-930588-47-9

Printed in the United States of America
10 9 8 7 6 5 4 3 2 1

Contents

Foreword

by Peter E. Palmquist

My first encounter with Lucy Thompson's *To the American Indian* was in the early 1970s. At the time, I was doing research on Emma B. Freeman (1880-1928), a photographer who had specialized in highly romantic and stylized images of northcoast Indians [see Palmquist, *With Nature's Children: Emma B. Freeman, Camera & Brush* (1977)]. Emma not only intermixed tribal artifacts and native lore (from all over America) with wild abandon, but her vision of Indian life was further tainted by ideas that she had winnowed from the saccharine kitsch then being published as poem and popular fiction concerning the "Noble Red Man." The result? A collection of photographs such as that of a proud young woman in a Navajo blanket surrounded by traditional Yurok basketry.

The woman in that photograph, and Emma's principal model, turned out to be Bertha M. Thompson, Lucy Thompson's daughter. As I sorted through Emma's life story, I discovered that Lucy Thompson was Emma's primary resource for whatever factual information about Indian life there was in her photographic studies. In fact, many of Emma's photographs featured native regalia obtained directly from Lucy's personal collection.

I wanted to find a copy of Lucy Thompson's book in order to get beyond Emma's cultural *whitewashing*. However, obtaining *To the*

American Indian was not easy. When I finally located a copy at an antiquarian bookstore, I was not prepared for the large number of typos and utter incomprehensibilities which tainted my first impression. I put the book down, only to pick it up again and again over the next few years. Behind the typos and inconsistencies, I came to understand and appreciate the importance of Lucy's opening comments: "As there has been so much said and written about the American Indians...which has been guessed at and not facts...[in] this book I will endeavor to tell all in a plain and truthful way without the least coloring of the facts..." Lucy Thompson clearly intended to tell the truth about her culture, and all I had to do was listen.

Listening meant being aware that Lucy was communicating to me in a language not her own, and using cultural metaphors and symbols which were totally foreign to her origins. The text bears ample evidence that she was having immense difficulty translating Yurok institutions and experience into English. Today we take for granted a terminology developed by anthropologists and linguists that bestows definition and that forms our way of thinking about Indian culture. Lucy either had no access to those terms or rejected them. Thus, for example, Wah-pec-wah-mow is referred to by anthropologists as "Earthmaker" or the "Creator." Lucy, struggling for the right English word, calls him "God," and to explain his divinity to others Lucy, using English symbolism, places him on a "mighty throne, high in the infinite realms of Heaven." The *Wo:ge* [*Wa-gas* in Lucy Thompson's orthography], a race of creator beings who inhabited the world before the coming of Indians and who established the institutions and rituals by which people live, are today generally referred to (and thought of) as "divinities" or "gods." Lucy, however, refers to these luminous beings as "white people." How revealing! That she was thinking of these creator beings as another kind of "people" tells us something important about Yurok religious thinking, something that the categorizations we are used to, fail to explain. The text is full of such odd and idiosyncratic renderings. While many modern readers will be disquieted, those with an open mind will find within this text an opportunity to learn something new and valuable, something not to be found anywhere else.

Left to right: Bertha (Lucy and Milton's daughter), Chief White Elk (Bertha's husband), Lucy and her husband Milton Thompson. The man at back left has not been identified.

The original manuscript, handwritten, misspelled, and ungrammatical, was the cause of further difficulties. It was evident that much of the lack of proofreading and copy editing could easily be traced to problems with the original manuscript, probably coupled with the bigotry, and/or indifference, afforded an Indian book in 1916. After all, who would stoop to proof an Indian woman's book? The book was typeset and printed by the Cummins Print Shop in Eureka, presumably a reputable business, yet there seems to have been no editing at all, so that gross errors in both spelling and grammar found their way into the finished book. Moreover, the typesetting was so slovenly that it seemed to have introduced still more errors, garbling and altering the text further. Even in the binding of the book, signatures (clusters of pages) were sometimes doubled up or eliminated.

The original book was published in a 6⅜ x 9½ inch, softcover format. There were a total of 214 pages (plus end sheets) and nine illustrations (eight photographs and one map). Publication of the book was paid for by Mrs. Amelia Carson, a daughter-in-law of a local lumber baron. Lucy's preface was dated June 1916, and the book was dedicated to her white husband, Milton J. Thompson. The book was copyrighted in Lucy's name. So far, I have been unable to locate any public announcement or review of *To the American Indian* in the local media. Nor do I know how many books were produced.

Several factors probably led Lucy to write *To the American Indian*. Indian life, as she knew it, was being decimated. And, there was a burgeoning (if misguided) interest in the subject within a *few* sectors of the white community. There was an increasing use of "Indian" words and terminology in everyday life. The Improved Order of Redmen, for example, borrowed "Indian" symbols at whim. This organization of white men formed a "wigwam," held its "pow-wows," elected its "chiefs," fined its "braves," and collected their "wampum." In addition to such misplaced glorifications, there were typically racist accounts in newspapers. Finally, there were the accounts of anthropologists such as Kroeber, who, one might guess, also failed to tell what Lucy knew of Yurok culture.

Despite technical problems, I felt that *To the American Indian* needed to be republished in order for Lucy's "truth" to become more widely available for those seeking to hear the voice of someone who had been raised Indian. The choices before us (as editors and publishers) were to treat this flawed document as a scholarly text, reproducing faithfully all the various inconsistencies and errors, or to take it upon ourselves to "improve" it somewhat; i.e., make it more readable. Since copies of the original book are available in scholarly libraries, we felt *To the American Indian* should be accessible to the general reader, while at the same time, retaining the original text's usefulness as an ethnographic record.

Editing of this reprint has pretty much been limited to corrections of spelling errors, repunctuating and recapitalizing in order to untangle sentences that were so involved and impacted as to be virtually incomprehensible. Consistent spellings of proper names have been introduced. (Note that an extensive index has been created which retains these variant spellings as well as providing a quick access to topics.) We are aware that such editing may have reduced the scholarly value of the work and perhaps in some cases introduced further errors, however, we feel that we are performing a task that should have been undertaken by the original printers some seventy-five years ago.

Those illustrations from the original volume which related directly to Lucy have been retained. Many historic photographs, relating to the northcoastal area generally, have been added to this reprint.

Perhaps the garbled text of the original is one of the main reasons why *To the American Indian* has never been reprinted, why it has been for so many years referred to, talked about, but seldom read. We hope that in this new edition this remarkable book will find, among Indians and non-Indians, the readership it deserves. Except for Sarah Winnemucca's writings, we do not know of any other book by an American Indian woman of this generation that so clearly reflects the pride, pain, and struggle of witnessing the degradation of a cherished culture.

What of Lucy herself? Biographical details are few. From what can be gathered from the book before us, the United States Census records, and a few other sources, we know that she was born in the village of Pecwan in 1853. In about 1875, at the age of 22, she married Milton James Thompson, a man some ten years her senior. Milton (Lucy called him "Jim") was born in Alabama, arrived in California in 1865 (at about age 22), and was employed as a timber cruiser. The couple apparently lived along the Klamath River for many years, for penciled into the margin of one of Milton's land maps is the notation: "Milton J. Thompson whom [sic] lived in land around Klamath Bluffs which is now Klamath Post Office for 29 years, was there when every government survey [for the Klamath and Hoopa Valley Indian Reservations] was made." These maps further suggest that part of Milton's livelihood included income from land and timber speculations. A surviving notebook mentions a timber claim, owned by Lucy, that she sold for $15 per acre.

The Thompson's moved to Eureka by 1910. They were credited with having three children, although only Bertha, then 23, was listed in the 1910 census as living in their home at 1557 Myrtle Avenue. It is perhaps significant that Milton, although a well-known figure in white society, was listed with his wife on an *Indian Population* enumerations form by the government census taker.

Notices from the *Humboldt Times* confirm that Milton died on December 10, 1930 (age 87), and that Lucy followed on February 23, 1932 (age 79). A passing mention in her obituary says that "she was a noble character and had a host of friends." Several eyewitnesses reported that whenever the Thompsons were seen on the streets of Eureka "they always walked hand-in-hand."

A grand niece fondly remembers Lucy's family visits and that she nearly always brought peppermint candy and other goodies to share. When asked to describe Lucy, she replied that she "stood very erect, with great dignity."

Perhaps to compensate for the lack of verifiable biographic information, there has been no end to the rumors about the Thompsons. One of the most serious, and one hears this again and again, is that Lucy could not have written the book because she was uneducated; her husband did it all. There are further claims that the original manuscript "does not exist," "was sold in 1960," "may be seen at so-and-so's house," etc.

In truth there are multiple copies of the handwritten manuscript, including a full-length example at the Beinecke Library, Yale University, and portions of it still in existence elsewhere. They are written in Milton's hand, so he must have had a part in the composition of this book. Yet the 1910 census confirms that Lucy was literate, and if she did not actually pen the words we are reading, she must have dictated them, for there can be little doubt that they come from someone who spoke directly from her heart, from her beliefs, from her sad and wise experiences as a member of a tribe whose culture she saw being extinguished before her eyes.

Peter E. Palmquist is an historian who specializes in the study of California photographers active before 1920.

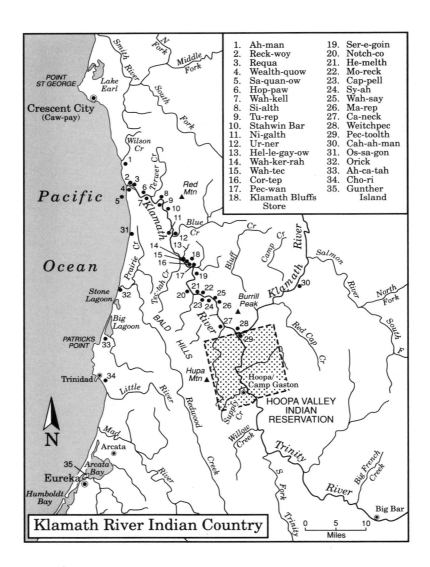

1.	Ah-man	19.	Ser-e-goin
2.	Reck-woy	20.	Notch-co
3.	Requa	21.	He-melth
4.	Wealth-quow	22.	Mo-reck
5.	Sa-quan-ow	23.	Cap-pell
6.	Hop-paw	24.	Sy-ah
7.	Wah-kell	25.	Wah-say
8.	Si-alth	26.	Ma-rep
9.	Tu-rep	27.	Ca-neck
10.	Stahwin Bar	28.	Weitchpec
11.	Ni-galth	29.	Pec-toolth
12.	Ur-ner	30.	Cah-ah-man
13.	Hel-le-gay-ow	31.	Os-sa-gon
14.	Wah-ker-rah	32.	Orick
15.	Wah-tec	33.	Ah-ca-tah
16.	Cor-tep	34.	Cho-ri
17.	Pec-wan	35.	Gunther
18.	Klamath Bluffs		Island
	Store		

Klamath River Indian Country

0 5 10
Miles

Introduction
by Julian Lang

It never ceases to amaze me that it has been a scant 141 years since Indian people in northwestern California witnessed the mass arrival of Americans seeking their fortunes in the last gold fields of the West. Once the miners departed, most of them empty-handed, other fields opened up: anthropology, linguistics, folklore, history and psychology. Volumes of published works were produced by some of the most renowned names in these scholarly disciplines. They recognized that within a relatively small 200-mile area of mountains and rivers, a unique aggregate of culture, language and ritual was evident. The indigenous people of the area were living a perfected lifestyle and possessed a worldview that is as interesting today as it was in the 1850s.

The culture found in the area is no less interesting for us, the Indians! We exult in our arts, laws, songs, cleverness, ceremonials and past. The linguists tell us that the three unrelated languages we speak are of diverse origins. The Hupa are Athapaskan, whose speakers are abundant in the Southwest and Pacific Northwest; the Karuk are speakers of Hokan, the oldest language family of northwestern California; the Yurok language is related to the Northeast Woodland Algonquian tribes. It is a rare instance worldwide to find such diversity, especially since each language has essentially been maintained with little cross-sharing by each tribe. From our standpoint we have maintained our identity. While we have sustained our linguistic diversity, we have certainly developed a shared culture. We share dances, material culture, economic system, many fundamental religious concepts and beliefs, and the story of creation. The bird's-eye view reveals cultural uniformity; a closer view, however, reveals distinct ways and subtle differences of meaning and purpose.

It seems necessary in order to introduce ourselves to those seeking understanding about northwestern California indigenous culture to say: "Forget everything you've ever learned about Indians before." One must start with a healthy dose of patience and a cleared slate in order to glimpse into our way of life. Our story starts at the beginning of time. Our knowledge stems from a race of Spirit Beings whose job *at the beginning of time* was to unravel the mystery, to discover the ideal way of life on the newly created Earth. By trial and error, intuition and feeling, they unlocked the mysteries one by one. The Spirit Beings were followed by, and their divinely wrought knowledge passed onto us, the Indian people of the Klamath River. In exchange, we assumed responsibility to Fix the Earth each year: to make the world over through ceremonial re-enactment of the Spirit Beings' first successful World Renewal; to set the world back on its axis. Many of us today still subscribe to this belief. For us the vision of the future is grounded in the responsibility of annually fixing the world. We cannot conceive of a time when stabilizing the world will become an irrelevant act.

Our determination to continue ceremonial practices today reflects a recurring theme in the unique book *To the American Indian*, first published in 1916. The author, Lucy Thompson, was an elderly Yurok woman of aristocratic birth. She was a direct descendant of many of her tribe's ceremonialists, oral historians and priests. *To the American Indian*, reprinted here, is one of those rare instances when the Indian version of history is presented, revealing the vast gulf in sensibility and fact between the textbook version of events and the traditionalists' view of forced change. Thompson contributed sharp insights into the settling of the lower Klamath River region of northwestern California. She reveals to us the struggle, people, places and events which occurred in the 67 years preceding the publication of her book. As she states in her short introduction, she is compelled to set the record straight about the Yurok people, to present the Truth and debunk the misleading, offensive and incendiary editorials and other written materials published around the turn of the century. She was the first California Indian woman to be published. Despite her obvious struggle at the literary craft, she presented her time and a way of life that was in pervasive transition. Through her words we see the first efforts by an Indian leader to provide an insider's cultural perspective of the effects of imposed social change and a glimpse at the cultural loss that such change blindly demands.

Her writing style is enigmatic, being closer to the oral tradition of storytelling than it is to literary craft. Reading her book is like sitting with an elder and listening as she relates her tribal and personal history in a seemingly (but not really) disorganized mosaic of experiences, anecdotes and reminiscences. This is the traditional form of relating knowledge. The listener is expected to listen from beginning to end. Among the Yurok, storytelling was an artform having a clear protocol. The listeners are students, the storyteller the teacher. Tribal mythology, oral histories and medicine and power formulas were learned this way. She utilizes this teaching approach in presenting her story in *To the American Indian*. She has, as well, at least a passing knowledge of the popular non-Indian literature of the day. The result of combining these sources is a curious blend striving to create a picture of her people's reality. The audience to whom she is writing is the local Anglos. The strains to which she is willing to go, using anachronistic Biblical and literary references in order to speak the language of the readers, is frankly painful for me. Yet, she is not diverging from her tradition. She is a Yurok aristocrat and is fulfilling her responsibility to present Yurok culture to those who had been unwilling to acknowledge it.

Thompson's writing will seem arcane for some. After all, she must use a second language, English, to convey the many intricacies of Yurok thought. So, she utilizes every form of verbal and written communication she is able to muster in order to convey the Truth to the fundamentalist Christian, the dewy-eyed Romantic, the steel-eyed yellow journalist and those seeking scientific understanding.

There is an innate emotional volatility that underpins her telling of Yurok history. She lashes out at her traditions and people as often as she denigrates American society's maltreatment of the elders of her tribe. In fact, anything and everything is a candidate for a good tongue-lashing. Taking one step back during these outbursts, one sees that she is not expressing disdain. She is concealing a broken heart. In the end and despite the grief, Thompson chooses to proceed with the story of her family and people. She does so in intimate terms and without reluctance.

The attacks she makes against her own find their origins in the dichotomy between the progressive, pro-assimilation Indian faction and the conservatives steadfastly clinging to the "old ways." For her the former are bad people and the latter the good. The old way stemmed from a divine prescription. It was the path to personal and collective spiritual enlightenment and wealth. In the eyes of tribal conservatives the Americans offer only one thing to the Indians: replacement of a successful way of life with undefined change and disregard for native values. For those Indians who chose the progressive path, Thompson used the Yurok term for sorcerer or Indian devil, *uma'a* [spelled *Oh-ma-ha* in Lucy Thompson's orthography]. Sorcerers lived, by their own choice, outside the accepted norms of traditional society, causing sickness, calamity and even death. The *uma'a* were considered "wild" Indians, lacking a need or desire for spiritual enlightenment. They lived apart from the towns in caves back in the hills. They were often wealthy, possessing the much-valued ceremonial regalia and dentalia-shell Indian money. Their wealth objects, however, were generally believed to be robbed from graves, and no act was regarded as more degraded or spiritually dangerous to all than "insulting the dead." The pro-assimilation Indians were regarded in her eyes on a par with the *uma'a*. Their disregard for the religious prescriptions of the First Spirit Beings doomed them to the same grisly and hellish afterlife as the *uma'a*.

Thompson, however, remains true to the Yurok pursuit of the

Middle Way, demonstrating her people's proclivity for dignified solutions to thorny problems. She asserted that the "wild" pro-assimilationist could, by utilizing the traditionalist formula, escape the debauched afterlife. She felt that the progressives had to live according to the laws and rules of the white man just as the conservatives had to live by Indian law. No hooliganism or renegade behavior were recommended because they reflected badly on the good Indian people.

Traditional Indian law was, in effect, a safeguard to the social order and to the right of the individual. Heinous crimes such as murder, rape and uttering the name of someone's deceased relative created the greatest furor. Lesser crimes such as poaching on another's hunting grounds, divorce and damage to property had specific penalties assessed against the law-breaker, thereby resolving the problem. Without resolution, the little problems were very likely to escalate into full-scale conflagrations, pitting individual against individual, family against family and, worst of all, village against village. There was little tolerance for lawlessness or taking the law in one's own hands. The constant pursuit of peace and balance was and remains the ideal.

The remedy for any and all legal transgressions was a cash payment to the injured party. Over the eons, a list of specific fines and monetary values was developed to cover every conceivable offense. The preferred currency was ceremonial regalia and "Indian money" (strands of rare four-inch tusk-shaped shells called dentalia). Traditional settlements continue today. In 1982 I witnessed the payment of dance feathers, dance arrows and finely decorated otter skin dance-quivers. It is perhaps most important for the ceremonialists to uphold such traditions. Thompson tells of the Indian law which requires the ceremonial dance leaders to pay heads of family when a family member has died within the year. The purpose of the payment is to "make the dance right." As Thompson leads us along the traditional path, we catch glimpses of Yurok ideals, making things right so that all can meet on the middle path. The Yurok way is to laugh and fix the world by expressing the happiness and abundance that the first Spirit Beings discovered was the key ingredient to efficacious ceremony making.

To the American Indian is a rare opportunity to hear an Indian version of history. We need only seek out the ethnographic, linguistic, historical and archaeological journals to get the scientific appraisal of pre-contact Yurok culture. Dr. Alfred Kroeber, the renowned expert on pre-contact Yurok culture, avoided discussing matters pertaining to the historic period (post-contact) because, as anthropologist Thomas Buckley has recently written, Kroeber "could not stand all the tears" the topic elicited from his informants. So, while Kroeber collected myths, material artifacts, and ethnographies, he never introduced us to the living people, focusing instead on the past. Thompson, on the other hand, swallows the tears and discusses this most painful subject with a forthrightness which unnerves both Indians and non-Indians alike. She unflinchingly indicts her tribal members on many counts, as harshly as she indicts the Americans for atrocities and double-dealing levied against Indians. It is paradoxical to me that she is so severe. During the Red Power movement of the '60s and '70s the book was regarded as reactionary! To the Red Power radical, native traditional culture was sacrosanct, no longer open for scrutiny by the "anthros" and other academics. They flatly disregarded the anthropological study of Indians by non-Indians, feeling it perpetuated falsehood, stereotypes and colonial attitudes in every respect. Thompson's book, written about Indians *by* an Indian, was the proper formula as prescribed by the new nationalistic fervor. To the dismay of many radicals, however, it was a somewhat embarrassing book since she, in fact, indicts her whole tribe on numerous counts of treason, betrayal and moral turpitude! The book, rather than being lauded as a true history or as the first book written and published by an Indian woman, was allowed to drift into obscurity. Ironically, it has remained a reference cited not by tribal historians and scholars seeking the Indian view of history, but by the anthros, and precisely because it is an Indian perspective.

The maturation of Indian political and cultural thought since the '60s and '70s casts a different light on Thompson's story, and allows for easier understanding of her attitude today. After all, she was witness (in her mind at least) to the end of her people. With the ensuing loss of conviction about the traditional way by her many contemporaries, she sadly concluded that most of them were not worthy to bask in the heroic backlight cast by Yurok myth and history. Today many Indian people face a similar dilemma. Those of us who have devoted our lives to the World Renewal tradition often feel alone and betrayed. The pressure to adopt "progressive" political, social, and legal changes, despite their contrariness to "Indian law," once again is finding significant support in our tribal governments and federal Indian policy. The old traditions are increasingly enigmatic in a system designed to assimilate differences and which promotes political compromise. Her book offers us insight into the struggle that currently plagues tribal communities worldwide to preserve their belief systems and cultural identity.

Thompson's story presents us with the thoughts and feelings of the elders who raised her: the masters of the Yurok way of life. She points out with relish the inconsistencies and obvious self-interest by which the whites conducted their legal affairs with her people, conduct which no upstanding Yurok of the old school would ever imagine adopting. According to her belief, greed and lawlessness is what motivated the *uma'a,* the Indian devils. The enlightened, "good" Klamath River Indian is ever helpful, never greedy, and of a pleasant disposition to all. We learn that mutual respect is both the warp and weft of the traditional Yurok cultural and social fabric.

Her strong sense of propriety, pride and purpose underscores an intensely emotional historical perspective. She steadfastly guides us along her people's course from the "good old (pre-contact) days" into the overwhelming American floodwaters. By her people's social standards, the American lifestyle was not spiritually clean. We feel her frustration and melancholy as she describes the great imbalance that grew from the onset between the traditional and American cultures. We sense it was her generation that was the seam separating the two cultures, the old way and the new, and that the seam was literally bursting apart as she wrote. The native language was still widely heard, yet many of the younger generations spoke English as their first language. The last elders who were born during the pre-contact period viewed a world in which their cultural values lay obliterated in the remnants of the long unused redwood-plank houses, tainted by their war-ravaged memories. By 1916 the Indian cultural landscape was covered with the white man's frame houses, clothes, economy, and regulation. The old way, at least on the surface, had been virtually acculturated. Yet, amazingly, first contact had only been 67 years earlier! From 1849 to 1916 the pace of change on the Klamath River had ripped through the traditional culture like a tornado.

It is easier for us today to empathize with the hardship faced by these old people. The first wave of *kiniyo: [Ken-e-ah]*, "foreigners" (the early Yurok word for white man), had been preceded by devastating epidemics. Many great Indian leaders, priests, priestesses, healers, and heroes had lain dying of smallpox and measles before their helpless survivors and kin. It is not so far-fetched to me that under such tragic circumstances, the Yurok regarded the first white men as the vanguard of the returning *Wo:ge [Wa-gas]*, the race of white-skinned Spirit Beings who had promised, according to Yurok mythology, to return to the people one day. According to the stories, they had mysteriously departed the Earth in ancient times, leaving behind their divinely wrought knowledge to guide the Yurok people. When the white man first arrived, the Yurok hope was that the *Wo:ge* were returning to set the world back in balance and scourge the Earth of the debilitating epidemics. It later became brutally obvious that the newly arrived ones were, in fact, another epidemic.

Within a very short time the rape of the Yurok people and Earth was evident everywhere. With each day the unrelenting subjugation of the faith, values, mores and traditions of the old Yurok society progressed. The old ones watched as the Earth was literally being flushed into the river by the white man in his frenetic search for gold. One can only imagine the impact to their psyches. For them the desecration of the Earth resulted not so much in loss of land, but, by their belief, the destruction of God itself. To the Indians of the Klamath River, the Earth *is* God. Where once-proud villages and spiritually ordained geography stood, now lay utter ruin and decay.

To Lucy Thompson the era marked the end of the enlightened native consciousness on the River. This consciousness had been embodied in a society the Yuroks called *Ta:L [Talth]*. The society was responsible for maintaining the "high" knowledge of the people, from which the ceremonialists and thinkers of the tribes had always been trained. Thompson wrote that she and her father were the last two *Ta:L* members to be fully trained in the esoteric knowledge of the World Renewal ceremonies. Today we know that the *Ta:L* society's influence was extant into the late 1940s, in both the upstream (Karuk) and downstream (Yurok) divisions of the Klamath River Indians. Despite this fact she fully believed that the *Ta:L* tradition would end with the passing of her and her father.

Nowadays traditional knowledge is possessed by a precious few men and women. Hope is not lost, however. A growing group of younger generation men and women have embarked on the same path of enlightenment as described by Thompson. It is my hope that the reprinting of this book will serve to reveal today's critical need to protect and assert ceremonial values, traditions and knowledge. Lucy Thompson's nightmare was seeing the exorcising of traditional knowledge from the minds of her people. Today it is the job of the traditional-minded to re-integrate that knowledge. In this light *To the American Indian* is a very important book.

During the early 1970s there was a movement among local tribes to revive the ceremonies which had been abandoned for years, resulting in a veritable renaissance of culture. Community efforts to rebuild language and culture have invigorated Indian life up and down the Klamath River. For the generations born within the last 50 years, progress at the expense of abandoning ceremonies was and is not acceptable. Fixing the world has become once again the cultural imperative. Nevertheless, the inequity, inconsistency, and self-serving motives of the "other way" plague our generation just as they plagued Thompson's. Federal legislation, court rulings, and policy changes stand before the traditional-minded like roadblocks and detours along our path to enlightenment. I wonder what Lucy Thompson's reaction might be to the fact that the "upstream division of the Klamath River Indians" (Karuk tribe) wasn't recognized by Congress as a tribe until 1979. Her own division, the Yurok tribe, was ordered to organize itself according to the accepted federal model by an act of Congress in October of 1988!

Thompson's story mirrors the plight faced by tribes across California. The book provides us with a window through which we can better appreciate today's dedication to traditional ways as positive and healing. Many tribes across the state are once again embarked on their own paths to enlightenment. The incisive point that we must all grapple with today is that *we are the descendants* of the old times. *To the American Indian,* if nothing else, captures the devoted, endearing love in which Lucy Thompson and her people held the Earth and all those who passed on before them. It is the guiding force for us, too, when we fix the Earth by ceremony.

Thompson's further contribution with *To the American Indian* is her vivid and detailed description of Yurok culture. She describes the deep awe in which the "Indian doctors" were held by the average Indian person. This awe was, in great part, due to the incredible physical and mental endurance prospective doctors were required to sustain during their initiation. They fasted, prayed and danced without sleep for days on end. They made annual pilgrimages to high mountain peaks located far back and away from the river. The great doctors of the Klamath River were regarded as individuals of incredible determination and iron-clad belief. Coupled with personalities of often unequalled intensity, doctors were able to amass great wealth and prestige for themselves, their families and villages.

Thompson explained, by anecdote, the traditional ideal of acquiring wealth. One achieved wealth through self-denial, prayer and fasting, just as the doctors acquired their healing power. So, we come to understand that Indian wealth was directly tied to a strict moral and spiritual code. Maintenance of the wealth required exact measurements of maturity, spiritual development and obeyance of traditional laws. There are many stories of individuals who "made medicine" to acquire wealth, and did so in the face of great spiritual and physical danger to themselves.

The Deerskin and Jump Dances, both adjuncts to the World Renewal ceremony, were the collective or tribal counterpart to individual ambition and expressions of the cultural ideal to make power. Thompson obviously loved these dances, their pageantry and purpose. She held the two ceremonies up to scrutiny by her non-

Indian readers without reluctance, fully believing in their sanctity, purity and perfection. The dances gave all Indians of the tribe the opportunity to help with the ritual fixing of the world. It was the means for villages from up and down the Klamath River to bring out their best "Indian treasure"—singers and dancers. The spectacular displays of wealth were displays of devotion and successful pursuance of the Way. Every aspect of the ceremony was imbued with meaning and portent. The spectators, dancers, singers, cooks, priests, priestesses and even the spirit world came together to remake the world. Each individual was a powerful element in the religious process. Each person's behavior and attitude during the ceremony reflected how one's life would go during the interval until the next ceremony. Great care was taken to pray for the priests and priestesses, that their arduous jobs go well, that their spirits be high, and that they gain "luck" by their effort. Their success would portend a bountiful harvest of water and plant food, no sickness, and happiness and spiritual well-being for all. It is believed that the Spirit Beings came to observe the people during these ceremonies, to see how they worked and prayed to rebuild the Earth, to witness those who were fulfilling their responsibility to fix the world. It is one of the most dangerous times, in a spiritual sense, exactly because the world is being visited by the Spirit People. At such times one must be aware and on best behavior lest bad luck befall one.

From 1849 until 1900, attacks against the Yuroks and Karuk people by the miners and settlers had disrupted the World Renewal ceremonies many times. After 1900, Indian ceremonials were being outlawed in some cases, and even when not outlawed were strongly discouraged. By 1916 some of the younger generation and non-Indians complicated furtherance of the dances by attending ceremonies as if they were social events like the white man dances which were very popular at the time. The ceremonial leaders were growing more intolerant of the decline in belief, with some village leaders abandoning the dances altogether. Thompson's era can only be characterized as confused, the confusion brought about by severely contentious belief systems. She wove her story around the Kepel [Cap-pell] village Fish Dam and Pekwon [Pec-wan] village Jump

Dance. The Fish Dam ceremony has not been held since the early decades of this century. With the current federally regulated control of the Klamath River and its salmon fishery, this ceremony may never be seen again. The Jump Dance was last held at Pekwon in 1936, having falling victim to progressive times. In September 1982, a determined band of young Yurok traditionalists, mentored by a *Ta:L* elder, Dewey George, resumed the World Renewal Jump Dance cycle at Pekwon. The personal sacrifice of the dance-maker families and those entering the sweathouse as prayer-makers and fasters was undertaken in order to build a renewed sense of stability, laughter and purpose.

The 21st century is fast approaching. Happily, the Indians of northwestern California are bound and determined to continue the quest of fixing the world. Perhaps with time society will catch up with us. Perhaps in time, the traditions Thompson justly felt were about to end will once again be common sights across the land.

Julian Lang, a member of the Karuk Tribe (called the "upper Klamath" by Lucy Thompson), is a traditional singer, dancer, and tribal scholar. He is affiliated with the Center for Indian Community Development at Humboldt State University, Arcata.

Lucy Thompson in her wedding dress. Photograph from the original edition of *To the American Indian.*

Lucy with a portion of her basket collection, 1916.

xxviii

Preface

As there has been so much said and written about the American Indians, with my tribe, the Klamath Indians, included, by the white people, which is guessed at and not facts, I deem it necessary to first tell you who I am, for which please do not criticize me as egotistical.

I am a pure, full-blooded Klamath River woman. In our tongue we call this great river by the name of Health-kick-wer-roy, and I wear the tattoos on my chin that has been the custom for our women for many generations. I was born at Pec-wan village, and of highest birth or what we term under the highest laws of marriage. I am known by my people as a Talth. My maiden name was Che-na-wah Weitch-ah-wah, Che-na-wah being my given name.

My father, being also a Talth, took me at a very early age and began training me in all of the mysteries and laws of my people. It took me years to learn, and the ordeal was a hard one. I was made a Talth and given the true name of God, the

Creator of all things, and taught the meaning of every article that is used in our festivals, together with all the laws governing our people. I can understand every word, every nod and gesture made in our language. Therefore, I feel that I am in a better position than any other person to tell the true facts of the religion and the meaning of the many things that we used to commemorate the events of the past.

In this book I will endeavor to tell all in a plain and truthful way, without the least coloring of the facts, and will add many of our fairy tales and mothers' stories to their children. I will also give the names of many things in my own native tongue.

Mrs. Lucy Thompson
(Che-na-wah Weitch-ah-wah)

Eureka, California
June, 1916.

To Milton J. Thompson

My beloved husband, with whom all of my married life has been so pleasantly spent, I dedicate this book.

Mrs. Lucy Thompson,

Che-na-wah Weitch-ah-wah.

Dedication from the original edition of *To the American Indian*.

Chapter I
Bill McGarvey's Store

The old Klamath Bluffs Store, or Fort, and in late years the Klamath Post Office, was built in 1855 or 1856 by a man named Snider. He conducted it as a trading post for Indians, soldiers and travelers alike. It was built of rough split lumber and strongly made of double walls with sawed blocks four inches thick placed between the walls, and was bulletproof, with portholes so that a few white men could defend themselves against many Indians. This store is located twenty-four miles up the river from its mouth, and is about eighteen miles down the river from Weitchpec or the junction of the Trinity River, and something like forty miles below Orleans Bar on the Klamath. Orleans Bar was at one time the county seat of Klamath County. The old store is on the north bank of the river on a bar that was formed in ancient times, and is high enough to make it safe from all high waters. It is a beautiful, sunny spot and on the line of travel up and down the Klamath River.

The north side of the river is mostly prairie along the bank, and the old Indian trail is on that side. The whites took up the Indian trails and improved them so they were traveled by all.

This old store is also the central ground for the lower Klamath Indians, as here close by is where they held the sacred White Deerskin Dance [Oh-pure-ah-wah], which is a worship of their God. Here for ages past have gathered the wealthiest and most prominent Indians, both men and women, of all the upper and lower Klamath Tribe, including the Hoopa, Smith River and our Indians down the coast as far as Trinidad.

White men have visited this famous old store whose names will go down in history, such as General Crook and many other army officers, besides many wealthy businessmen. All of them liked to linger in this beautiful spot where the sun shines warm and the pleasant seabreeze fans it all through the summer months. There is a trail to this place from the north, Crescent City, Reck-woy and other places. This is not a mining country as there are no mines below the mouth of the Trinity, except in the river gravel or in the low bars that have been washed down from the upper Klamath and Trinity Rivers where all the rich gold-bearing mining placers are found. These mines were the cause of the old store being a central stopping place for the men in the early days going to and from the mines. In the fall of 1876 I counted upwards of three thousand Indians there at a White Deerskin Dance. There were five different languages spoken among them: the lower Klamath, upper Klamath, Hoopa, Smith River and Mad River. Some of them could speak two and some three, while others could only speak one. So it can be seen that this old Klamath Bluffs Store (or Klamath Post Office, as it is now called) has been the scene of many and not a few murders, and this store will be mentioned often in my writing.

In about the year 1861, Snider sold the stock of goods to Bill McGarvey, a jolly Irishman. It was Bill McGarvey that named me Lucy, yet he always called me by my Indian name, Che-na-wah. Bill McGarvey kept in stock plenty of whiskey, always in the flat pint bottles, which he sold at a dollar a bottle to the whites and Indians alike. He would only bring out one bottle at a time in selling it to the Indians so that any time they became quarrelsome he could tell them that it was all gone. Bill McGarvey had many ups and downs in the way of his trading there among them, and I will tell of some of his experiences.

Three Indians came to the store one day, bringing with them a fine-looking young Indian girl, and wanted to borrow thirty dollars and leave the girl as security. He talked it over for a while. The Indians said that they had to have this amount to make a settlement with some other Indians, that they would come back and pay him and take the girl in thirty days. So he decided to let them have the money without due consideration of how he would take care of the girl. After they were gone be began to think of the situation that he had placed himself in, as he was a bachelor. So he made up a room for her; and when it came to cooking he thought he would have her wash the dishes and sweep the house, but she would do no housework unless he paid her for it. McGarvey tried to argue the case with her and told her that he had to furnish her food and cook it, also furnish a room and a bed to sleep in, and that she ought to clean up the house. She answered by telling him that he was doing only what he had to do and that she would not work unless he paid her for it. McGarvey had to absolutely wait on her for the whole thirty days as completely as if she had owned him as a slave. She could go and come as she liked, always coming back in time so he could not make a complaint, telling him that if he said so, she would stay in the house all the time. He said that the experience was in after-years a lesson to him in dealing

Bill McGarvey's Store (Illustration from the original edition of *To the American Indian*.)

with the Indians. When the thirty days were up they came with the money, paid him and took the girl.

Another time he wanted to get in his winter supplies, and at that time he got his goods from Crescent City (Caw-pay). And he went to Cor-tep village, which is about six hundred yards above the store and on the same side of the river, to see if he could hire them to go down the Klamath and out to sea to Crescent City with their canoes, as they had a large new one. He hired five of them, all Cor-tep Indians, to go and bring his goods into the mouth of the river and store them there until they had them all in before the ocean would get too rough, as the winter months were coming on.

Early in the morning the five Indians of the Cor-tep village (this was a town village of the Klamath Tribe) started down the river and on arriving at the mouth never stopped to take a view of the weather, but put out to sea. The ocean was very rough, the waves were rolling high, and when they got into the breakers their boat capsized and all five of them were drowned. This brought on serious trouble for Bill McGarvey. The relatives of the drowned Indians talked it over for three or four months and then decided to go to McGarvey and demand pay, the most of it to be paid in Indian money. McGarvey said that after counting it up it would amount in our gold to about fifteen hundred dollars. He refused to pay it, telling them that he was not responsible for the drowning, that he had only hired them to bring in his goods by water, that their getting drowned was not his fault and he would not pay. At this they went away.

Two or three days after, late in the evening, he heard small stones striking on the shed roof of the kitchen at the back part of the store. He listened, but heard no more, so he went to the door of the kitchen, enclosed with a high, strong picket fence, and opposite the kitchen door was a gate in this fence; and as he looked out of the door there stood a tall, slender, fine-looking Indian woman, one who had always been a friend of McGarvey, and not only to him but to all the whites. This woman was my close kindred, which gave me the opportunity of knowing it correctly. She beckoned to McGarvey to come, and as he came up to her she told him to make preparations for himself and the other two men that were in the store to defend themselves, as the Cor-tep Indians would be there very early the next morning and would kill him unless they could manage to hold the Indians off. Then the Indian woman stealthily crept away and back to her home while McGarvey and his two friends, Jack Paupaw and George A. White, began at once to prepare for their defense as well as they could. They got in as good a supply of water as they had vessels to hold it in, closed the doors and bolted them from the inside, and opened the portholes. Under the store was a large cellar just on a level with the ground from the outside.

Sure enough, early the next morning there came twenty-five or thirty of them, with their faces blackened with war paint and yelling the war-whoop. But McGarvey and his friends were ready to keep them at bay for a few hours, until a young Indian who was a great friend of the whites and a lifelong friend to McGarvey came, and as he walked up to the door of the store he asked to be let in. They opened the door and let him in. This Indian, named So-pin-itts (Solomon), lived close by and is yet living. After he was in the store a while he went out and talked it over with the Indians and called a stop till the next day, during which time McGarvey tried to make a settlement with them, finally telling them that it was too much money, that he never kept so much money in the store, and that the only way he could pay that amount was to send to Crescent City and get his friends there to help him. Finally the Indians consented to this and all of them went home.

McGarvey wrote a letter to his friends in Crescent City, asking them to help him, telling them of the situation he was in, and asked them to intercede in his behalf or the three of them would be killed by the Indians. He also wrote a letter to the government officer in command of the Smith River Indian Reservation, telling him of his predicament and asking him to send a squad of soldiers to his assistance, and then dispatched the letters by an Indian in posthaste. The Indian, not knowing the contents of the letters, went with all speed to deliver them to the friend of McGarvey at Crescent City. The friend, after reading them, also made haste to deliver the one to the commanding officer, while the officer in turn arranged to send ten soldiers with an officer to the McGarvey store. They arrived at the store on the morning of the fifth day after the truce had been given. At daylight the soldiers came down the hill to the north of the store, whooping and yelling at the top of their voices after a long and tedious march of almost day and night over rough mountain trails, uphill and down, through brush and timber, with only part of the distance in the open ground, traveling for about fifty hours.

On the arrival of the soldiers the Indians were dismayed, knowing that they had been out-generaled and that McGarvey had sent for the soldiers instead of sending for the money to pay them, and had done it by sending one of their own men to deliver the message. At this turn of affairs the Indians quieted down and abided their time, as they never get in a hurry to make a settlement.

After the soldiers had been there for a few days they received orders to remain until further notice. It was then that McGarvey hired some men to build an addition to the store. This was erected at the west end of the store, about twelve feet wide and eighteen feet long and eight feet high to the eaves. It stood out over a steep bank of a small creek that comes down close to the west end of the store. This made comfortable quarters for the soldiers where they would be sheltered from the hot rays of the summer heat and the rains of the winter months, also privacy from the prying eyes of the inquisitive Indians. Here the soldiers remained for about eight months, having all sorts of a jolly time, as Bill McGarvey had plenty of whiskey to supply their thirst at a dollar a bottle after each pay-day. McGarvey on some occasions would take quite freely of the whiskey himself, becoming intoxicated and boisterous. On these occasions his friend Solomon, the Indian, would go into the store and keep him straight, locking the doors and letting no one in.

Jack Paupaw and George White went to their own homes. Jack Paupaw was a blacksmith by trade and was working in Crescent City. He was an old pioneer of Crescent City and the Klamath River. He returned to Crescent City while White went up the river to a place known as Big Bar, thus leaving McGarvey with the soldiers, as everything was now quiet. Things proceeded smoothly while the soldiers were there, and all thought that the trouble was forgiven and forgotten, and the soldiers were ordered back to their command.

But the Indians of the Cor-tep village began to scheme for another plan for revenge of their lost relatives, but gave up McGarvey and chose this time a man by the name of Bryson who was the superintendent of the Klamath Bluffs Mine,

Sugarloaf Mountain, *segwu tektani,* at Somes Bar. Mistakenly identified in the original edition of *To the American Indian* as "View of the Klamath River near Pec-wan." This site is the Karuk ("upstream Klamath") center of the world, called in the Karuk language *Ka'tim'iin.* Photo by A.W. Ericson, 1896.

View of a sacred granite outcropping where tribal doctors sought their power.

situated only about two hundred yards up the river from the store. Bryson had a miner's cabin which he lived in while working at the mines, up from the river out of the way of high water. The mine was down close to the river. He was coming up the trail to his cabin for dinner just about twelve o'clock when one of the Cor-tep Indians shot him down in his tracks with one of the old muzzle-loading rifles; this Indian was named Lotch-kum. Then all the Indians left for the timber to get out of the way of the whites and friendly Indians. This started the row going again, and McGarvey barricaded his store until the friendly Indians came to his assistance. The first family to come was Weitch-ah-wah (my father) and his brother (my uncle).

At that time they were camped at the mouth of Tec-tah Creek, some four miles down the river from the store, and as soon as they heard of the killing of Bryson they started for their home at the Pec-wan village about one mile above the store, and on going home went by the store, and stopped to learn the particulars of the killing. McGarvey made arrangements with Warrots (my uncle) to go up the river and give notice to the whites, T.M. Brown, the sheriff of Klamath County, and to the soldiers stationed at Camp Gaston in Hoopa Valley, some twelve miles up the Trinity River from its junction with the Klamath. After Warrots had delivered the message at all points, he stealthily returned to his home at Pec-wan in the night so the other Indians would not find out he was on this errand against them. On the day following War-rots' return, the sheriff and other white men came among them. George A. White, who was a cripple as has been stated, started to walk on the front porch of the store when some of the angry Indians said to him, Melasses White you can't fight, you are crippled (Melasses was his Indian name).

White went back into the store and got one of the first makes of Henry rifles (the one Warrots had let McGarvey have to defend himself with, and the one my brother had brought from Oregon while he was up there with the white men; it was also the only one to be found on the Klamath of the kind and make at that time). As soon as the Cor-tep Indians saw the rifle they knew at once that Warrots had given it to the whites to shoot them with, and it caused them to swear vengeance against Warrots and his brother. Upon further inquiry they also found out that Warrots had been up to Hoopa and told of the killing of Bryson.

T.M. Brown, having been the sheriff of Klamath County a number of years and also a pioneer of the Klamath River, was quite well acquainted with the habits and customs of the Klamath River Indians, and he counseled with the friendly Indians and agreed to pay them for their services if they would bring in the guilty Indian Lotch-kum dead or alive. So Warrots set out to find Lotch-kum and kept watching different places to find where he was hiding. The country being heavily timbered, Lotch-kum kept out of sight for nearly a year, but at last Warrots found where he was hiding in a creek some eight miles down the river from the store and about one mile up the creek from the river in the heavy redwood timber, in a large pile of drift logs. He first heard Lotch-kum's little fist dog bark, and on watching patiently for a while saw Lotch-kum come out. At this he went back to his home in the Pec-wan village, then visited with the Ser-e-goin village and told them that he had found the hiding place of Lotch-kum. When they got ready, three of them (the other two being from the Ser-e-goin village, Mermis Jack and Marechus Charley), with Warrots leading the way, arrived close to Lotch-kum's hiding place. They commenced to keep a close lookout for him, as they could see his tracks in the soft dirt and sand in the bed of the creek, and had to keep up the watch for about ten days. Finally they saw him come creeping out to the creek, where he began to bathe himself. Warrots raised his rifle to his shoulder, took aim and fired, Charley and Jack firing next. Lotch-kum fell to the ground but kept rising up and falling down again, trying to get away, when the three of them ran up to him as fast as they could, drew their long, heavy knives and severed his head, put it in a sack, and carried it back to the old store in triumph. Inside, they rolled it out on the counter, which satisfied the whites for the killing of Bryson.

Bryson was buried in a pretty spot a little northeast of the store, with hardly a mark to show the place where he was to sleep, and all settled down to peace and quietness again between the Indians and the whites. But the Pec-wan Indians were divided between the Indians and the whites; some of them were friendly to the whites, while others took sides with the Cor-tep Indians. Warrots was a Pec-wan Indian and full brother to Weitch-ah-wah. The sheriff and government officers gave to the three Indians who had killed Lotch-kum letters of very high recommendations for their services and to the good graces of all the whites. (I have seen these letters with the signatures many times in my girlhood days.)

Now the Cor-tep village and part of the Pec-wan village began to make plans to kill Warrots, and as he was considered to be a good and faithful friend of the whites by these Indians, it must be done in a way so as to deceive the whites and not to let them know it was being done as a revenge for the part he had taken in killing Lotch-kum. So they bided their time waiting for a good chance, but all the time Warrots was hearing of their schemes through his friends, and he went to the sheriff and government officers and told them that Lotch-kum's friends were planning to kill him, and all of them promised him that no one would be allowed to harm him. Sheriff Brown sent him word to meet him at Trinidad, as Trinidad was at that time in Klamath County. Warrots came and laid the facts before him, and the sheriff promised him protection, and Warrots went back home.

After about three weeks his brother Weitch-ah-wah and all the family except myself (I was about eight years of age) went away; thereby, Warrots' enemies got their chance to carry out their plans. Early in the morning Warrots went down to the creek, which was only a short distance, to bathe, and there he met a little boy, the son of Pec-wan Ma-hatch-us. He spoke to the boy, bathed in the creek and went back up to the house, when he saw another Indian coming up the river trail from the Cor-tep village; and as he passed the boy, Warrots saw him stop, talk to the boy and give him a piece of bread, which he ate. The boy then came up to the Pec-wan village while the Indian, who was from the Cor-tep village, kept on up the river. As the boy got to his house he became ill, and in about thirty minutes died. Evidently the Indian had given him a piece of poisoned bread which had killed him. They gave no attention to the one that gave the bread but instead laid all the blame on Warrots for the death of the boy, and as soon as the ceremony and burial was over they pounced upon Warrots and shot him at the door of his sweathouse, killing him. The next day Warrots was laid to rest in the graveyard of his own folks in Pec-wan village.

None of the whites ever made any attempt to punish any of the Indians or stop them from killing him. This is the reward he received for being a faithful friend to the whites in times of need. His brother with his family was forced to leave their home in Pec-wan village and move to Ser-e-goin village, where lived the friends and helpers of Warrots, Mermis Jack and Marechus Charley. After living there for a while we moved up to Hoopa so as to get farther away from our enemies and where we could have a better chance for protection. I took a position with the agent which they said I filled with credit to myself and satisfaction to them. Mermis Jack and Marechus Charley lived for many years but were never friendly with the friends of Lotch-kum. Mermis Jack finally died suddenly, and in a manner that pointed strongly that he was given poison in his food. Marechus Charley died a natural death in 1886.

In 1876 Bill McGarvey died in the old store that went by his name so long. He had not been feeling well for some time. In the large room at the west end of the store building he had a large stone fireplace, put in many years before, and he used this room as his bedroom and also a sitting room. In this room he was taking his bath in a tub when he fell over dead in front of the fireplace. The same evening, his Indian lady friend died in her home, which was just a short distance from the store. McGarvey had outside shutters to his windows which fastened from the inside, and these he had fastened, and in the morning as he did not open the store, his Indian friend Solomon waited until late in the morning for the opening of the store, when he became suspicious of all not being right. He pried open the shutter of the window on the south side of the store, which would give him a view of everything in the room where McGarvey slept, and there before the large stone fireplace lay McGarvey cold in death, and beside him was the tub in which he was taking his bath. When the Indians heard of his death they all said Bill McGarvey and Mollie have both gone over to the other side together. (Mollie was closely related to all my folks.) Bill McGarvey was laid to rest by the side of Bryson, on the flat above the store, and the store passed into the hands of James McGarvey, a brother of Bill.

James McGarvey made the claim that he was the only living brother, which was afterwards said to be false, yet he got the store and ran it for several years. He kept whiskey and sold it to the Indians and the whites. The Indians would get drunk and have fights and kill each other until he finally got mixed up with them by having a row over one Indian finding a pistol in the trail that belonged to a white man by name of Jim Douglas. McGarvey thought he would make the Indian give up the pistol in short order, and he went into the Wah-tec village, which is situated but a short distance from the store, and as he got within a few yards of Ray-no, the Indian, he drew his pistol and commenced to shoot at him. McGarvey's shots went wild, and the Indian drew his pistol and shot McGarvey, striking him in the back on the left side, just missing the backbone and went clean through the body on the striffin of his stomach, and he fell to the ground. The white men went to his assistance and carried him to the store, and the Indians that were in the row left and went up the river to other villages with the pistol in their possession. This raised quite a furor, and the whites were counseled with by the Indians that were friendly to both sides, and they were asked to bring back the ones that were in the shooting of McGarvey and to bring back the pistol to the rightful owner. The next day they came back and returned the pistol to James Douglas, and he gave them five dollars to be given to the one that found it.

In some three weeks Jim McGarvey was up and walking

Weitchpec c. 1910, along the Klamath River near the confluence of the Trinity River. *Pec-toolth* is the spit of land shown just beyond the tree in the center of the photo.

Mill alongside the Trinity River near Hoopa. Photograph taken in the 1880s.

around and in a short time went to Orleans Bar, where there was a justice of the peace, and tried to swear out a warrant for the arrest of the Indian; but the warrant was refused by the justice, who told him that he had commenced the row himself by shooting first, while intoxicated. Several years before this, Klamath County was taken off the map by being absorbed into Humboldt and Del Norte Counties, leaving this old Klamath Bluffs Store in Humboldt County.

Jim McGarvey was selling whiskey to the Indians and causing so much trouble among them that it caused a number of killing scrapes. After this trouble was settled and Jim McGarvey got well of his wounds, he sold the store to Peter Kane and moved down the Klamath River to within about three miles of the mouth of the river and settled at the mouth of a small creek close to the bank of the river, taking with him all of his ill-gotten gains and his beautiful little Indian woman that had lived with him for years and to whom he had never been married by any law. She was neat and tidy and a good cook, but McGarvey got mad at her for crying over the death of her mother and struck her on the back of her head. From this she began to lose her mind and he finally abandoned her, and she became a raving maniac and died, leaving no children. Her body was taken back up to her birthplace and laid to rest with her kin in the family graveyard, while Jim McGarvey lived on his place for a few years and then died.

Peter Kane now had the store, and he also kept whiskey and a rough house. He would sell whiskey to the Indians and get drunk himself, having trouble all around. He said one fall that he had two five-gallon kegs of whiskey and that the Indians close around there had four hundred dollars; and that he would get it all out of them for the two kegs of whiskey. His selling to them was the cause of four of them getting killed. Peter Kane had an Indian woman belonging to Redwood Creek. She spoke the Hoopa tongue and bore him three children. One day one of the little girls, about seven months old, was crying, and Kane grabbed her roughly by the neck, held her out, shook her at the same time he walked out through the kitchen and threw the child flat on the ground with its face down, then turned and walked back into the store cursing the child and its mother. The next morning the mother got her things together and started for her home on Redwood Creek. Arriving at the Klamath River, which she had to cross, she proceeded to cross over with her children, and had almost reached the other side before Kane found that she was leaving. As soon as he discovered that she was leaving he ran into the store, grabbed his rifle and ran down the bank to the water's edge and began firing. He fired several shots at her, the bullets striking close by, but failed to strike her. She went to her home in the night, some twenty miles away, over a rough mountain trail and through heavy timber most of the way. She never came back. The Indians preventing him from following her that night was all that kept him from killing her.

It got too warm for him, and he sold the store to C.H. Johnson and afterwards went to the Indian woman on Redwood Creek and remained there with her. This brute took the same little girl by her legs and dashed her brains out against a large redwood post, so everyone said. The woman again had to flee for her life. She left for Hoopa Valley, where she could get some protection, and Kane did not dare to follow her there. He drifted down on the coast and lived for a number of years, but finally took sick and died in the county hospital. The woman he had lived with and bore him children remained at Hoopa and raised the other children. Can you expect children, born to such fathers under such conditions, to grow up to be good and respectable men and women? Many of them are a credit to their Indian mothers, while those who have good respectable fathers and are born under wedlock, having a birth that they can be proud of, over the average make the best of men and women.

I have strenuously fought the whiskey traffic carried on by the unprincipled white men for years, and did all that I could to stop it, and made bitter enemies in doing so. Yet it is going on just the same under the very eyes of some of those who are employed by the U.S. Government to put it down. It looks as if they were paid to keep their eyes closed and not see it.

When C.H. Johnson took over the store he cleaned it up, built an addition to it and put in a large stock of provisions, made friends with the Indians, and did not keep any intoxicating liquors. And he allowed no one to drink around the store. He gave the Indians good advice so that all looked up to him as a friend among them; and he never meddled with any of their wives, but treated them with respect, so that all could come and go, trade and chat with perfect ease and freedom. Many of them would lay their troubles before him, and he would listen patiently and always try to give them good advice and keep down trouble among them as far as it was in his power to do so. Mr. Johnson kept this store for over twenty-five years, and the Indians never at any time made a threat against him or offered to harm him in any way. He began with the help of the settlers and succeeded in getting the government to establish a post office at the store which he named Klamath Post Office, while he was the postmaster. He ran the post office with the store and made a good official, striving at all times to do what he could for the patrons of the office. It was very few times that any complaint was made for mislaying mail. He ran the post office for about twenty-two years, and during this time many of the Indians sent letters and received others; and he used to read their letters for them and did much of their correspondence for them. He kept the office until he died. Mr. Johnson used to keep quite a stock of patent medicines and acted as doctor to the Indians if any of them were sick, often going to see them and give them medicine if he thought by doing so he could cure them. In serious cases he would advise them to go to a white doctor, which they would sometimes do.

As Mr. Johnson never kept any whiskey, being opposed to selling it to the Indians, his neighbors now took advantage of the whiskey business and began to get it in quantities and sell it to the Indians and mixed-bloods, which still kept the quarrels going. It looks as if it will still continue so to the end. It is a well-known fact that Mr. Johnson made money at the store, and when he became sick he was attended by white men until he died. It was said that no money was found above a small sum. The stock of goods was run down until there was but little left. The reader can guess how this happened, as Mr. Johnson never made a failure and always paid for his goods, his credit being good for whatever he ordered. He was the father of one daughter, her mother being a Klamath Indian woman. This daughter he always claimed as his child, and made arrangements for her to have all he possessed at his death, but she will never get but little. He was buried upon the flat beside the grave of Mr. Bryson in a deplorable manner.

A man by the name of Oscar Chapman, after the lapse of several weeks, was sent up to take charge of the store until the estate could be settled. The post office was moved from the store, and Chapman continued to run the store about one year, and kept whiskey to sell and ran gambling tables in the store. He meddled with the women, both married and single, for which he was shot dead in ambush. The coroner was sent up from Arcata to take charge of the body, and brought it down to Arcata for burial.

Then a man named William Lawson was sent up there to take charge of the store, and remained a few months and would not stay any longer. The order was given to him to sell all he could and box up the remainder, and take what was left down to the mouth of the Klamath by boat and store it there for safekeeping until some future time. Thus, the old store at Klamath Bluffs is dismantled and now stands there unoccupied.

After the death of Mr. Johnson the government put two lady matrons on the Klamath River to look after the interests of the Indians. They at once began to look after this store and made reports against it. The order came that no one could buy it or start it up as a trading post without first giving a bond in the sum of ten thousand dollars; yet it had been run by different men, sold a number of times, and none had ever given any bonds for over fifty years.

Around this store there are many tales woven, and I will tell quite a number of them, using this place as a center to start with, as this is where the lower Klamath Indians have their White Deerskin Dance, and a short distance above the store is where one of their sacred lodges is located. They have the true name of God, which is used in the lodge only in a low whisper and outside of the lodge when three or four of them are out in a secret place, and then only in a whisper when they are burning certain roots and herbs that give sweet and pleasant odors to their God. While the festival is being held, all difficulties are settled. Those of lower birth at the present time are pretending to carry out the worship, but for the past few years have made a sorry affair of it.

Marriage

In the high marriage of the Talth the woman is most beautifully dressed on her wedding day. A buckskin dress all strung with beads and shells that clink and rattle with her ever graceful step. Her hair is parted in the middle, brought down on each side and rolled with the skin of the otter. This skin is nicely dressed or tanned and then cut into about one-inch strips, thus holding the hair so it hangs down to their hips or lower, according to its length. Around her neck are strings of most beautifully arranged beads, of high value; they hang down to her waist, almost completely covering her chest. A buckskin, dressed and made as white as it can be made, goes over the shoulders and fastens around the neck and hangs down covering the back. This makes her very beautiful. She is so quick in movement that one has to keep eyes on her closely to see all of her actions, while she speaks low and softly. These high marriages are very few, and this beautiful sight of the bride is seldom seen. The girls born of these marriages were always looked up to by the Indians. When these girls came along or were met by any children of other births, the latter would always get out of the trail and let them pass.

The Klamath Indians never had a chief like the other large tribes but were ruled by these men and women of such births that became members of the order [Talth].

Another system is the "half-married" one, the woman

taking her husband to her house to live with her. By this marriage she is the absolute boss of the man and has complete control of all the children. She has the power to correct her husband in all his actions and can send him out to hunt, fish or work just as she deems proper, he being a slave to her, as they usually both belong to the class that are slaves. It amuses one to hear them use the term against white men that marry white women, the man having no home of his own, and the woman taking him to her home. They say that white man is half-married just the same as our people are half-married, and that the white man cannot walk out at any time as he is not boss, for the woman owns everything. They have a third form of marriage that belongs to the middle class. These marriages are considered by the whole tribe as good marriages, and the children born by these marriages have a good standing in all walks of life. The marriage is performed by a part barter and trade, such as giving in exchange a boat or fishing place or any other property of a personal nature. This ceremony is more of the common than the imposing way. Since the coming of the white man, he has brought this marriage around to a simple form of buying outright by giving a price as one would for a horse, cow or any other purchase. The old Indian law was an exchange of valuable articles, and often the woman did not go to the man she married and live with him in his own home until they had been married one, two or three years.

The Klamath Indians were, at the coming of the white man, a very large tribe, there being several thousand of them. It taxed every resource of the country in which they lived for all of them to obtain a subsistence; therefore everything was owned in the same way that it is now owned by the white man. The land was divided up by the boundaries of the creeks, ridges and the river. All open prairies for gathering grass seeds, such as Indian wheat, which looks similar to rye, besides other kinds of seed; the oak timber for gathering acorns, the sugarpine for gathering pine nuts, the hazel flats for gathering hazelnuts and the fishing places for catching salmon.

The most frugal and saving of the families had become the owners of these places and their ownership undisputed, and these ownerships were handed down from one generation to another by will. In time this left a great many of them owning no property by which they could make a living, and many of their own people became slaves to the wealthy class. They made the slaves work and kept them from starving, and by this there came about the "half-married" system. There are some of these Indians that were born slaves living yet, and they are the ones that are always ready to tell the white man all of the Indian legends in a way to fit their own cases. They cannot tell the true legends at all, as they are ignorant of such facts. The wealthy ones would see that the men got wives and that the girls got husbands, build them houses; and some families were very kind to their slaves. When they were sick they saw that they had doctors and the proper care. Some families were mean and overbearing to their slaves: giving no care to the sick, letting them die, and going so far as to throw them into a hole, leaving them there to suffer and starve until they died. This sort of treatment was looked down upon by the ones that had better humane feelings, and they sometimes prevented such inhuman actions.

Most of the doctors are women, and they exercised great power (especially those who had a high standing as to family) and the art of curing most all diseases or cases of sickness. A few of the doctors were men, and they used roots and herbs of different kinds, and they are hard to beat as doctors in a great many kinds of sickness. They can cure the bite of a rattlesnake, not one of them ever dying from the bite. I knew many of the people that were bitten by the rattlesnake at different times, and they were cured and lived to be very old. For this cure they use saltwater out of the ocean and the root of the onion of what you call kelp and which is taken out of the ocean. They pound the onion of the kelp and make a poultice out of it, place it over the wound and keep it wet with the saltwater, at the same time letting the patient drink all he can of the saltwater. The patient is kept perfectly still and not allowed to move about more than is necessary. They bind the limb or place where the part is bitten to prevent the free circulation of the blood through these parts.

In other things they are equally as good. In childbirth they prepare a woman for giving birth to her child, and at the birth of the child they have an old woman to take care of the mother and child. After the birth of the child the cord is cut and tied; then they take the black part of a large snail, which has an oily substance, and place it over the navel. They put a bandage around the child which is kept there for some time. I have never known an Indian of the old tribe to be ruptured, and yet they do not know anything about surgery. If anything of a serious nature happens to a woman during childbirth they are at a loss to know what to do to save her.

If the woman gives birth to twins and they are a boy and girl, they try to raise them both; but if it be two boys or girls they pick one of them and raise it while the other one is neglected and starved to death; and when it died they went through all the forms of sorrow by crying and mourning over the loss of

27

the child just the same as if they tried to raise it. If anything happens to the mother that causes her death at childbirth or after, and the child is yet an infant, they take sugarpine nuts or hazelnuts and pound them into fine flower and mix this in warm water, making a milky substance out of it. They can raise a child on this preparation as well as if it was nursed at the mother's breast. Every family in the olden times was very careful to keep a good supply of pine and hazelnuts on hand.

The Indians were preservers of the sugarpine timber which grew on the high ranges of mountains on the north side of the river, and there was a very heavy fine and also death to the Indian that willfully destroyed any of this timber. The sugar from these trees was also used by them as a medicine in different cases of sickness. The saltwater mussels that they gather which cling to the rocks close to the seashore is an article of food for them, and they gather and eat them while fresh by boiling them. They also dry them and take them up the river to their homes for winter use. In the month of August and a part of September these mussels become poisoned, in some years worse than in others, with phosphorus. Sometimes whole families would get poisoned by eating them out of season, and in this case they use the sugar which is taken from the sugarpine tree, and which is a sure cure if taken in time. This made the Indian prize the sugarpine tree very highly, and put to death even a member of their own tribe who harmed a tree in any way.

In the early days when a white man arrived among the Indians, he took an Indian woman, and in the fall of the year she would want to gather some pine nuts. The white man would go with her, taking his axe, and cut down the tree, as he could not climb it; and told the woman there they are, what are

Wah-kell Harry, a downstream man of wealth, displaying his regalia used in the "jumping" dance. (See page 216.)

Martin's Ferry, c. 1910, site of present-day bridge. This was the main fording place across the Klamath River between Weitchpec and Pec-wan. Photo by A.W. Ericson.

you going to do about it? At first the women complained, and finally said that the white man would spoil everything. Then the Indians began to cut the trees. In the last few years these trees have become very valuable in the eyes of the white man, and it has become the complaint of the white man that the Indians ought to be arrested and punished. Some of them have gone so far as to say that the Indians ought to be shot for cutting down this fine timber for the nuts. I leave the reader to decide which one ought to be punished for the cutting of the great number of these fine sugarpine trees.

The Indians also took the greatest of care of the hazelnut flats, as the nuts are used in many ways. The nuts were gathered and stored away, as they could be kept for a long time and could be pounded into flour, put into warm water and made a good substitute for milk which could be used for weak, sickly children, also in some cases for sick persons that needed nourishment and had weak stomachs. The hazel is used in all of their basketmaking, as the frames of all the baskets are made of the hazel sticks. In taking care of the hazel flats, they go out in the dry summer or early in the fall months and burn the hazel brush; then the next spring the young shoots start up from the old roots.

On the following spring in the month of May, when the sap rises and the shoots start to grow, the women go forth and gather these young shoots, which are from one to two feet in length. Some of these sticks grow up to a height of three feet and are gathered for making the large baskets and also the wood baskets. They gather these sticks by the thousands and take them home, where the women, children and men all join in peeling the bark off the sticks. They take up a handful in the right hand, then place the butt end of one of them in their mouth, taking hold of it with their teeth and the left hand, giving it a twist so as to peel the bark around the end; and as they get the bark started they give the stick one quick jerk and the bark peels off at one effort. After they are peeled they are laid out in the sun on a smooth place, in thin layers and allowed to bleach and dry. And when they are dried they gather them up and sort them out according to their size and length, and tie the different sizes in bundles and lay them away for use, sometimes three or four years later, before they are made up into baskets. The small sticks are used for making up the very fine baskets. The reader can easily see by this why the hazel was preserved and not destroyed, as it had a great value to them in many ways. They made withes of it for tying their boats and other things.

The oak timber they were very careful to preserve, as they gathered the acorns from it late in the fall, October and November. The oak tree furnished them with the staff of life, as it was from the acorn they made all their bread and mush; and this bread they could take for use on long journeys on their hunting trips. They would wrap up a large lump of dough and, placing it in a cool place, keep it for several days before it would begin to spoil or sour. From this dough they made their mush by taking a piece about the size of a teacup and put it into one of the baskets, fill it nearly full with water; then take some wash-stones taken from the river or creek and put them in the fire until they were hot and often red-hot, when they would take two sticks and lift them out, drop them into the basket and stir the whole briskly with a paddle made for this purpose. They would soon have it boiling, and by putting in another stone, and with a little more stirring, they would soon have the basket of mush cooked. They call this mush Ka-go, and it is very nutritious and gives great power of endurance. After the basket of mush has been set aside for thirty or forty minutes, it is then dipped out into small baskets made for the purpose and of size to fit the stomach. One person serves, handing out the mush together with a piece of dry salmon or venison or different things that may be prepared for eating. The acorn furnishes the bread to all the Klamath River Indians.

All the oak timber was owned by the well-to-do families and was divided off by lines and boundaries as carefully as the whites have got it surveyed today. It can easily be seen by this that the Indians have carefully preserved the oak timber and have never at any time destroyed it.

The Douglas fir timber they say has always encroached on the open prairies and crowded out the other timber; therefore they have continuously burned it and have done all they could to keep it from covering all the open lands. Our legends tell when they arrived in the Klamath River country that there were thousands of acres of prairie lands, and with all the burning that they could do the country has been growing up to timber more and more.

The redwood timber they use for making their canoes and building their houses. In making a canoe they took a redwood log in length and size to suit the canoe they wanted to make, and split the log in half, shaping the bottom of the canoe first, then turning it over and chipping off the top until they get it down to the right place, when they would start shaping the guards; after this they dug out the inside, leaving it a certain thickness, and this they gauged by placing one hand outside and the other inside, moving both hands slowly along—and it is surprising how even the thickness is in all parts. They cut out the seat in the stern, with a place to put each foot on the side in front of the seat so one can brace himself while paddling it with a long and narrow paddle (pointed at the end so they can paddle or push the canoe with it). They are certainly expert in the Klamath River with a canoe, either the men or women.

They have no keel on their canoes, just a round smooth bottom, with a rounded bow and stern. A large hazel withe is put through holes in the corners of the bow and drawn very tight across it so as to keep the canoe from splitting in case it strikes the rocks very hard, which often happens, as they [the canoes] grind upon the rocks in the rough places in the river. These canoes will carry heavy loads, much larger than they would seem to carry, sometimes from forty to one hundred and fifty sacks of flour at a load. In making a canoe, the Indians always leave in the bottom and some two feet back from the front or bow a knob some three inches across and about two inches high, with a hole about one-inch deep dug into it; and this they call the heart of the canoe, and without this the canoe would be dead. When I was a young woman no Indian would use a canoe unless it had the heart left in it to make it alive, as it was not safe to use if not thus fixed, something after the fashion or notion of the sailors as to a vessel being christened.

The redwood canoes are being used for a distance of one hundred miles up the Klamath River, but the redwood is used only for a distance of about thirty miles up the river for houses; after this distance they use red fir for houses. The redwood is a soft, easy timber for working and not susceptible to being sun-cracked, and is an ideal wood for making a canoe. After they have finished making the canoe, they take the shavings and some dry brush and burn it both inside and outside, and then brush off the dry parts, which leaves it very light and dry. After using the canoe for a few days, if any light cracks start in it they take it out, dry it perfectly and go over it with pitch taken from the fir tree. In doing this they first put the pitch on the cracks, then put hot rocks on the pitch, which melts it and it fills up the cracks. After this treatment the canoe will last for years.

Their tools for working timber were very crude, and they had to work very slow. For axes and wedges they used the elk horn. They would cut the horn to the length preferred with flint, and then use a granite rock where the quartz would adhere to it, making it very rough; and with this they would whet the horn into shape. After this they put grease on them and lay them up so that the fire would dry the grease into them, until they became very tough and could be used for years before wearing out. For their malls or hammers they took a granite rock and by pecking on it, could work it down to about one foot in length; then work it down so that at one end it would be about four inches across the face of it and the other end about two inches across it, while in the middle they would bring it to about one inch, making it so one could hold it with ease, using the large end for the mall part.

With these crude tools they cut trees, made their canoes and houses, by the aid of the fire to help in many ways. They could split up a log into slabs and get some nice-looking lumber, only rough and of different thickness, and in this way they could build a very warm and comfortable house.

In building a house they leveled off a piece of ground from thirty to forty feet square; then, beginning in the center of the square, they dug down about five feet and from twelve to twenty feet across. Surrounding this part, they dug a trench two feet deep, and in this they set the slabs or boards up endwise, being careful to put thick ones at each of the four corners with holes burned through the top ends. These boards were about eight feet long, which would leave them about six feet above the ground on two sides. To this they tied with hazel withes a heavy pole of the same size across the two gable ends on the same level of the side poles. They tamped the ground in tightly around these boards the same on all sides. At one corner of the gable end they had a very wide plank about four feet in width and about four inches thick; they cut out a hole in this plank about two feet across, and around this they put in about two feet from the corner setting it down in the trench, tramping it very solid, for the door. Then they put across the top from four to six very heavy poles for rafters, the two top poles being only about three feet apart, with one a little lower than the other so as to give it a slope for the water to run off when it rained. Then they tied all this with hazel withes until the whole thing is fastened solidly together; and after this part is finished they put on the roof, using the same heavy slabs, which are about eight feet long, doubling them so as to make it rainproof, while the center part or comb of the roof is short slabs about four feet long; and in the center they leave a large wide plank so they can raise it to a slanting position so as to keep the rain out and at the same time let the smoke out.

After the roof planks are all placed they put the large poles across the top, over the joints, and tie them down to the ones under with the hazel withes, making it all quite substantial as to strength. Then they make a hole in the center of the basement about one foot deep and side this up with stones to fit for a fireplace, making it very smooth, then put gravel in the bottom of the fireplace to the thickness of four inches in depth. They then put a plank wall all the way around the house or basement part, holding them firmly to their place, after the fashion of the white man's wainscoting. After this they take a good quality of clay, wet it with water until they get it to suit, and plaster it over the floor of the basement, tramping it until they get it plastered over about four inches thick. While it is drying they keep very close watch of it, and where it starts to crack they go over it with more clay, filling in the cracks. They keep the cracks filled until the floor becomes very dry and hard, and this makes a very smooth floor. They smooth off the upper floor, which is irregular in shape, and place a slab or post at the four places which come opposite the corners of the house, back about one foot from the wall and under one of the rafter poles, so as to give support to the rafters. Then they put in an inside partition in front of the door, letting this come back some ten feet on each side of the door, reaching up to the roof and an inside door, which is like the white man's door. This is a place fixed in all the houses for keeping their winter's wood in, while the rest of the place is for storing away their provisions for the winter months, such as dried salmon, eels, acorns and the other kinds of food which they store in large baskets. Some of these baskets are large enough for a man to lie down in.

Some of the girls make their beds in this upper part of the house for the summer months. In a house where there is a large family, this upper part of the house is well filled with baskets holding the different articles of foodstuffs, some of which have been stored there for a number of years. They have shutters to both the outside and inside doors, and the roof projects well out all around the house, which makes the house warm in the wintertime and cool in the summer. Going down into the basement they take a log about one foot through and cut the right length, cut notches in it for footsteps, and set it in place, and the little Indian children can go up and down this like squirrels with less accidents than the white have on their stairs. The whole family eats in the basement, and all the cooking is done there, and at night things are cleared away, and all the women and girls sleep in this basement, while the men and boys all go to the sweathouses to sleep.

Outside, in front of the door, they make a sort of porch, the floor of which is made of smooth rocks, thus completing the house. In going through the doors they have to stoop very low, and almost in a crawling position, and raise straight up on entering the inside. The inner door is high, and they can stand up on going through it. The doors in most cases face toward the river.

One of these houses will stand for fifty years and with some repairing will stand a great while. There were from ten to forty of these houses in a village, and the villages were from one-half to three miles apart, some on one side and some on the other side of the river. Generally there was a sweathouse to each dwelling, but sometimes there was only one sweathouse for two houses. The men and boys visited from one sweathouse to another for a social time and to remain overnight. The Indians that traveled up and down the river used to stop with old friends or relatives and would get in the sweathouse, exchange news and smoke their pipes until a late hour in the night. There is no law forbidding the women from sleeping in a sweathouse, but the men say the women have too many fleas on them and the women say the men talk too much, so the women let the men sweep, get the wood and make their own fires in the sweathouses. Sometimes an Indian will take his wife or favorite daughter to the sweathouse to sleep if the weather is cold, but the women prefer to sleep in the dwelling houses as they are very comfortable there and can be kept very warm with a small fire. The women make a sort of mattress of the tules that grow in the swamps. They gather this tule, let it dry and bleach it, then take strings of their own make and, commencing in the middle of the string, they lay one of the stalks of the tule and plait them closely together. They weave the tules close together, putting about six strings in a mat about three or four feet wide; and have the mat five or six feet in length, sometimes making them three and four thicknesses, which they can fold up and put out of the way in the daytime and take out and unfold at night. These mats are quite comfortable to sleep on. The old women sleep on the basement floors, while the young girls sleep on the upper floors in the warm months and on the lower floors, with the old women, during the cold months.

My people were in the habit of eating but two meals a day: the first meal or breakfast came about eleven o'clock; and in the evening, after dark, the women prepare the supper, the menu differing according to the season of the year.

As soon as it begins to get cold, the men would go out and get large loads of small limbs and brush, tie it up in a bundle which they placed on their backs and held with both hands; and as they came in, they sang a song for luck in whatever they might wish for, such as making money, good health and many other things. With this wood they make a fire in the sweat-house, and the smoke coming out of the crevices would make it look as if the house was afire for a short time, when the wood would burn down to a bed of coals and the smoke all disappeared. And then the men and boys would strip and creep into them, one at a time, and in about thirty or forty minutes would all come crawling out of the small round door, steaming and covered with perspiration, weak and limp, appearing as if they could hardly stand up. After crawling out they lay flat on the stone platform that is fixed for the purpose and sing the same songs, only at this time in a more doleful way.

They lay in this way for thirty or forty minutes, then get up and, still looking weak, start off down to the bank of the river, one at a time, and plunge into the cold water and swim and splash for a time. Then all go back to the dwelling-house and go in where the women folks are preparing the evening meal; take their seats around the basement floor, out of the way of the women while they are cooking; and all will join in laughing and talking until the evening meal is over. Then the men and boys go back to the sweathouse for the night and prepare for a big smoke, all laughing and talking about different topics and telling amusing tales. Some of the older ones would discuss points on Indian law; others tell how things are changing, how this and that used to be and is different now, how they fought the other tribes, when they were victorious and when they were defeated; praising one that was the leader or condemning another, one that was a good general; and many other things. And some were very interesting talkers. They talked until they were ready to go to sleep for the night, and then they would place the wooden pillows under their heads. Some of them would not use any kind of covering and would be almost naked, as the sweathouses would keep very warm for at least twelve hours after a big fire had been built in them.

Early in the morning they would come out and each take his own way for the day, such as hunting, trapping, fishing or getting something that might be needed for the family. The old men dressed deerskins, many of which the hair was left on, and these were for the women to use as blankets and for shawl-like coats which they wear; for moccasins (noch-i), they take a dressed deerskin and smoke it and then make it up into moccasins. They make dresses and many other things out of skins. Others would dress furs which they use in many ways. They use the fisher skin for quivers to carry arrows in; also the young panther skin. The freshwater otter they dress very nicely for the women to tie their hair with. Some would make mawls and wedges for future use, and others were making bows and arrows, while a few would give directions to the others. The women went about their work, such as pounding acorns, soaking the flour and preparing it to make bread or mush, some cutting fresh salmon and preparing it for cooking; others go out after wood for their part of the living and cooking quarters, and others made baskets for cooking purposes. Some made hats and baskets they used for storing away food, while others made fine dresses for wearing and anything that was to be done, but few of them being idle, unless it was some of the old women that were very wealthy.

The Klamath people have the same kind of tobacco that grows over a large part of the United States, which, when it grows up, has small leaves. They prepare the ground and plant the seed, but will not use any they find growing out of cultivation. They are very careful in gathering the plant and cure it by the fire, or in the hot sun; then pulverize it very fine, then put it up in tight baskets for use. It becomes very strong and often makes the oldest smokers sick, which they pass over lightly, saying that it is a good quality of tobacco. The women doctors all smoke, but the other women never do. Their pipes are made out of yew wood with a soapstone for a bowl. The wood is a straight piece, and is from three to six inches long, and is larger at the bowl end where it joins onto the stone. It is notched in so it sets the bowl on the wood, making the pipe straight. They hold the pipe upwards if sitting or standing, and it is only when lying on the back that one seems to enjoy the smoke with perfect ease; however, they can handle the pipe to take a smoke in any position. Some of these pipes are small, not holding any more than a thimbleful of tobacco. My people never let the tobacco habit get the better of them, as they can go all day without smoking or quit smoking for several days at a time and never complain in the least. The men, after supper, on going into the sweathouse, take their pipes and smoke, and some take two or three smokes before they go to bed. The old women doctors will smoke through the day, and always take a smoke before lying down to sleep. All inhale the smoke, letting it pass out of the lungs through the nose.

Women doctors are made and educated, which comes about in a very peculiar way. They are usually from the daughter of wealthy families. Most of them begin quite young, and often the doctor will take one of her daughters that she selects along with her and begin by teaching her to smoke and help her in her attendance on the sick, and at the right time will commence with her at the sweathouse, while others will have a dream that they are doctors, and then the word will be given out. And in either case along in the late fall all will be made ready, the day being set.

The sweathouse (which is the white man's name and does not have the same meaning in our language; we call it Ur-girk) being selected, they take her to it, dressed with a heavy skirt that comes down to her ankles and which is made of the inner bark of the maple, with her arms and breast bare. They all go into the sweathouse, there being from fifteen to twenty men and women in number, she having a brother or cousin, some-

Dancers holding white deerskins preceding to the dance ground at Pa-nam-niik (Orleans Bar) in Karuk territory, c. 1900. The men in the foreground are holding ceremonial obsidian blades.

Modern clothing and a traditional baby basket—a family in transition. Photo by
A.W. Ericson.

times two, that look after her. All begin to sing songs that are used for the occasion, dance jumping up and down, going slowly around the fire and to the right. They keep this up until she is wet with perspiration, as wet as the water could make her, and when she gets so tired that she can stand up no longer, one of her brothers or cousins takes her on his back with her arms around his neck and keeps her going until she is completely exhausted. Then they take her out and into the house. There she is bathed in warm water and then allowed to sleep as long as she wishes, which revives her and gives her back her strength. On awakening she appears rested and vigorous, with a beautiful complexion. She can now eat her meal, such as is allowed her.

While she is training for a doctor she is not allowed to drink any water or eat any fresh salmon. All the water she gets is in the acorn mush or in the manzanita berry, pounded to a flour and then mixed with water, made into a sort of mush, and warmed. They are allowed to eat all other kinds of food. These dances are kept up at intervals all through the winter months until late in the spring, when they will take her far back on the high mountains and keep her there all through the summer, never allowing her to drink water, only as mixed with mush, nor eat any fresh salmon. In the fall they bring her back home to the river, when she will go through the same performance in the sweathouse.

Sometimes she will be from three to ten years before being ready for the final graduation exercises, when she will be taken back to some almost inaccessible place on a high peak or on a very high rock where they will smoke, pray and fast for from three to five days. While at this place none eat or drink, and on leaving it the pipes are left secreted so as to be found on the next visit. On this trip there will not be more than three or four with her, and always one of them is an old doctor so as to care for her, and on coming back, after they get down the hill part way to a suitable place, they make a stop and all eat and take a rest.

The young doctor bathes herself, loosens her hair and washes it, then dries it and combs it with a bone knife. These knives of deer bone, about the size of a table knife, have a hole bored through the handle and a string tied through it, and fastens around the wrist; and in carrying it the point of the blade is up and lays against the arm so that a person would hardly know that she carried it. This comb is beautifully carved and checkered with black stripes. She gently strokes the hair with it until it is dry; then she thrusts the point through it, close to the head, gently pressing the blade down through it. She keeps the comb in motion until the hair is perfectly straight and glossy, and then she parts the hair in the middle of the forehead; then takes stripes of otter skin and ties it up, letting it hang down on each side of the head and in front of each shoulder.

This girl is a virgin, as perfect in stature and active in movement and health as God can make her. She can bear hardships and punishment without complaint or murmur that would make a bear whine. After all have rested they start for home, which will perhaps take them two or three days to reach, and all the time her health is looked after to see that she is in good spirits and does not become wearied. And on arriving home she is allowed to rest for two, three or four weeks, when all is made ready to give her the final degree, this time preparing one of the large living houses for the purpose by taking off a part of the roof and fixing it so that all can come and get a chance to see the whole performance. The time is set and word is sent all up and down the river, and at the appointed time they will be there, some coming for many miles to see and take part in giving the young doctor her final degree.

At sundown the fire is made in the center of the living room, and at the commencement of the hour of darkness she is brought in, goes through the door and down into the basement, takes her place, when the others that are to help her take their places, forming a circle around the fire, and all start singing in a low and monotonous voice, jumping up and down, the young doctor taking care of herself at first and taking instructions from the old doctor who sits close by but takes no part other than to instruct her. After keeping this up for two to four hours, the young doctor becomes very warm and fatigued, and they keep close watch of her until the time comes, when one of the men takes hold of her and holds her up and helps her to stand, still wearing her down, until two men take hold of her by each arm and in this way keep her dancing until she is helpless and so limp that she can no longer go on. Then they lay her up and out of the way, still keeping on with the ceremony until daylight in the morning, when all repair to their places to sleep for a few hours, then arise, go forth, bathe and eat and go back to their homes. The young doctor does not always go through this ordeal and come out safely, as sometimes she became so warm that she would never recover from the effects of the severe punishment, but this seldom happens.

After going through this, she is pronounced a doctor and can begin practicing her profession. She is now allowed to get married if she so desires, and the most of them do and raise large families and live to be very old. They wield a big influence among the tribe if they are successful as doctors, and some of them are very successful as doctors, while others are of the ordinary class. These women doctors are seers, as when they are called to doctor the sick, they claim to tell what is the cause of the sickness and what will cure it. They suck the body where the pain is located and sing in a sort of chanting way for a while, then suck the body again and keep this up for four or six hours. If it is a serious case there will be two doctors and sometimes three, and in this case they will not agree as to the cause; if the patient gets well, there will be one of them that gets the credit for the greater part of it and sometimes all of it. When there is a case of sickness, the relatives of the sick one decide on the doctor, and the amount of money or other valuables, or all valuables just as they may; go to the doctor, and lay it before her, at which she will accept or refuse the offer. But if it is satisfactory she will prepare to go with them, and if it is rejected she will demand more; and sometimes she will call for some valuable relic which she knows the family has in their possession, sometimes an article that has in years gone by been in the doctor's own family, and she will strive to get it back again. If the sick one should die while she is trying to get more, they will make her pay to them all that they have laid down to her, but if she accepts the money and goes and the patient dies, then they make her return all that was given to her. If there was two or three doctors, then they all have to return all that was given to them, and then they will debate among themselves as to which one of the doctors is the best. Some of the doctors were very successful and hardly ever lost a patient, and accumulated great wealth, owning the best fishing places and large tracts of land where they could gather acorns, hazelnuts and grass seeds, besides many slaves. They were great talkers and always had a ready answer to every question, and were almost habitual smokers, using a large pipe and smoking often. They had a wonderful constitution.

To give an idea of the power of one of these most successful doctors, I will give a sketch of one and her methods. This doctor was born at Cor-tep village and of a wealthy family who had been for many generations back. She married a man that was born at Pec-wan village, also of a wealthy family, and would be called after marriage in the Indian tongue as Peck-wish-on, but not in this case as she was called by the tribes as Caw. She became famous among her people and would come out of her house and sit on the porch of the stone platform in front of her door, take off her cap, stroke her hair down over her face and eyes, and sit this way for hours at a time; and all, young and old, would become afraid of her and say: look at Caw; she will make someone sick. And there would be such a dread of her that there was sure to be someone sick in two or three days. Then they would say that Caw made them sick; and if they could get her to doctor the sick one, she would cure the sick one, as she seldom ever failed to cure any of her cases. She doctored and took all the wealth of her mother and father into her own hands, besides all that her brothers and sisters and other relatives had, for doctoring them. She lived to be quite old and had raised a family of boys and girls. She had lots of slaves, land and fishing places, and money. Her son was the richest Indian in the whole tribe and was known as Pec-wan Colonel. I knew a girl that this doctor took for a doctor bill and who was to be the wife of one of her grandsons. But as the grandson and girl grew up to be of marriageable age, he did not want her for his wife and the money was returned, which freed her; and she married another man, one of choice.

These doctors never act in cases of childbirth, nor do they

ever attend or have any part in these cases. An old woman that is always very pleasant takes these cases, taking charge of the woman that is about to become a mother and prepares her for the task of giving birth. She has a medicine which she prepares and gives to the woman which does not fail to do its work in a very short time. This is the pitch or gum of the fir tree that has by fires or otherwise dropped into the waters of the creeks or streams and laid in the water for a long time, which makes it very brittle and hard. They take a piece of this and, after pounding it until it becomes as fine as flour, put it into a cup of water and let the patient drink, which in most cases brings her out in good condition. This is not the only remedy they have, for they have many for use in the different condition of the patient; the baby is also cared for by these women. They wash the child and dress it in soft furs, such as rabbitskins or other soft kinds of fur. They now pound hazelnuts into flour, put it into warm water, which makes a kind of milk, and then feed it to the child; they also take milk from the mother's breast and give to the baby. They do not let the baby nurse at the mother's breast until after the first ten days, at which time the child is allowed to do so until time to wean it. The baby is provided with a basket made for the purpose, and the child is placed in this in a sitting position. It has a strap fastened in the back so that the mother can swing it across her back, set it up against the wall or lay it down flat just as she may choose. The baby if in health will doddle its feet and laugh when any one takes notice of it. The baby baskets are changed in size as the baby grows older and larger; the older baskets are burned. These granny women are called Na-gaw-ah-clan.

The Klamath Indians have men doctors, and they use many kinds of roots, herbs and some minerals; and when it comes to wounds, bites of poisonous reptiles, chronic diseases, women ailing with such disease as falling of the womb and many other kinds of sickness, they are called in [by] rich families; and they too are paid in advance, and if they fail to cure they have to return the money, or if they refuse to come and the patient dies, they have to make good all that was offered them. These men doctors hand down their secrets of the different kinds of medicines they use, and for what each kind is used, to their sons or close relatives, and before one begins to practice he goes back on the mountains to some distant and secluded place where there is a large rock or high peak, where he can look over the whole surrounding country all alone. There he prays to his God for health, strength and success. He does not drink water or eat, and punishes himself as much as he can, and stands up under the strain. He is gone from eight to twelve days, and on his return he bathes himself, rests and sleeps, smokes his pipe for three or four weeks, and then is ready to take up the calling of the doctor, and will go with the old doctors for quite a while so as to make sure that he makes no mistake in handling the cases or in the uses of the different kinds of medicine to be used for different cases or diseases. These men doctors are called Pe-girk-ka-gay, the women doctors being called Kay-gay.

Most of the men doctors are of the highest birth and are often members of the highest families and are often members of the secret lodge. It is only them that stop the women doctors and make them take [back] many of their accusations or retract their sayings, thus keeping them in bounds of reason, though they are very lenient with them and often let them go too far before they stop them. These men doctors help to start and to make the settlements for the White Deerskin Dance, and this is the time when all troubles between individuals, clans and villages are settled, so the whole tribe is in peace. If any of them are not willing to settle their difficulties they are strictly forbidden to attend the worship, and if they should attend they would lose the respect of the whole tribe, besides they would be dealt with harshly. So in case there be some that cannot make a settlement, it is best for them to remain away for this is a time and place where all is free and the best of good cheer and behavior must prevail.

The White Deerskin Dance they hold every two years unless something of a serious nature happens and which sometimes did happen and so crippled the people that they could not hold them for a number of years, such as contagious diseases or other calamities. In years that everything was all right, these men doctors would get together about the last of July or the first of August and have a talk and settle the question and give out the announcement that they were going to have the Deerskin Dance. The word would be sent out to all the Indians up and down the river, to the Hoopa and Smith River Indians and down the coast as far as Trinidad; and any and all of them of the other tribes could come and see the dance, and none of them would ever be molested. Now they would begin to settle all of their quarrels among themselves by paying; this was done by arbitration in most of the cases, as they would select the ones that were friends to both sides of the ones in dispute. They would argue the case and bring them to a settlement if possible, and if they could not make a settlement they could not come to see the dance. This way things would move along, and all kinds of sayings would be learned and disputed, as those that had no authority would be guessing and oftentimes give out something as coming from some of the head men. All would believe it to be true until it got far enough when the head ones would pronounce it as not authoritive and the false sayings would stop. Another false story would take its place, and this would go on until about the middle of August, when the Talth would get together and set the time for the dance to start. They always put in the fish dam first, it being a part of this great festival.

The one that handles the putting in of the fish dam is known as Lock, and the fish dam is called La-og-gen. Lock selects one other of the high priests and one girl of equal high birth, and the three go to a secluded place out on a high mountain from which place they can have a good view of the surrounding country, and there the girl makes a small fire and is given instructions of how and what to do. The other man is also directed what to do. Lock unrolls his emblems, which is a closely woven scroll that is absolutely waterproof, and takes from it the roots that he burns slowly over the fire that the maiden keeps burning. These roots are burned as an incense and have a sweet odor as they burn, and while they are burning Lock prays and sings to God to give him health and power to carry through all the hardships of putting in the dam. They remain here for two days and nights, then go back down the river to where the fish dam is to be placed. There they land with their boat and stop at a very large rock which is close up to the water's edge and [by] a large creek of clear pure water which enters into the river just at and a little below this large rock.

In the middle of the night the maiden gets wood and starts a small fire and fixes things for Lock and his helper. This girl is a virgin of purity. She goes across the river and bathes herself and dresses her hair, using her Indian knife like a comb, which she carries fastened to her wrist, until her hair is dry and glossy; then she lets it hang loose, wearing a band around her head made of beads which keeps the hair from falling over her face, just coming to the jaw, and if at any time the hair comes over her face, she strokes it back with her Indian comb, but she never touches her hair with her hands. After she has bathed and dressed, she goes to the lodge and lies down and sleeps until late in the morning, when Lock and his helper come to the lodge and lie down and sleep until late in the morning, when Lock-nee and his helper come to the lodge, when the three of them all take a bath, and then eat for the first time since they started. None of them are allowed any water and will not be allowed to drink any for many days yet. Some of these people would start in looking fine, and when they came out they would often look like a walking skeleton; they would soon regain their flesh, although sometimes they never would regain their normal condition.

These three keep themselves secluded, and no one has seen or heard of them, but all are anxiously waiting to hear the word. After they have had their meal, Lock and his helper go back across to the large rock; then Lock unrolls his scroll, burns some more incense and gives his order to his helper to go out to all the villages and call on as many to come forward and help to put in the fish dam as is needed, and this is the time for them to appear before Lock. Sometimes there will be from one hundred to two hundred young men; no old or sickly ones are wanted. After they all appear before Lock, he assigns to each lot of eight or ten of them the part and amount that they are to do. After this they go home, fix up their provisions and camp outfit, and in about thirty hours' time the river bars in and around this place are alive with Indians and the air is filled with merriment and jokes.

Early in the morning they all start out without eating and cut the small pines that are from two to three inches through at the butt ends. Some will make a fire, and as the others are cutting and packing in, they will take the green pine poles and run them through the fire until they are scorched, then take them out and the bark is peeled off easily. While they are yet hot they split each one in two and four pieces; then others get long hazel withes and run them through the fire, and while they are hot split them in two pieces. Then they take them and the pine pieces and plait them together like mats, leaving the pine sticks about one and two inches apart. These mats when set upon end are about nine feet long, with five or six hazel withes about fourteen inches apart. After they get a mat put together they roll it up, making each mat so that one man can pack it on his shoulder, and at a given time they all carry them down to the river to the place where the fish dam is to be put in. Others get the posts, which are about eleven feet long and five or six inches through. They are all sharpened at one end and made very smooth, all the bark being taken off. Some get the long pole-beams or girders, which are from twenty to twenty four feet long and about six or seven inches through, with the bark taken off.

The girl that carries the true name of God is, during the day, in the lodge or house that is used only on these occasions. This house was kept in good condition at all times, but no one lives in it, except on these occasions, also the sweathouse that Lock sleeps in while this work is going on. In the evening, about dusk, after all the workers have retired for the day, she quietly goes out and crosses the river, as Lock's helper at this time is watching for her and takes the canoe over to take her where

Lock is concealed under the large rock close to the bank of the river; and she gathers a quantity of dry wood by which Lock keeps a small fire burning all through the day, and on which he burns incense. Lock keeps out of sight of all the workers, as they do not want to see him and avoid doing so. Lock gives orders to his helper, directing him so that he can deliver the orders to the different companies of workers. This helper is one that has the birth but has not the secret of the true name of God. Lock gives him all the orders in a low whisper, and this helper is called Lock-nee.

As soon as the girl, whom they call Nor-mer, has finished, the three cross the river to the south side, and after landing they all bathe, there being a secluded place close by where the girl takes her bath; and when they have finished, they proceed to the Lah-wah-alth or house where Lock's wife and his help-er's wife are preparing the only meal that they eat every twenty four hours. After the meal is finished, Lock and his helper go to the sweathouse for the night in which a fire has been started by an old man who was selected to get the wood, and thus the place was warm for the night. Lock and his helper take a smoke and then retire.

Very early in the morning there is a fire made in the sweat-house, and Lock and Lock-nee take a sweat and then go back across the river, Lock going to his secluded place and keeping himself hid so that none can catch even a glimpse of him. The girl also keeps secluded by keeping in the house where the wives of Lock and Lock-nee are, and she is busy fixing her dresses, combing her hair and keeping herself very neat; and what spare time she may have after this, she is making a new dress or skirt from the inner bark of the wild maple that grows on the river. The bark is bleached until white, then plaited and hung to a band that goes around the waist, making it as a skirt, coming down to the ankles. All the workers, which are called Nah-quirlth, are ready to work like beavers getting everything in readiness. No one eats more than one meal a day, and all must be in good health and young before they are accepted to work on the fish dam. The day that it starts and until it is completed must not exceed ten days.

The girl, Nor-mer, now sends Lock's wife or Lock-nee's wife (either one can go) to select for her ten girls, all of which must be of good birth from the middle class or rich, and not more than ten; but if ten cannot be secured, a less number will do. These young girls now come and are called Wah-clure, but they do not see Nor-mer. They remain with their kindred and are drilled and fixed up to be ready for the last day and final finish of the fish dam. Now Lock-nee has selected from the Nah-quirlth, or workers, either five or six to act as managers over the different parts of the work, and these take the bark of the madrone and make a hat which looks very much like an old style plug hat that the white man wears. This is striped and painted in a novel fashion, and these workers are very noticeable as they go from place to place giving instructions to the workers. These plug hat men now select twelve or less boys and put them to making ribbons of bark which they strip off very flowery by painting and carving, also making fancy Indian pipes, carving and painting them very artistically. These boys are called Char-rah, and the pipes and ribbons made by them are put on the top of long slim poles from twelve to fifteen feet long, and are to be used at the finish of the fish dam. These poles have the bark taken off and are clean and white.

All this time Lock has kept himself secreted from the eyes of all the workers, and on the morning of the fifth day, very early, he and Lock-nee go up the mountainside and select the first one of the long beams or stringers that is to be put in on the north side of the river, starting just above the large rock under which he keeps himself secluded up to this time. And when he has selected the one that suits him, he makes a small fire at the roots of the tree and burns his incense, then sits down by the fire and prays to God to give blessings to the whole people with health and plenty. Now all of the workers, knowing the time, and the boys and the men have followed up and are all looking for the posts, twenty two in number, and the rest of the string-ers, which are ten besides the one that Lock selects, making eleven altogether. After Lock has finished with his prayer to God he commences to cut the tree, Lock-nee helping him, and together they cut it down; and when it falls with a crash all the workers shout loudly, "oh-oo," and the whole side of the moun-tain echoes with their voices.

Lock-nee begins to trim off the branches and peel the bark while others come in and help. All the workers are scattered off in different places, each squad looking for posts and the rest looking for stringers and cutting them down, and as each tree fell, they all holler "oh-oo." They take the bark off and trim and sharpen the posts. All these pieces are completed in one day and taken down to the river's edge by evening and before anyone can eat or drink water after all the pieces are finished. Lock and Lock-nee take the lead with the stringers, a rope tied around the large butt end, which is quite heavy timber, and start down the mountain with it, Lock all the while talking in prayer to God; and if the timber stops he prays and talks good, and as he has all his life been so good, that God causes the timber to move along easily. As Lock starts, all the rest follow with their timbers, and all arrive about sunset on the north bank with all the heavy frame-part for the fish dam.

These people while they are working all day are full of jokes, laughing and telling funny stories, and if one has done a mean trick of any kind and others know of it, he is twitted about it; they poke fun at each other continually, yet they all keep good-natured about it, and they are all very witty in their answers. They all smoke during the day, each one using his own pipe, and all have their own buckskin sack to carry his pipe and tobacco in. Now all the timbers are in the water and tied to the bank and left floating, ready for morning. Men and boys now bathe themselves and clean their hair, when all depart for their different camping places, parting with jests and jokes, and eat their only meal in twenty four hours. Lock addresses the girl as "my child," "my daughter" and other endearing terms. After the meal is over Lock and Lock-nee go to the sweathouse to rest and sleep for the night, and in the morning, early, all are out and ready and go down to the river and across in their canoes, they having many of them on such occasions.

Lock now gets the rock for driving the post. This is of granite and flat, from twelve to fifteen inches across and from two to four inches thick, and weighs from fifty to sixty pounds. Only those who use this rock ever have a chance to examine it, and it is said to have been made many generations ago. It is kept hidden in a secret place and only brought to view for this purpose; and all the other tools that are used for every part and purpose in putting in the fish dam (La-og-gen) are hidden in a secret place, not all being in one place, and there are never more than two persons (Lock and Lock-nee) at one time that know where to find them, being handed down from one to another. This rock they call Milth-me-ah-lisi, and in calling for it they say, "Say-yah." The other tools are called by their different names; the hammer they call Tec-wan-ore.

Lock and Lock-nee drive the first two posts, which starts the fish dam; the first one is driven nearly perpendicular. And now the workers have to put up a staging, which Lock climbs upon as the post is long and has to be driven quite deep into the ground. Lock-nee holds the post so as to keep it in place, while Lock takes a mall, and as he raises it he talks to God, using words for lots of salmon and to bless all; and at this he come down with a hard blow, and keeps it up until the first post has been driven to the proper depth. He does not strike his blows fast; each blow is struck slowly. The second post is set at an angle on the downriver side of the first one, set to make a brace against the current of the river; and also the top ends come together so as to leave a fork or crotch at the top which is tied securely together with hazel rope, leaving it so beam-poles can be placed in the crotch and tied securely.

Now when Lock-nee has the second post properly set in place, Lock commences as on the first and drives it down to the proper depth, and after this is done Lock and Lock-nee take the hazel withe and tie it to the first one, leaving the crotch. This being done, Lock passes the mall over to the other workers and drive the rest of the posts, the next two of which are set angling down the river, and the third two are set angling up the river so as to make it in a shape like the old style of a worm fence made of rails; this is also done for the purpose of bracing the whole structure against the current of the river. As soon as the posts are all driven, Lock and Lock-nee place the first long stringer in its right place, which is on the north side of the river; then the workers soon place the rest of them and tie them with hazel withes. Then smaller posts are driven at the corners for each trap. At the corners two posts are driven, one angling down the river, and they are placed so as to leave the crotch, in which a pole is placed. The traps are about twelve feet wide and fourteen feet long, commencing so the center of the first trap will be in the center of the first worm of the main framework, and this is started first on the north side of the river.

Then the posts are all driven for the traps (which are many of them) for the corners and side, and also to brace against the current of the river. The top pieces are placed and braced; then poles are withed to the sides and ends all around each trap. The mat or woven work of small split poles are taken in and placed, unrolled, letting them close up, close to the framework of the structure. These traps are set on the downriver side of the main structure so that all of this mat-work has to be put on the inside of the framework of the traps. Then all of this matting is tied with hazel withes very carefully. These traps are not put up close together; there is a place of about six feet left between each trap so that a canoe can be run between them. This matting is placed all the way across on the upper side of the main frame, except on the south side of the river where there is an open place of about twenty feet in width; this only has the main beam over it and is left so all can pass up and down the river in their boats, and also [provides] a chance for many salmon to pass upriver. They place boards along the main fish dam so as to leave a good footwalk all the distance across the river from one bank to another. They put in a gate at the lower end of fish traps and one at the upper end of each trap, and at this time the water begins to roar so that when close to the dam it is deafening. Now there are so many families to each trap, so the upper gate is closed down and the lower gate is opened.

We are now up to the noon hour of the tenth day, when there is a long pole some twenty to twenty four feet long set just at the south side and end of the fish dam and just on the lower side. On the top of this pole all of the fancy work that the boys have been making is tied, and there is a mound of sand heaped around the foot of this pole to a height of three or four feet and from eight to ten feet across.

Now it is about four o'clock in the afternoon, and Lock and Lock-nee are with the Nah-quirlth, busy as bees putting the final touches to the fish dam. And of all the tribes, the women are the most anxious and are from place to place asking the others how the girl Nor-mer is, if she is well, can she go, and if she is going, when out comes Nor-mer from her place where she has been kept from view all these days. She has in the palm of her right hand a small basket in which is a small piece of acorn dough, and she goes in a swift run on a broad smooth trail in an easterly direction for a distance of five hundred yards to this pole, which she runs up to, facing it; then going around to the right, she sets the basket on top of the mound, close up to the pole. All are watching for her, and as soon as one sees her they all shout at the top of their voices. Then Lock runs to hide, as he does not want to see her at this time. Now she turns and goes back at the same swift speed, and at this time all of the girls that she sent for are in their place where they dance. The ground is all fixed, having been scooped out, leaving a depression some four feet deep and twenty feet across, gently sloping to the center. Nor-mer comes up to the dancers and passes on in a westerly direction down the river until she comes to a woman who has been a Nor-mer before her, and tells her where to turn to the river, where she bathes herself; then turns back and walks to where the girls are dancing, and sits down in front of them and urges them to sing louder and dance faster.

These Wah-clures stand erect, moving the body forward and backward by the action of the knees, raising first one foot and then the other. Nor-mer keeps watch of the sun, and as it is getting low and it is getting time for all to come, she raises to a kneeling position and bids the Wah-clures to sing louder and dance faster. They then move very lively. Nor-mer is the absolute ruler of her people as she is the child of God's own purity. Then comes Lock with Lock-nee closely behind, and thirdly comes the boy, Char-rah, with the same basket that Nor-mer left at the pole and which is now full of water, and as Lock walks up to Nor-mer the girls all drop down and hover over Nor-mer. Then Lock and Lock-nee drop over them; then the boy who has the basket of water lowers his hand and throws the basket, water and all, as high up in the air as he can, and the water comes down over them in a shower. As the boy throws the basket and water up in the air he and all of the boys drop down over the others, hovering over Nor-mer like a swarm of bees hovering over the queen. This is done for her protection, for now come all the workers, each one having a long pole on the top of which are tied the bark ribbons and fancy, carved Indian pipes that the boys made; and as they come running up they form a half-circle around the heap, letting the long heavy poles fall over them with a crash, which is done so quickly that it is very hard to see how it is done; and just as quickly the whole heap raises up out of this place and place themselves in fours for the next move. At this time, if Nor-mer was silly enough she could command every man, woman and child to lie flat on their abdomens and go without eating for another twenty four hours, as all must obey her commands, no matter what they might be.

Now the fish dam is completed and all go to their camps. Nor-mer goes to the lodge with Lock, while Lock-nee secures and takes to her the first salmon taken from the fish dam; and Lock-nee cuts out from the middle of this salmon enough for her supper, while no one else can eat of the salmon until the next day. Everything now becomes quiet for an hour, as they are all taking their evening meal. Then first one, then another will begin to inquire about Nor-mer and her health. Now all depends upon Nor-mer. If she is strong enough she quietly goes out and cleans off the ground this same evening, but if too tired she puts it off until morning. After making her plans she then gives her orders to Lock, and he in return gives it out to the people, and they all begin to prepare. After Nor-mer has cleaned the ground she makes a small fire just in front of the dancers and on which she places the incense roots. Then as the dancers come up and take their places she sits there with her hair hanging loose, down on each side of her face, and with beads over her neck and hanging down over her breast. She has on a white buckskin dress trimmed with beads and shells, all of which are made by her own hands, as we use only of our own make. She does not use feathers of any kind. Nor-mer sits there, a model of beauty with the teachings that have been handed down through the many generations: that if she should, while carrying out her duties, lose her virtue, or disobey any of the laws of her God, that she would be struck dead for doing so.

Now the dance starts, and this is the beginning of the White Deerskin Dance. This place is about ten miles up the river from the place where the White Deerskin Dance is held but is started first at this place after the finishing of the fish dam. Nor-mer starts it here and then all go home, but Nor-mer, Lock, Lock-nee, the girls and the boys remain here, Lock and Lock-nee taking charge of the fish dam, and all stay here as long as the fish dam holds intact, except the last day of the White Deerskin Dance when Lock calls all of them and asks if they want to see it the last day. If they decide to go, not one of them must eat the last day, and all go together and return in the evening, when they all eat. Now all is fun and mirth with all of them that remain at the fish dam, Lock and Lock-nee leading them all in the plays and fun of every nature. Nor-mer stays with Lock and Lock-nee but she now goes out and plays and jokes and has her share of the fun, and all have their regular meals.

This place where the fish dam is put in is called by them Cap-pell, and is a bar of some twenty or thirty acres, high enough so the river never overflows it, and yet it is very level. It is a pretty place, being situated on the south bank of the Klamath River. There are two villages on this pretty spot, one being Cap-pell, which was very large in the ages gone by and which contained a very large number of Indians. The other village was called Sy-ah and was very ancient, being the place where the lodge was situated. The house they stay in is called Lah-wa-alth, and the house where Lock and Lock-nee sleep is called Ur-girk.

I will say to the white race that my people, or any other Indian tribes as far as I know them, do not use the name of our Creator when using profane language, as we would feel it a disgrace to do so, even to think of such a thing. We never use the sacred name of God only in our prayers.

The following are a few expressions sometimes used: "Kee-mol-len-a Ta-ga-ar-a-wah-ma" (bad talk). Pointing the right hand with the fingers extended toward a person and at the same time saying: "Woo-saw-ah," means that the person is badly born, and they never forgive you for this. Another is "Char-reck-quick-cal-lah," and means: "I wish you were in hell," and for this also they never forgive.

Chapter II
The Creation of the World

In a vision, the Indian through his mysterious eyes
Sees yonder in the distant skies,
A scene sublime of the past ages,
That for aye will enchant bards and sages.

On His mighty Throne, high in the infinite realms of Heaven, sat the great ruler of the stars and endless skies, Wah-pec-wah-mow (God). As he peered down through the darkness of a cheerless and lonely space, He created a new world, the earth on which we live. He first made the soil of the earth and placed it in a buckskin sack. He opened the sack and shook the soil from it; it fell down into the chasm of darkness, and Wah-pec-wah-mow could not see anything but the intense darkness. He commanded that the rays of light should penetrate the awful darkness, and there should alternately be night and day, the sun to shine by day and the moon to shine by night, to break the awful stillness of this once dark and cheerless world.

Gazing down from His Throne on high, Wah-pec-wah-mow saw the world he had created was a desolate waste without human life, or life of any kind. He now began the transformation of the new world, and lo, the once barren surface of the earth was clothed in verdure; forests lifted their giant branches skyward; tranquil streams flowed and great rivers wended their way to the ocean.

The first living thing placed upon the earth was the white deer (Moon-chay-poke). The white deer roamed over the hills, mountains, in the valleys and on the plains. He was the pride and dignity of the animal kingdom. This is why the Klamath Indians revere the white deer that is so sacred to their hearts and use the skin as an emblem of purity in one of their greatest festivals, or worships, which is termed in English as, "The White Deerskin Dance." In the Indian language it is called "Oh-pure-ah-wah," which does not mean dance but means one of their most sacred religious festivals.

The next living creature that Wah-pec-wah-mow placed upon the earth was the red eagle, Hay-wan-alth, who has ever since ruled as the monarch of the skies. The Indians prize the feathers of this eagle very highly, and use them in their great festival. In the decoration of their headgear, they take a single feather, fasten it in the hair at the back of the head, arranging it so that it stands straight up. They also use the feathers of the bald eagle, Per-gone-gish, and the gray eagle, Per-gish, sometimes as a substitute for the feathers of the red eagle.

After the white deer and red eagle was placed upon the earth, Wah-pec-wah-mow now created all the other animals of the earth. Some were to roam upon the plains, others in the forests, some to eat grass and others to devour other animals, etc.

Wah-pec-wah-mow did not give our people any single day during the week or month as a day of worship, but gave them a certain season of the year in which to hold their religious ceremonies. This season of worshipful ceremonies usually begins in the month of September, and lasts for several days. It is the season of the year when the water of the rivers and brooks ebb lowest, and the summer is almost ready to wane into the glories of autumn. This season is called "Kne-wal-la-taw," the eighth month of the year, according to our way of reckoning time.

When Wah-pec-wah-mow had finished creating the plant and animal life of the earth, He then created the first real man. He made the first man of the soil of the earth, and placed him in the beautiful valley of Cheek-cheek-alth. This valley was located in a far off northern clime. When the first man was created and he became a living being upon the earth, Wah-pec-wah-mow said to him, "You are a living man." God named this man He-quan-neck. Inspired with the breath of life, He-quan-neck first saw the light of day in this sweet valley of sunshine, flowers, fruits and herbs. Among the growing herbs was the herb walth-pay, which has a forked root. God saw that the man was lonely in this sunny valley, and he was not pleased with his work. Wah-pec-wah-mow now requested He-quan-neck to blow his nose, which he did, and immediately the forked root, or walth-pay, turned into a living woman, Kay-y-yourn-nah. Man now became blessed with a living companion, and for a time they dwelt together in the chaste life of peace and happiness.

Our tradition has been handed down through the long centuries. The first dwelling place of man and woman was far away in a northern clime. It would seem a distant land across the waters from the North American continent that is located in the northern part of the world, which we call Cheek-cheek-alth.

Man and woman in the valley of Cheek-cheek-alth knew no sin; two pure souls were they in this valley of perpetual sunshine and flowers.

The loneliness of two human beings dawned upon Wah-pec-wah-mow, so he decided to have the earth populated with people. He now caused He-quan-neck and Kay-y-yourn-nah to fall asleep, and while they slept He caused the snake to crawl across the woman's bare abdomen. That awakened the sleepers, and this opened their eyes to their nudeness, and thereafter they knew sin. The finer senses of the woman awoke, as she became deeply humiliated at the sight of her naked self; and she began to fasten leaves together from the herb, Cur-poo-sa-gon, out of which she made an apron to clothe herself. Thus the first garment that woman wore was from the leaves of this wonderful plant. This plant grows in abundance along the lower Klamath River and its surrounding regions, and the little Indian girls up to this day like to gather these leaves, rub their face and hands with and wear them upon their heads under their caps. These leaves have a very strong and unpleasant odor.

Wah-pec-wah-mow commanded the man and woman to go forth and bring children upon the earth. A curse fell upon the woman, that she should bear children with pain; therefore every woman after her, through all the long centuries, has had to endure this hardship. The first children were born, some with light hair and fair skin and blue eyes, and some with black hair, dark skin and black eyes; and as they married they would mate with black hair, the others with light hair. And when they left the old land Cheek-cheek-alth they were not so dark; many of them were light-haired, fair and blue eyed.

Wah-pec-wah-mow put a curse upon the snake that it should crawl upon its belly as long as the earth should last.

God's laws were that every man and woman should marry and bring forth children. These people were taught to obey the laws and be honest. They increased in number until they became very numerous, and at that time, they all talked the same language. As time sped by they became very numerous and Wah-pec-wah-mow now caused our people, the Indians, to start on their long journey, away from their native haunts and childhood's land, Cheek-cheek-alth. We do not know how long, but they wandered thus in search of a new land, leaving behind them only a memory of the old land, a land that claims its own no more in life, and like a people in exile they wandered on.

View of a well-traveled Indian path. Photo by Ruth K. Roberts. *(Courtesy Humboldt State University)*

72

Chapter III
The Wandering Tribe

From the land of Cheek-cheek-alth, the mystic Eden of long ago, came our wandering tribe of people who long since inhabited North and South America; for we are all one people. Among them were our leaders, the men who possessed in their secret breasts the true name of God. These men and women in our language we call Talth, and were the High Priests and great rulers who ruled our people. Therefore, we were one of the tribes that was never ruled by a single chief, but by our Talth, or High Priests. Upon leaving the old land the Talth carried with them the forked root, walth-pay (the root from which woman was made), and the stalk of this root as a divine rod of strength, endurance and courage, being used as a saviour of the tribe. With it the Talth would command food for their famished members and bring peace and rest to their weary bodies. The walth-pay stalk kept perfectly green, and blossomed all the while, and the High Priests carried it with them on their long journeys and years of wanderings.

The Talth were the mediators between man and God during their years of hardships and wanderings, and could command for the tribes anything that was needed for human existence. These Priests all possessed the true name of God and were members of the ancient order sometimes termed as "The

American Mysteries." The only members left to survive their ancient order at the present writing is my father, Weitch-ah-wah, now past the century mark several years, an unlettered man who can speak no English, and the other member is myself. In my infancy I was taught all that was good and all that would make for a true and noble womanhood; that there was a God in Heaven who ruled over all; and during my researches throughout I have found nothing better.

When these last two members finish their earthly reign, with us perishes the true name of God to my people. With it has perished from the earth our true Indian laws, our sublime religion, our deeds of chivalry, as rich as the civilized world has ever beheld; also our glorious manhood and womanhood. Immoral, corrupt, tottering, downtrodden and debauched by a superior race, we have perished in that winter night of the transition period. At a single blow our laws were torn asunder; loathsome diseases we had never known crushed out the life and beauty of our physical bodies and demented our spiritual minds with lowly passions. Poisonous spirituous drink has set the brain on fire, degrading man and womanhood. Thus as a race we have perished, and this great land, the richest the world has ever known, the land of our forefathers for so many thousands of years. Now another race is struggling on where our reign has ended. Already our great rulers are at rest, and forever; laureled with the glories of the primeval ages that have passed away in silence. As a nation, like the ancient Egyptians, we have grown old and passed away; we have seen a great civilization rise to the highest of its splendors and pass away to another land beyond recall. Today we see another civilization endowed with a splendor of its own, rising over the debris of the eternal years.

We are all one tribe from the source of the Klamath River to its mouth, and down the coast as far as Trinidad (Cho-ri) and up the coast as far as Wilson Creek, which we call Ah-man. We are classed in two divisions, and term ourselves as Po-lick-la's along the coast and up the river as far as Weitchpec, designated as the lower division of our tribe. From Weitchpec on up the river to its source we term as Pech-ic-la, the upper division of our tribe. We intermarry to a great extent, having the same marriage laws and religious ceremonies, and all our traditions and teachings are the same. We call God Wah-pec-wah-mow, which means in our tongue the father of all, and we do not consider Him as a "which has been so much of the white man's allegory, but as an Invisible Omnipotent Being, who rules this great universe with an all seeing eye, He is everywhere."

Wah-pec-wah-mow is the common name applied to God, used by all classes of our tribe, as the real and true name of God is never spoken. Our high priests, born of the royal marriages, are initiated in the Holy Lodge and are given the true name of God, but they never speak it outside of the lodge; it is only spoken inside after they have gone through a long and secret communion, and then the name is only whispered in the lowest whisper from mouth to ear. This true name is only used by the Talth with profound reverence to the Great Creator in the sacred lodge and in the hallowed lonely places far back on the high mountains where they go to worship in the profound solitudes, away from the gaze of curious people. Our religion has been too sacred, too sublime an ideal to quarrel over; hence we have remained silent through the gloom of so many years and borne patiently the insults on royal society as being heathens. This true name of God, as great as the universe, will never be spoken again. If it should be uttered in a loud and harsh tone of voice, it is said that the earth will tremble, ignite in mighty flames and pass away forever. Ever thus, since the creation of the world, the Talth have handed down our religion and traditions from the old land of Cheek-cheek-alth, from generation to generation. It is the duty of every Indian child to be pious and worship the Great Creator. Our sacred religion is Oh-pure-ah-wah (the White Deerskin Dance), where all the members of the tribes [join] in unison and worship, and entertain our guests with much hospitality.

In our recollections of the past we left the land of our birth (Cheek-cheek-alth) many thousands of years ago with our leaders, the Talth, who were given the true name of God in the old land, and carried with them the forked root, or walth-pay. With this divine rod they commanded food, comfort and peace during their long years of weary wanderings. After we left the beautiful valley of Cheek-cheek-alth, for years we wandered down a European land, always moving toward the south, having our origin in the far north. Over this land we wandered like exiles, we know not how long, as it might have been centuries until we reached the rolling waves of the ocean. Upon reaching this salt water we made boats or canoes, and paddled over the waves until we reached the opposite shore, having crossed the straits in safety.

Having reached this opposite shore, upon this new continent we continued our weary years of wandering, ever on, far on, down this land, always going south as before. We carried the memory through the long ages: the perils of the far north, the huge icebergs, the regal monarchs of the North that floated like ghostships at night on dreamland seas. The splendors of the aurora borealis flickered across the snowy fields, and

through this land of the midnight sun came our brave forefathers. In this land of the frozen North some of our people
were left, the Esquimau [Eskimo]; they were given a language
as they were separated from our sturdy band and emigrated
over the snowy fields, and have long since from this time on
inhabited the land of perpetual ice and snow.

Our tribe would often become weary with travel and become very dissatisfied and would quarrel much among themselves. The Talth would stop after hearing so much grumbling
and build a lodge where their members would hold a meeting
and offer up worship to God, that He would guide them aright,
endow them with power to bring peace among their people,
comfort them in their wants and give them food. After the
lodge meeting and prayer, the Talth would command with the
rod of walth-pay food for their people. The food came to them
in the form of acorn dough, out of which they made bread or
pop-saw. The Indians would never see pop-saw falling to the
ground, but they would find it where the Talth told them to
look, and each one would be compelled to gather up their own,
or they would go hungry. As long as they remained camped in
the same place the pop-saw would come to them, but when
they would break up camp and travel on, the pop-saw would
cease to come and the tribe would grow very hungry and begin
to quarrel again. The Talth would stop after days of fatigue
and hunger, and build another lodge where their members
would worship at the sacred shrine. After the worship, food
would come again in the form of the acorn dough, commanded
with rod of walth-pay. Sometimes the Talth would leave the
camps for several days, during which time the people would
become very restless and discontented, and some of the people
would try to perform the duties of the Talth in their absence,

and some of them would pray to the sun, some to the stars and other idols. The Talth would be very much humiliated upon their return to find their people so corrupt in their worship, and it would take much faithful work to assure peace and order among them again. The Talth would plant the herb, walth-pay, at their stopping places during their travels, and it would readily take root and grow. At almost every stopping place, some of our people were left, and God would give them a language; they would inhabit the locality permanently and branch out to other localities, while our part of the people traveled on until they reached their final earthly home on the Klamath River, which we call Health-kick-wer-roy; and here we found the white race (Wa-gas), and which will be told of in another chapter.

Thus we traveled on down a great continent, leaving behind at our stopping places a portion of our people, which were given different languages. Thus were our languages confounded among the tribes of America, and our tribes became numerous, being scattered over the land of the midnight sun of perpetual ice and snow, over the continent of North America to the equator and regions of perpetual sunshine; and beyond the equator, over the continent of South America to its farthermost southern borders, where we merge into the regions of ice and snow again, our tribes have been scattered. Over this great land we are all one people; however, some of our tribes were far superior to others. We know not how many centuries we wandered, or when we reached our last stopping place on the Klamath River, and where we decided our long journey should end, and that we would make this our final home.

The Wah-tec, Wah-ker-rah, Cor-tep and Pec-wan villages were among our first camping grounds on the Klamath River.

Here we spread our camps and built our first houses long ages ago, and have resided in them and kept them in repair from generation to generation. Some of these primeval houses yet remain in these old villages, haunted with the romance of centuries and the inspiring history of past ages. Upon our first arrival there were a great many of our people, and we began to divide off into different villages and locate along the Klamath River and down the coast as far as Trinidad (Cho-ri), and up the coast to Wilson Creek (Ah-man). The other tribes were placed by Wah-pec-wah-mow in different localities, that all the people might sustain themselves with plenty of game and food, and be kept comfortable.

The Talth kept the walth-pay in commemoration of God's creation of woman and their travels, and planted it in a few selected places back in the lonely mountains. The Talth all know where to find this wonderful herb growing, but it is also fading with the remote ages, as there are only a few Indians left who know where to find it. With them passes away the sacred rites and laws of an ancient nation forever, and the primeval art becomes a thing of the mystic ages.

(Top) *Reck-woy* (old Requa), at the mouth of the Klamath River. (Bottom) Woman being ferried across the Klamath in a white man's boat. Note that the oar locks are not in use, and the boat is being paddled like a traditional dugout. Both photos by Ruth K. Roberts. *(Courtesy Humboldt State University)*

Chapter IV
Traditions of the
Ancient White People

When The Indians first made their appearance on the Klamath River it was already inhabited by a white race of people known among us as the Wa-gas. These white people were found to inhabit the whole continent, and were a highly moral and civilized race. They heartily welcomed the Indians to their country and taught us all of their arts and sciences. The Indians recognized the rights of these ancient people as the first possessors of the soil, and no difficulties ever arose between the two people. Their hospitality was exceedingly generous in the welfare of our people, and all prospered together in peace and happiness, in their pursuit of human existence. After a time there were intermarriages between the two races, but these were never promiscuous. For a vast period of time the two races dwelt together in peace and honored homes; wars and quarrels were unknown in this golden age of happiness. No depredations were ever committed upon the property of their people, as the white people ruled with beacon light of kindness, and our people still worship the hallowed places where once they trod. Their morals were far superior to the white people of today; their ideals were high and inspired our people with greatness. After we had lived with these ancient people so long, they suddenly called their hosts together and mysteriously disappeared for a distant land, we know not where.

We have no memory of their reason or cause why they abandoned their ancient homes where they had dwelt for untold centuries. Wars did not drive them forth, for we loved them more than brothers, and difficulties were unknown between the two people. On leaving they went toward the north from whence we came, and disappeared from our land beyond the northern seas. It was a sad farewell when they departed from this land, for our people mourned their loss, as no more have we found such friends as they, so true and loyal. In their farewell journey across this land they left landmarks of stone monuments on the tops of high mountains and places commanding a view of the surrounding country. These landmarks we have kept in repair down through the ages in loving remembrance. I have seen many of these landmarks myself and often repaired them that they left as a symbol of the mystic ages and the grandeur of a mighty nation that passed in a single season. Oh, how little we know of the depths of the ages gone; how wide, how profound and deep is the knowledge we seek. A monument of stone, a stone bowl, a broken symbol, a hallowed unknown spot, a lodge of ruins: all this makes a golden page glittering with diamonds that trills the emotions with mysterious longings for truth and light in the depths unknown.

When the Wa-gas left this land, they assured my people that they would return to them at some future time. Thousands of years have elapsed since then, and they have not returned; we have waited in vain perchance, for it seems that our cherished hopes are fading. However, some of our people are still looking for the return of the white man. The traditions handed down lead us to believe that the Wa-gas returned to the land of their birth, in the far north, the valley of Cheek-cheek-alth, as their traditions were given to us that their origin was in this same land of Cheek-cheek-alth, as they came down from the North when they came to this land. When the Wa-gas first arrived on this continent they handed down the traditions to us that it was inhabited by a giant race of people when they first came. These giants were represented by the Wa-gas as being very swarthy in complexion, and they used implements so large that no ordinary man could lift them. It was an age when large animals roamed the earth, and it seems the birds and fowls were all very large in size. It appeared to be the first age, and was the age of the giants. The recollections transmitted by the Wa-gas were that these giants were very cruel and wicked. It was said that God became displeased with them and destroyed them and they all perished from the earth. It was also said that God appeared to the High Priest of the Wa-gas and told them that he was going to destroy the giant race and that the Wa-gas themselves would survive upon the earth as a new people. Smaller birds and animals would appear upon the earth for the use of man. Thus the age of giants perished, but the Wa-gas do not hand down any tradition of how they perished from the earth, as my people have no recollections of ever seeing giants. My mother says that our people in ancient times have seen many relics belonging to these prehistoric giants, such as huge stone bowls, stone slabs and other implements so great that our people could not move them. During the ages of rains and wearing away of the earth, these implements have been buried so deep and have sunk into the earth, is the reason we cannot find them today. The Indian name for the giant race is Pah-pel-ene, which means people that have all died and passed away.

When the Wa-gas returned to Cheek-cheek-alth it is supposed they found a ladder in this beautiful valley which extends from earth to Heaven, and climbed it to Werse-on-now (Heaven), where they dwell with God. All the half-castes with the exception of a few went away with the Wa-gas, and nearly all those that were three-quarters Indian remained with our people. This is said to be the reason why some of our people are very fair. Some of the Indians are still looking for their return to the earth. When they come back it is believed that peace and happiness will reign supreme again over this great land, and all evil will be cast out. When the present race of the white people made their first appearance upon the American continent, we believed it was the Wa-gas returning, and a hearty welcome was extended to them; and there was great rejoicing among our tribes. But soon the sad mistake was discovered, to our sorrow, when the men began to debauch our women, give whiskey to our men, and claim our land that our forefathers had inhabited for so many thousands of years; yet not a single [white] family has ever been driven from their house on the Klamath River up to this day. We no longer termed them as Wa-gas, but as Ken-e-ahs, which means foreigners, who had no right to the land and could never appreciate our kindness, for they were a very different people from the Wa-gas. They had corrupt morals that brought dissolution upon our people and wrought the horrors of untold havoc.

When the Indians first reached the Klamath River there were large prairies and vast tracts of grassy land, which have since grown up in timber and underbrush. Many of the prairies were set on fire and burnt off every year during the dry seasons, which kept the timber from growing up every fast.

The Klamath emptied into the ocean at Wilson Creek, about six miles north of where it now goes into an ocean at Reck-woy. There were high bluffs of rocks between the river and the ocean all the way from Reck-woy to Wilson Creek which kept the river in its course to Ah-man (Wilson Creek), where it emptied into the ocean. The river was said to have kept in this course until our Christ caused the mighty rocks to split open, and the waters of the river rushed ahead to the ocean at Reck-woy, where it has ever since flowed into the ocean.

The traditions handed down say that the land north of Redwood Creek, where it goes into the ocean, extended far out into the sea to the large rock that is now known to the white people as Redding Rock; has continually washed away [and that it] leaving this rock jutting up from the ocean depths, [to] be seen for many miles over the surrounding area of land and sea. This rock is located at a distance of about ten miles from the shore and is called by the Indians Sa-quan-ow. This name translated into English means an acorn pestle, a conical shaped stone, carved out of granite and used to pound acorns and grass seeds into the finest flour. Long ages ago Redding Rock extended up from the ocean to a great height, and from a distance appeared to be a huge Sa-quan, or pestle, hence its name. After ages of erosion the massive rock became surrounded by water, and the receding bluffs left it alone out in the ocean, where its greater portion has crumbled and fallen beneath the waves as it is seen today. The Indians still call it

Sa-quan-ow.

There has been but little change in the channel of the Klamath River, except at its mouth, since our arrival in this land. In olden times the channel of the river was very deep and clear and much narrower than it is now, and large bars of alluvial soil composed its banks, where luxuriant grasses grew; and upon these lowlands during the winter months great herds of deer and elk would graze, coming down from the snow-covered mountains. The channels of the large creeks and tributaries of the river, such as Blue Creek (Ur-ner), Tec-tah and Pec-wan, have practically never changed, as they still flow into the river in the same places. Where the Trinity River flows into the Klamath River, it has made but little or no change during the passing ages as has been handed down to us.

We have no word of severe earthquakes in our regions, but have had slight shocks from time to time throughout the centuries. We have no tales of any great damage ever done by earthquakes, and our people never held any fear of tremors of the earth. But my people tell of great tidal waves that have swept our country. They say a long time ago one swept up the Klamath River to the mouth of the Trinity River, a distance of over forty miles, and did great damage, as it swept away houses; and thousands of our people were drowned and carried away by the rolling waves of the ocean. So few of our tribe were left that they were well-nigh exterminated. Many smaller tidal waves have swept over the coast where the destruction was not so great.

They tell of epidemics that came up the river and laid us low in the devastation of life. Thousands of our people would pass away in a single season; they would die so fast that they could not be buried, and many of the bodies would be thrown into the river. The only way we could keep the whole tribe from complete devastation by the ravages of these dreadful diseases was to abandon the dead and leave the river and go back into the high mountains; and there we built bark houses and remained until the snow and cold would compel us to retreat to the lowlands again. In our mountain home we subsisted on wild game, berries, pine nuts, roots and herbs. Some of our people would have such a terror of the fatal diseases that they would refuse to return to their homes and would brave the fierce storms of the cold winter until they were convinced that all dangers had ceased. In our traditions of the passing centuries, many of these epidemics have almost devasted the land of human life. During one of these contagions it was said that the children would go down to the river to swim and would lie down in rows from six to twelve in number upon the sand, as if they were alive and had been placed there by careful hands; but they would be in their eternal sleep, contagion having overtaken them.

Hoopa Store, c. 1883. By supplying the basic necessities for survival in the white man's world, stores such as this one also served as gathering spots, post offices and social centers. Kerosene lamps, shoes and clothing were sold along with food.

Chapter V
Time and Names

We have ten months for one year, and four seasons, as follows:

1st month:	Caw-cha-witch.
2nd month:	Nan-ah-wetch.
3rd month:	Nachk-sa-witch.
4th month:	Chaw-na-ah-wertch.
5th month:	Mere-i-yaw.
6th month:	Cauh-chow.
7th month:	Chere-wer-ser-a.
8th month:	Can-na-wal-at-tow.
9th month:	Cher-mick.
10th month:	Wealth-ah-wah.

Spring:	Key-atch-ker.
Summer:	Kis-sa-no.
Autumn:	Ka-yock-ka-muck.
Winter:	Cah-mah.

We lose time in our count each year, so we throw in or stop counting until the time comes around to start again. The Klamath Indians are good in counting and can count up into the thousands. We count ten, and ten tens for one thousand. All of our counting is done by whole numbers; we have no fractions. All the women have to count and count closely in weaving baskets in order to make the designs come out correctly. We have astronomers, called Haw-getch-neens, and they keep close observation of the sun, which we call Ca-chine-wan-now-slay. Day we call Ca-chine; the moon, Nas-cha-wan-now-sloy (this means the night sun).

English Names	Klamath Indian
An old woman	Ca-par-a
Young women	Way-yun
Little girl	Wer-yes
Baby	Oaks
Boat or canoe	Yatch
House	Och-lum-ilth
Come in the house	Och-la-may
How do you do, my friend?	I-ya-quay Nec-tor-mer
Me or I	Neck
Yes	A
Fire	Metch
Mother	Calk
Father	Tat, or Tatus
Grandfather	Peach
Grandmother	Gooch
Old man	Ma-we-mer
Young man	Pay-girk
Large boy	Che-na-mouse

Small boy	May-wah
Mother-in-law	Cha-win
Father-in-law	Par-ah
Sister-in-law	Netch-nah
Brother-in-law	Weitch-tay, or Tay
Uncle	Jim
Aunt	Tool
Klamath River	Health-kick-wer-roy
Redwood timber	Keilth
Mermaids	Squerth-tuck
Silver Salmon	Nep-puoy
Steelhead Salmon	Squalth
King Salmon	Ah-pus
Hookbill Salmon	Cha-goon
Grizzly Bear	Nick-witch
Sea or Ocean	Pis-calth

The Bald Hills we call Cho-lu contain many hundreds of acres of open land, high up where one can see as far as the eye can reach in all directions.

There is another species of the Salmon caught in the Klamath River, the English name of which I do not know, but we call it Ra-gawk.

In the year 1850 my people had never heard of the present white race, and we were then making our fires with two pieces of wood, one the willow and the other of hardwood.

My mother and father never learned to talk English, so I talk to them only in our own language.

Oregos, rock at the mouth of the Klamath just downstream from *Reck-woy*, believed to be a transformed Spirit Being. Photo by Ruth K. Roberts. *(Courtesy Humboldt State University)*

Chapter VI
Death and the Spirit Land

There is a large and silent river that flows through the shadowy vale of death. On the banks of this awful and mysterious river dwells an old woman, called Sye-elth, and she keeps at her side a large dog, Chish-yah (the common name for dog).

When an Indian dies, if he has led a dishonorable and wicked life, a broad path leads his soul down to the banks of the river to the very door where the old woman lives in her house. When the wandering soul reaches her door, the Chish-yah tries to drive it back to the dead body, but the old woman fights the dog off. And if she is successful in her efforts, she takes charge of the miserable soul and sends it on to the opposite side of the river, in the shadowy land of endless anguish. If the dog is successful in fighting the soul back, it returns to the dead body, where life is regained and the person lives again. This seldom occurs, and only where the body lives in a state of coma and is supposed to be dead, but after a few hours comes out of that state and revives into life again. The Chish-yah is seldom successful, as a case rarely occurs. This is why the Indian never likes to scold or treat the dog badly.

The old Indians do not like to look at a photograph or to have their photographs taken because they say it is a reflection or a shadowy image of the departed spirit, O-quirlth. They do not like to see spirits, but they say they have often seen them. This is the reason they turn their backs on the camera and object so strongly to having their pictures taken. Often have my people been ridiculed for their strange actions, but they have a reason for every one of them. If the civilized man could only respect the reasons and simple ways of the highest type of primitive man as much as primitive man venerates his civilization.

When the spirit comes back to the tired and weary body, and that body lives again, that person is said to meet a very unfortunate existence. It is said he is never satisfied with earthly things again. He is very restless and unhappy, as nothing can satisfy his longing soul, and always meets death suddenly.

On the shore of this mysterious River of Death awaits a young man, Pa-ga-rick, in his canoe; he is always ready to receive the soul from the old woman as she hands it into his care. His canoe is similar in shape and size to the earthly Indian canoes, with the exception that, one may note carefully, all the [earthly] canoes contain in the bow a knob in the center, some three feet back from the bow, which is the heart; and they say it is the life of the boat. Also, the canoe the Indians use is burned inside and out, and polished smooth. The canoe that Pa-ga-rick uses for the crossing of the souls is neither burned or polished and has no heart; therefore it is called the dead boat, Merm-ma. In olden times no Indian would venture out in a boat upon the water that did not contain a heart, as they said it was lifeless and would be sure to sink or some disaster befall it. We call our canoe here on earth Yatch.

Sye-elth [stands] just on bank of this dark River of Death,

Char-reck-quick-werroy, where she gets the souls away from the dog. She takes it to the water's edge and gives it to the man in the dead boat. He takes the soul into his canoe, paddles it across those silent waters, the awful stillness, the awful fear of death. When the canoe, Merm-ma or Nee-girk, either name, touches the opposite shore, Pa-ga-rick takes the soul, O-quirlth, and banishes it into exile, exile without an end or example in story, and leaves it in a wilderness. In this wilderness it is damp, a constant gloom is cast, dark and fearful clouds forever flit, cold winds forever howl and shriek the agonies of hell.

In this terrible wildness, the souls of the condemned men and women sustain their misery upon bitter berries, bitter grasses and roots, and cannot die. They had never lived but a wasted life upon earth; therefore they can wait to die, as souls never die. These wretched souls [have waited] since Time began, and I think the time is sad and heavy through all the weary ages, since they go wandering, hollering, moaning, weeping and wailing, grieving grief without an end, and suffering pain, intense pain that knows no ending. Thus Wah-pec-wah-mow, the Great God, has seen fit to punish his disreputable children until the judgement day.

Sye-elth, this old woman, is the Satan of my people; Chish-yah, the dog, is our Guardian Angel. This old women is our evil doer who is always trying to influence the Indians away from the path of rectitude. She hovers about them in life unseen, seeking out their weak points, that she may lead them [to] evil ways and vindicate her cruel wants upon their death by taking their souls down the broad path to the wilderness of anguish. Fearing her powers, fearing the Unhappy Land, the Indians struggle to live simple and peaceful lives, and never quarrel over their religion.

The wretched souls banished into the wilderness of anguish do not quarrel with one another, as they are too wretched in their own agony to concern themselves about others.

The Indian seeing a vision of the Unhappy Land tries to live the simple and honest life, near to nature and their nature's God. However, there is not a tribe, however well-guarded, but some and sometimes many stray afar from the path of rectitude and is led into the wilderness of anguish by their cruel Satan, Sye-elth.

My people believe that there will sometime come a chance for them to become regenerated, or reborn, so that many of them will be given the opportunity to recompensate for the wickedness of their former lives and [be] given a chance to live good clean lives in their second birth. Thus, given the opportunity by God when they die again, they will be rewarded in going to Heaven, Werse-on-now. However, if the ones given the opportunity of being saved, do not live lives of integrity after their second birth they are cast off and destroyed forever.

The Indians who had always lived the life of integrity on earth, when they die, their souls or spirit travels a narrow and winding trail which takes the soul north, to a land far away from their native haunts. This far northern clime is said to be the old land of Cheek-cheek-alth, where the spirit finds a ladder that reaches from earth into Heaven. As the spirit climbs the ladder to Heaven, it reaches God on that infinite shore, where it dwells forever in flowery fields of light, staying together with the Master in peace and love, and joining the spirits of those that have gone before them.

Can you of the Christian faith comprehend why we take so

Yurok woman in front of traditional plank house at *Reck-woy*. Note that the house is being propped up and is probably in disuse. Photo by Ruth K. Roberts. *(Courtesy Humboldt State University)*

97

Dance ceremonies such as this attracted spectators from the mouth of the Klamath far up the river from present day Crescent City (the Tolowa) and from Hoopa Valley (the Hupa). Spectators wore their best clothes, the dancers their finest feather regalia. Photo by Ruth K. Roberts. *(Courtesy Humboldt State University)*

kindly to your own belief? Yet we think that ours is the most perfect; and yet you call us savage. We love our God almost akin to sadness and are always ready with a prayer-offering, be it midday hour or in the hours of the silent night. The Indian in all his savagery could never blaspheme the sacred name of his Creator in man's builded houses or in his daily life, as he is a child of nature, akin to nature's God, [believing] that the Divine Being is the beacon light of his soul, showing him life beyond the grave and [leading him] into the flowery fields of light and love, on that infinite shore, into the glories of Heaven.

The Indian through his long centuries of barbarism battled with the environments of barbaric man. In his childlike nature, he taught his sons and daughters to be kind, courageous, self-denying, industrious, and above all [to have] integrity that could not be questioned. Fathers, brothers and cousins guarded the mothers, daughters and sisters, that not one of them may stray into a life of shame by the passions of designing men. Woman was manifestly the upholder of her race, loved as the unassuming creature who gave to the race clean-limbed and vigorous men. But ah, the sad knell, the approach of civilized man, and his crushing hand of debauchery, to the sorrow of our race; and our laws have long since been demolished, and with it our true religion, our life-blood, our all. Out of the gloom of saddened years, rising in scattered remnants, like the children of Israel that have lived without a country for many weary centuries, we are struggling to gain our own once more: freedom to worship God in our own way and to be allowed to become citizens of this, our own glorious country.

When an illegitimate child is born, mother and child lived in disgrace, and after death could never reach the kingdom of Heaven, but traveled that broad road which leads to the wilderness, being forever lost. During their life, the mother is always addressed as Caw-haw, a name that reminds her always of her disgrace every time she is spoken to, and the child is always reminded of its unwedded mother. Sometimes the unfortunate mother may marry, but she is always known as Caw-haw as long as she lives and cannot take the name of the man she marries.

Those who sought unscrupulous brawls were low and disgraced; all traveled after death the broad road to Satan and are never given an opportunity to go to Werse-on-now. There are many of the miserable souls who lived a wasted life on earth, only to enter in the Spirit Land, the wilderness of anguish.

In marriage the wife takes the husband's name and the husband takes the wife's name, just as an exchange of names and the family names are handed down from one generation to another. This is done by giving the name to a daughter, son, cousin, etc., either the mother or father's name on both sides of the family. Sometimes the generation dies out and there are none left of a near kindred. In this case they sometimes give the name to a close friend; this custom is followed more by the high families. As an example, some years ago an old man lived in the Pec-wan village; his name was Ta-poo-sen. He died some thirty years ago. And at this writing a middle-aged man is living in the Cor-tep village who adopted his name after his death, and he is known to everyone as Ta-poo-sen. There are quite a number of Indians living at the present time who have taken the names of deceased relatives or friends. The deceased has been laid at rest for at least one year before anyone takes his or her name.

The Klamath Indians are very much prejudiced against one taking their own life. They look down on the act, and if one should take his own life, which we call o-motch-ser-mer-yer, there is no chance for them to be saved. And they go down the broad road that leads to the old woman, and she gives them over to the man in the boat, and he takes them over and leaves them in the wilderness, where they live in misery until the judgement day, and then are destroyed forever, there being no salvation for them. And the family will be looked down upon for many generations to come, and held back in taking part in any of their social functions. The children will be shunned by their playmates.

The Indian seldom commits suicide, and will avoid self-destruction by wishing that some wild animal will take them while they sleep; and of such cases they tell some very weird and touching tales. There was a girl taken by a wild animal, of which reference is made in another chapter. Another was a young man of good family belonging to the Pec-wan village, and he wanted to marry a girl of the upper division. The young woman refused him, and this nearly broke his heart, so he went back into the mountains all alone. And there he busied himself by trapping and hunting until he had accumulated great riches of valuable furs and other things, and was there for a number of years when he returned to his home. He never married, and lived to be an old man, and all the children called him grandpa. As he became old he also became blind, but the children all loved him, and any of them were always ready to lead him wherever he wanted to go; and he was always ready to give blessings to the newly married couples and to newly born babies. He always wanted to visit where there was a newborn baby. This old man would sweep and keep clean the village, even down to the creek and river, feeling and sweeping the whole day long, and when he was tired some of the children would lead him home; and he thus lived to a good old age. So this is the way it would go in accordance with their belief in the hereafter. A Klamath Indian would never commit suicide, if there was any way to prevent it, on account of the stigma it would place on the family.

The Klamath Indian grave is made about two-and-a-half feet deep. They take redwood or Douglas spruce boards which they place in the oblong square, as they never nail or fasten the boards together. Placing one wide board in the bottom and boards on each side, with short ones fitted in across the ends, the coffin [is] made ready to receive the corpse.

At the time of death the body is washed with the branches of the wormwood dipped into a basket of water and brushed over the entire body, never allowing their hands to touch the body at any time if it can be avoided. After the body has been bathed in this manner, it is clothed in the regular clothing and laid out for burial, wrapped in a blanket and placed on a wide plank, where it is left for twenty-four hours. After it has been laid out, friends and relatives gather around it in prayer, and the director of the funeral is given a large bunch of flag-grasses which he takes in his hand and holds over the blaze of the fire to ignite; and with flaming grasses, he stands over the body, waving it back and forth [and] sprinkling the falling ashes over the body. This is the final blessing, given with solemn prayer, the same as anointing the body with holy water.

The Indians remove the corpse from the house (the reasons being explained in another chapter) by making an opening in the wall on the left-hand side of the door by which they go out, as they never carry a corpse through the door. The personal belongings and bedding, also the dishes he has used during his illness, are taken out through this opening upon the removal of the body, and everything is burned in a large fire made outside of the house.

With great ceremony and mourning, the corpse is carried out of the house on the same plank it was laid out on. At the grave they unroll the corpse from the blanket, the clothing being cut open down the front, the body washed again, this time without the removal of the clothing. This final bath is a solution of the ho-mon-ah roots pounded fine as powder and then put into a basket of water. This shrub or plant is much different from the wormwood, and it is considered one of their best herbs for fumigation and disinfecting purposes. After the bath is completed the body is again wrapped in the blanket and laid carefully down in the grave. The funeral director, as before, burns a bunch of flag-grasses over the body, allowing the ashes to fall over the remains. Articles they wish to place in the grave with the body are put into the grave, and the plank that the body was carried out on is fitted into the top of the coffin as the top covering. Three or four persons take part as pallbearers in taking the body to the grave. The body is laid with the head directly to the west, as they say when the judgement day comes, all the Indians will rise up out of their graves facing the rising sun, and those who are worthy will rise in glory to the splendors of glory, to the Heavenly Father above.

In this grave, things of little value are placed, things usually belonging to the deceased. When things of value are placed in the grave, it is broken up, which destroys the value of the article.

The coffin is covered over with earth, and after this, being completed, they take two stones about eighteen inches long by twelve inches wide; one is placed at the head and the other one at the foot of the grave. On the top of the stones, directly in the middle of the grave, they place another wide plank about six feet long and eighteen inches wide. Stakes are driven on each side of this plank, in the middle, and with a rope an Indian made they tie the board to the stakes so it cannot be removed without some difficulty. After this has been completed, some dry sand is sprinkled around the grave, covering it completely to the sides of the wide board; this is done so the Indians can immediately detect if anyone has molested the grave. The reason why the Indians always have their graveyards near the village or dwelling-places is to keep the wild animals away from the grave. Sometimes the mourners place large baskets on the grave, sometimes two and often many more; there is no certain number to use. They are turned upside-down, close-up to the sides of the plank and on the ground around the grave. These baskets are made secure by driving a stake through the center of them and into the ground. On top of the plank they lay basket-plates, also acorn baskets. Around the grave a picket fence is made by driving the pickets into the ground. A strong hazel withe is tied around them about twelve inches below the tops. At the middle of the head and the foot of the grave a strong post is driven into the ground that stands much higher than the tops of the pickets. To these posts a crossbeam is fastened or tied, and on this a number of deerskins are hung. These skins are dressed whole, with the hair left on, and the body and head are stuffed with weeds. The head is elevated almost perpendicular, with the body and the legs left hanging straight down. Some of the clothes that have been worn by the deceased are also hung on this crossbeam, which makes quite a display and would lead one to believe very strongly that many valuables were also placed in the grave.

During and after the burial is completed, all the close relatives of the deceased weep and wail mournful songs, saying, "Good-by child," or calling out whatever relationship they were to the deceased. The mournful wail of an Indian mourner is so intensely sad that the surrounding sky and earth seem weeping with the sorrowful ones.

After the burial rites have been completed, those who had taken part in the burial go into the family sweathouse, where they wash their entire bodies from the basket of water containing the ho-mon-ah solution, and sweat themselves in the sweathouse. After this they all go to the river, taking the basket of solution with them, and bathe with it in the river. Upon returning to the house they all change their clothes, except the one who dug the grave; he puts on the same clothing and wears it for five days longer before he is free from the burial rites. His duty now is to kindle a fire, which he keeps burning about a couple of hours each evening close by the foot of the grave. This fire is made between the hours when the first long shadows are cast and the twilight gathers into the darkness of the night. They say the flickering of the firelight keeps them from seeing the O-quirlth, the spirit of the departed one, which is said to hover over the grave and around the home for five days after death. After five days have elapsed, the spirit departs either to Heaven or to the wilderness, according to what kind of life the deceased has lived. The friends and relatives of the deceased will weep, wail and pray that his spirit will go the narrow road, to the old land, Cheek-cheek-alth, where it will find the ladder and climb to Werse-on-now (Heaven). Sometimes a bitter enemy of the deceased will pray and hope the departed spirit will go the road to Sye-elth, where she hands him over to the man in the dead boat, [who] takes the spirit across the river and banishes it into the wilderness.

The light of the fire keeps the Indians from seeing the spirit when it leaves the grave, as they never wish to behold spirits. However, they claim, in spite of their caution, the spirit is sometimes seen by the Indians. They say when it leaves the body it looks like a shadow image of the person passing off. They claim a photograph resembles the spirit of the dead, and the old Indians never want to look at it, as they never wish to be reminded of the spirit.

The walls and the floor of the room which the person used is scrubbed everyday with the ho-mon-ah solution; also, whatever furniture there is in the room is gone over very carefully with the disinfecting process, and [this] is kept up for five days until the spirit departs. The family lives in the same room as usual, but Cah-ma-tow, the gravedigger, has his own separate bed in the room. He fixes a small board for himself on which his meals are served separate from the family, and dines by himself. The morning of the fifth day he arises earlier than usual, making a broom of the boughs of the Douglas spruce, and sweeps the floor of the house nice and clean. He burns the roots of the ho-mon-ah, which fumigates the house; and with solution made of the same plant, he scrubs the floor and goes over all the woodwork in the house for the last time. After this is finished he gathers up all the things he has used during the five days, the baskets of solution, his small board table, etc., and takes them all to the sweathouse. Here he takes the solution and washes his hands and entire body; and after he has finished bathing, he takes the baskets and clothes he has worn up the hill away from the river to a thicket and hangs them all up in a small tree, where he leaves them to the elements to decay. He then comes back and sweats himself thoroughly, afterwards plunging into the river, and comes out cleansed of any foul disease he may have contracted in handling the dead body.

The Indians get or hire anyone who is willing to do the burial, as it is not necessary to be a relative or even a well-known friend of the family.

During the five days the opening in the house where the dead body was taken out is left open, as the family and friends never use or go near the regular door of the house during this period. After five days have elapsed the opening in the wall is sealed up tightly, leaving no trace that an opening was ever made in the wall. They never leave the gap for another case, as the Indian never wants to be reminded that another death may occur in his household.

It has often been expressed by the white man that when a funeral is held, every man, woman and child in the village attends the funeral. This is far from being true, not any more than the funeral of a white man. Near-friends and relatives of the deceased may attend, while a great many others in the village will go about as usual, not even pretending to know that a funeral is being held. Of recent years, the white man is allowed to help with the burial if he chooses. Valuable articles of the dead are not buried with them, as is generally believed by the white theologist; instead only mere trifles of either little or no value are placed in and upon the grave.

When an Indian is very wealthy or rich, and has a family of several children, he sometimes divides his fortune equally among them, of course always making provision for his wife as long as she lives and remains single. Sometimes he had a favorite son or daughter to whom he leaves his entire fortune, disinheriting his other children. The Indian legacy is bequeathed to whom he chooses, and his will cannot be broken. In some cases the wife's wealth is just as great or even greater than her husband's. She divides her wealth among her children as she chooses, the same as her husband.

When husband and wife have been wedded a number of years and have reared a large family, upon the death of the husband the wife cuts her hair close to her head and burns it. She keeps her hair cut close to her head, and is called Ca-win until some one proposes marriage to her, when she lets it grow out to its natural length again. If she refuses the offer of marriage, after her hair has grown over two inches in length, she is addressed as Care-rep. This name explains itself, that she is a widow and has had an offer of marriage but has refused it. The sisters and daughters of a deceased man sometimes cut off a part of their hair during their period of mourning for him.

Chapter VII
Through the Pearly Gates
of Heaven

Long time ago a mother and father resided in Cor-tep village, in the house of Metch-cher-rau, located about a half-mile up the river from the old Klamath Bluffs Store. They had two good children, a boy and girl, the girl being the eldest. Brother and sister loved each other divinely; their devotion was more divine than human hearts had ever known. Their parents were very wealthy, and were married of a good marriage ceremony of the wealthy class. Metch-cher-us-ah-may, the sister, was the most lovely of all the girls of the tribe; besides her rare beauty she possessed a kind and loving disposition beyond comparison. When she had grown to womanhood, she went to the Talth, or High Priests, and asked them if she might join the sacred lodge. But the High Priests sadly shook their heads, and said they could never admit her to the sacred lodge, as her parents were not of high birth, and that she was not of the Talth marriage. Her pleadings were in vain, and she turned away from the lodge deeply grieved, realizing that she had been barred forever from the sacred altar of the High Priests, and that she could never become a Talth, or mix with the Priests. It would be useless to plead again; she was denied their solitary ways of worship, and she could never sit in their lodge and kindle their sacred fires. Her proud spirit was grieved and wounded almost beyond human endurance; a great battle now waged within her heart: that God Himself might take her above her humble birth and station in life, that she might rise in greatness beyond the glories of the High Priests, as she would walk in Heaven, and they on earth, until death claimed its own.

She would rise from her bed about four o'clock every morning while the village was yet dark and sleeping, and go to gather wood, praying as she gathered the branches in her basket; and when it was filled she would return to her house, praying all the while, and leave the wood there long before anyone was astir to see her at work. After this task was done, she would go to a high rock on the hillside in a small creek, a short distance from the Cor-tep village, where she would spend the entire day on top of this rock, praying to God and weaving baskets. There was a small basin of water in this solid rock, close by where she sat, which she used to keep her basket materials wet as she worked them. The rock was very high when she sat upon it long ages ago, but it is nearly covered with earth at this present writing. At eventide she would return to her home. So earnest were her prayers, so patient was her humble soul in waiting, that she prayed a number of years on top of this rock, ere her prayers were answered in Heaven. Praying in the great solitudes of a vast creation, she never faltered, but prayed on to the Heavenly Father that he might give her strength and courage to become far more pure than any that had ever lived on earth before her, that she might rise as a virgin of purity above her people, leaving in her footsteps the holy halo when she had passed from the earth away to the realms of Heaven above.

This beautiful woman, made far more beautiful in her purity, the sublime whiteness of her soul shining forth, transfigured beyond the glories of womanhood. After these years of faithful prayer, dark suspicions and intrigues rose from the people of the village, as her actions seemed so strange. And why should one so beautiful always be solitary? No doubt some youth was yearning for the beauty of her arms to encircle him; the sweetness of her smile had fascinated all, as her sweetness was so perfect. She was always alone, and there did not seem to be anything to prevent it. Day by day the village folks grew more restless in their surmises, in their doubts and fears for her safety, and they brought the tale to her parents, who accused her of clandestine meetings with some unscrupulous man who no doubt had ruined her virtuous womanhood; and [they said] that they would soon cast her from the village in disgrace if she persisted in her lone walks to the woods in the early morning and kept her solitary place on the rock during the day.

How unjustly we sometimes accuse the innocent; how deep the wounds we thrust that we mourn after years in sad regret of our cruel words spoken when God has taken them away and they no longer soothe our dark afflictions. Rising in wounded pride once more, she proclaimed her innocence, that her soul was free from this preposterous accusation. So long she had been patient and true, so long she had denied herself the pleasures and passions of earth, directing her thoughts to lofty ideals she could proudly verify when the time came for her to go to the Throne on High, when the Heavenly Father would call her to the Eternal Home. She said she could not tell her parents and the people her reasons and account for her actions now: why she would always get up so early in the morning to get her wood, and why she spent the entire days upon the rock. But she assured them that they would all know at a future time why she spent so many hours of solitude; this time would be when God called her Home, and they would repent for their cruel accusations.

During these years of patient prayer, brother and sister met in loving companionship of sympathy, and in exchanging the prayer of their ambitions. Metch-cher-us-ah-chene, the brother, knew the secret prayers of his devout sister, and by them his thoughts were directed to higher ideals. Pledged by solemn vows, he would never make known her secret prayers until she herself was ready for him to do so. They prayed together, he alone at his fishing, she alone on the high rock at her basket-weaving, their prayers united. However, his faith in God was not so strong, and his prayers were not so earnest as his sister's; and the future years left him alone on earth to mourn her loss.

Metch-cher-us-ah-may heeded not the warnings of her people, as she continued to rise in the early morning hours to gather her wood before the light of day, so that no one would feast their unscrupulous eyes upon her while she was at work. After this task was done, she would go as usual to the high rock and weave baskets the whole day through until evening, saying her prayers all the while.

Springtime had come when all the leaves of the trees and shrubbery had grown up, and the sap of the maple tree was full. Metch-cher-us-ah-may peeled the maple tree of its bark and took the inner layers that grow upon the surface of the hard wood of the tree, and out of this bark she made a dress of beautiful fringes, softer than silk itself, as it hung in ripples about her body. From the yellow-hammer she plucked its beautiful golden feathers and made a cape in which she wrapped her shoulders and arms. Springtime waned and midsummer came; it was the last summer that she would spend on earth, as her faithful prayers had been answered and she was now ready to be taken to Werse-on-now (Heaven). Ah, she could now mount to the glories of Heaven without passing through that dark and shadowy vale of death. The High Priests, who had turned her away from the sacred lodge, together with the other people, would all have to die, and the earth would give them a grave. Their hands would never touch her body, the earth would give her no grave; but instead, her body would be carried through the winds and storms until she reached that Infinite Shore, where she would dwell in the flowery meadows of Heaven.

The evening before the day of her departure she brought all of her baskets she had made to her home and gave all of her wealth to her brother, telling him to watch for her in the early morning, as she was departing for a far better throne than she had ever known upon earth. In the early morning hours, ere the sun was shining over the mountains of the Klamath, she bathed her body with sweet scented herbs, put on her new maple dress, and draped her shoulders with the gorgeous dyes of the yellow-hammer feathers; her long raven locks were combed and left flowing about her shoulders. Bidding her brother good-bye, he beheld her mount the rock where she had sat so many years in devout prayer; he alone saw her rise from the earth to go to the realms above. Swift as the lightning from Heaven she mounted the rock. Bowing to the great creation of the world with her arms outstretched and her beautiful hair flowing, she stood erect with her face to Heaven in the north with her eyes closed. Out of the north, on his mighty wings, rose the red eagle and came to her feet on the rock. Dipping her hand to the west, to the land of the setting sun, she bade the

world farewell and mounted the eagle's back. With outstretched wings, gorgeously tipped in crimson, he rose from
the rock with his fair princess mounted securely upon his
back, and flew with her to the far north from whence he came.
In the early dawn of the rising sun, in all the glories of Indian
Summer, her brother saw her mount the eagle and fly away to
the Kingdom of Heaven, passing not through the gates of
death.

She sat on the eagle's back through the long journey, with
her eyes always closed, her arms raised above her shoulders,
and her hands folded at the back of her head and neck. The
eagle, on his long journey north to the land of Cheek-cheek-
alth, commanded her not to open her eyes, though the storms
from Heaven may feel severe against her face and body.
Rising from the earth she felt the heat of the still Indian
Summer beat like fire upon her. Far away they soared, and
the eagle said, "You will now feel the mighty winds of Heaven
sweep around you in piercing gales, but do not open your eyes."
Far up through the winds they soared, and she opened her eyes
not. Far on they flew and he said again, "You will feel the rain
pouring in torrents upon you, but you must never open your
eyes." Through the rain they went until he again said, "You
will now feel the cold fall like piercing blades of ice, but you
must never open your eyes." Through the piercing cold they
flew, her eyes always shut, until he said again, "You will now
feel the snow fall thick and fast upon you, but you must not
open your eyes." Through the mighty winds and the cold,
fierce storms of Heaven they had flown, until the eagle at last
exclaimed, "You will feel the warmth of pleasant summer
again, open your eyes and I will leave you in that sublime land
of Cheek-cheek-alth." She opened her eyes for the first time

during her long flight through the airy regions and beheld the
beauteous land of Cheek-cheek-alth, the old land that gave
birth to our people long ages ago. She now stood upon the
banks of the most sublime river the world has ever known,
with its hallowed charms and brilliant gems of fortune, its
mystic waters of transparent brilliancy flowing sweet and
peaceful through the valley of Cheek-cheek-alth. On the shores
of this wonderful river she beheld millions of the dead turk-
tum (short shells of the Indian money) shining from the sands
of the water. From this river long centuries ago, when the
Indians first left their native land in search of the new world,
they brought with them the cheek, or Indian money. They say
this money is found in no other clime except in the old land of
Cheek-cheek-alth, the land of their birth. They do not use the
dead turk-tum washed upon the banks of the river for money,
but fish for the live cheek in the river which they catch the
same as fish, and out of these live shells make their cheek or
money. This money through the long evolution of centuries has
been handed down from one generation to another.

In the land of Cheek-cheek-alth, this divine princess found
the ladder that goes to Heaven and climbed it, round by round,
until she reached Heaven. All of her tribulations of earth were
finished; the false accusations of cruel friends could no longer
thrust their wounds into her blameless soul as she now sat
glorified on a Throne of Eternal Splendors, truly a Saint in
Heaven.

Several days had elapsed since the departure of Metch-cher-
us-ah-may, and the people began to inquire why she returned
no more to the house at nightfall. They went in search of her,
and found the wood baskets she had used here on earth left on
top of the high rock where she had taken her flight. Her

brother then informed them that his sister had gone to Werse-on-now, as he had beheld the vision himself. The parents, recalling to mind the harsh words spoken of their dark sus-picions concerning their saint-like daughter, wept and wailed most bitterly and were bowed down with heavy hearts and sad regrets, that one so true could no longer stay on earth; that God should so early call the divine and true to His Eternal Home.

The brother who had loved his sister so devotedly recalled to memory the tender devotion of her trying years of patience. Heart wrung with the strange, pathetic life of his sister and the charm of its beautiful ending, he wept until his proud heart seemed broken asunder, weeping tears of blood, it seemed, from the heart that loved so much; for the gentle hand that touched his brow, the hallowed form, the low voice and cheering smile was gone forever.

After a few days, the bitter wailing of her parents and the intense grief of her brother was answered by the gentle Saint herself. Her spirit came earthward in a shadowy image, or O-quirlth, and appeared before her loved ones, soothing them with gentle words of compassion in their dark hours of grief and sad regrets, assuring them that she dweleth safely beyond the Pearly Gates of Heaven, in the infinite meadows of beauty and light. Their misgivings no longer wounded, for her spirit survived in peace and happiness and [allowed] them to weep bitterly no more. Her spirit faded from the earth, leaving her parents assured of the eternal years of her greatness, a Saint in Heaven.

Her brother, Metch-cher-us-ah-chene, could not be com-forted long, as he had only known a sister's love and tender devotion. Day by day he grieved more and more in his lone-liness, [with] a sorrow that knows no comfort when the loved one has gone to realms beyond. His grief became so great that he could not long endure it, when her spirit answered him in his loneliness once more. This time she appeared before him in her living form as she had lived on earth, and brother and sister met in sweet earthly communion for the last time, as she would return to comfort them no more. She lifted the heavy veil of sorrow from his heart and gave him courage in earthly things again. She instructed him go to a riffle on the Klamath River, opposite the old Klamath Bluffs Store, and fish there for twelve days, at the end of which he would catch a small fish about the size of one's little finger, and [told him] that this fish would have many white rings encircling its body. This fish, as soon as it was caught, was to be put in an elkhorn Indian purse, which is beautifully carved out of the elk's horn and polished smooth on the internal and external surfaces. They sometimes carve and color very artistic designs upon them, cutting out a small oblong lid in the middle of the purse which they fit on it after putting the money in, wrapping the lid on securely with a strip of buckskin.

Metch-cher-us-ah-chene fished on the riffle for twelve days as directed by his sister, and at the closing of the twelfth day he caught the small fish, which he put in the elkhorn purse. And then the raven, or qua-gawk, came to him and said for him to mount his back, which he did; and then the raven commanded him to close his eyes and keep them tightly closed until he was told to open them. The raven flew with him through sunny regions, rain, cold, sleet, snow, and over icy fields, taking the same route that the red eagle had flown with his sister. Over the icy fields he could feel the ice with his hands. Then after this the raven sat him down in a warm place and commanded him to keep his eyes closed, and the raven flew on and left him alone for a short time. While alone he began to feel around, as he could not open his eyes. He felt in the sandy soil around him, and felt that it was covered with cheek (the shell of the Indian money), and he began to rake it up in heaps around him. When the raven returned he said that he must leave the cheek where it was found, as it was too heavy to carry so far. Metch-cher-us-ah-chene mounted the raven's back again, and away they flew to the land of Cheek-cheek-alth, which was only a short distance from where the raven had first left him. Upon arriving in this land, the raven set him down on the banks of the wonderful river, Wer-roy, where the climate is always warm and pleasant, the valley forever green, and the fruits and flowers forever blooming through one long perpetual summer day. On the banks of this glorious river the raven said for him to open his eyes and fish in its brilliant waters for one of the living cheek, or little shellfish. Fishing in this river of sublime beauty, he caught this rare and precious shellfish which the raven said he must put in the elkhorn purse with the other fish his sister had told him to catch in the Klamath River. He put the two fishes together as he had been instructed, and lo, vast riches soon followed. The fish he had caught in the Klamath was the female fish, while the one he had caught in the river of Cheek-cheek-alth was the male fish.

Metch-cher-us-ah-chene mounted the raven's back again, the raven instructing him to keep his eyes closed as before, and they flew back to the Klamath River, back to the Cor-tep village. When they reached the Klamath River the raven instructed him to make twelve of these elkhorn purses, as large as the horns would permit, and he made twelve of the largest kind that he could. And as the male and female cheek would breed little cheek in the small purse, he would take the young cheek just as soon as they were large enough and place them in one of the larger purses. He kept on breeding cheek in this way until he had all of his large purses filled with money, or cheek, and he now began putting the cheek in a large basket. His riches were growing so large that he did not know what he was going to do with so much money. Finding himself so lonely in the midst of his vast riches, he wooed a wife from the Pec-toolth village, where the Trinity River flows into the Klamath. Following the custom of marriage, his name was changed to Pec-tow, adopting his wife's name and she taking his name. After they had been married but a short time, his ambitions died within him and he lost interest in his work and neglected the teachings of his sister. Now the two fishes made their escape from the breeding purse and turned into a worm or bug, about an inch long, with white and black stripes on their bodies and two long horns on their heads. These worms can be found along the riverbanks around the large rocks, and the Indians always consider it good luck to find one of them, as they catch and put them away in a purse to keep them for good luck. After the escape of these fishes, he no longer had the power to accumulate vast riches, and ill luck followed.

His wife gave birth to a handsome boy, but it was said that God was displeased and caused the child to die. A second child was born to them, this time a beautiful baby girl, but it died also. A third child was born, another beautiful baby girl, but God too took it away as he had taken the others. A fourth child to this unhappy couple was born, a boy; it was still said that God was displeased with his marriage, and the handsome babe followed its brother and sisters in Heaven. At the death of the fourth child, Metch-cher-us-ah-chene became very sad and thoughtful. So sad and heavy was his heart that earth

A photographic study by Emma B. Freeman, 1915. This image was part of Emma's Northern California Indian Series.

120

seemed to him but dreary waste without the noise and prattle of his beautiful babies. He thought long and could not understand why God took the innocent and pure away to His Heavenly Home so soon.

Rising in the early morning, he would weep as he went up the mountainside to gather a load of sweathouse wood; and with this on his shoulders he started to the sweathouse in the village, singing and weeping as he went, "I-a-quay, tus," saying he was very sorry for his children. The mourner sat down to rest, putting the load of wood on the ground and resting his back and shoulders against the load. When he had rested sufficiently, he tried to rise with his load in the usual manner, but there was a heavy weight on his load and he could not rise, as if someone was holding him down. He looked around but saw no one, so he tried again and was able to rise with the wood. He sat down a second time and rested with his wood, and as before when he began to rise up he could not; but after looking around and seeing no one, he was able to get up all right. He sat down and rested a third time, when the same thing happened; and upon reaching home he made a fire in the sweathouse and sweated himself in the usual manner, after which he went to the river and took a cold plunge in the water. Coming out of the plunge, he went back to the sweathouse and seated himself in front of the door and gazed far off in the distance, imagining that he could see the spirit, O-quirlth, and at the same time his wife was calling him to dinner. He continued to sit there gazing far beyond the earth. He did not answer her calls; his spirit had gone to join his sister in Werse-on-now, where she resided in Heaven with God. There you may see brother and sister staying together in the infinite meadows of Heaven, and about them his beautiful babes, the pure buds of the blooming meadows.

After the death of Metch-cher-us-ah-chene, his wife returned to her native village at Pec-toolth, where the Trinity and the Klamath Rivers come together. She took with her the large basket with cheek (money), and after a time married a man of the Weitchpec village, which is located on the north side of the Klamath River opposite the mouth of the Trinity River. From her second marriage she had one son, and all the cheek she had brought with her made these two villages very rich from this time on.

Chapter VIII
Burial Customs:
Why the Dead Are
Never Taken through the Door

Many generations ago, there was a woman born and reared at a village called Os-sa-gon, which is located some six or seven miles south of the mouth of the Klamath River, on the ocean shore. Some years ago this place was a very large village of the Klamath Indians.

When this woman had grown into beautiful womanhood, she was wooed and won by a young man of the Wah-tec village, which is located near the old Klamath Bluffs Store and near the White Deerskin dancing grounds. They were both of wealthy families, and celebrated their nuptials of good ceremony of the middle class. During their wedded life they were very happy together. Three little ones came to bless this happy union: one boy and two girls. After the third child was born the husband became very ill and entered into the shadowy valley of death, leaving his young widow and children to mourn his untimely departure.

Up until his death, it had always been the custom of the Indians to take the dead body out of the house through the door, and as they carried it through they would take the ashes from the fireplace in the house and throw them through the door as the body was carried out. The ash dust was allowed to remain until the wind had swept it away. This had been their custom from generation to generation. They had performed the same rite with him, but in this a strange coincidence happened which changed their custom in removing the dead from the house.

After his burial was over and his wife had once more become reconciled to her daily routine of work, she would sit and weave baskets with her face toward the door, which was contrary to the Indian teachings, as one should never sit facing the door but must always sit with their backs turned upon it. She did not think this teaching of any importance, and always sat with her face toward the door while at work on her baskets; and at short intervals she would look up from her basket and glance at the door.

Nearly a year had elapsed, when one day while she was sitting weaving her basket, thinking intently of her husband, how happy their wedded life had been, how devotedly she had loved him in life and how deeply she mourned his loss, seemingly his departed spirit answered her from the unknown world. Glancing up at the door, she beheld his spirit, and dropped her basket with a sudden cry of joy and sprang to the door that she might take him in her arms, that he might nevermore leave her in her loneliness. Instead of her husband, the loved one, she caught in her arms the post which stands as a supporting column on the outside of the inner door, or between the inner and outer door of the Indian house. Her conscious self left her, as she thought he was trying to get away from her, and, thinking that she had fastened her hold upon his leg, instead she was clinging to the post. Her once supple body and limbs became as rigid as iron when her children and folks gathered around her and tried to make her let go of the post; but their efforts were of no avail, for she only clung the tighter. At last they were compelled to cut away the post before they were able to move her to a bed, where they did everything possible to restore her. She remained in this state of unconsciousness for several days, when they decided to take her down to the river and put her into a canoe. They took her down as far as Blue Creek (Ur-ner), some eight miles, and then turning back and coming up the river to Notch-co, some eight miles above the Wah-tec village, making sixteen miles in all. In these sixteen miles the river changes its course from due north, swinging around in the different bends west to nearly south. They kept taking the woman up and down the river the whole summer, until late in the autumn, and kept her alive during this period by nourishing her with the marrow fat from the leg bones of the deer, of which they applied to her lips and breasts by rubbing. When she had fully regained her consciousness she would, during all her spare time, weave baskets. The main frame or rib-work of the basket are hazel switches, which is called ho-lealth. In drawing or weaving the work in and out over the switches they turn to the lefthand side; and the basketmaker always keeps a basket of water within her reach, and at short intervals dips her hand into the water, moistens the switches and straightens them back into their proper places, thus building the basket up straight. This woman never straightened back the switches of her basket; therefore, they were made into a round twist. The children would say to their mother (Calk), "Why don't you straighten the switches on your basket?" She would always reply, "Never mind, that is all right," and tell them to stop talking so much about her basketweaving. She kept on weaving baskets in this manner until all of her children had grown up into man- and womanhood.

One evening as the twilight was fast gathering into darkness, she was sitting working on her baskets as usual, with her basket material around her. She simply said, "My time has come, my husband is waiting for me." She picked up her basket she was weaving and placed it on the fire, saying her spirit, O-quirlth, would have it to use while she was leaving for the world beyond the grave, and died. Her children and her husband's folks had gathered around in her last dying moments.

The Indians now keep the dead body for one whole day (twenty-four hours) to satisfy themselves that life has actually departed. They bury the body and after it is laid in the grave, they say that the spirit, O-quirlth, remains hovering around the living and near the newly made grave for five days. When five days have elapsed the spirit departs, and if the individual has lived a good moral life, his spirit goes to Cheek-cheek-alth, there finds the ladder and climbs to God, where he dwells forever in eternal happiness. If he is a mean and degraded wretch, his spirit goes the broad road to the old woman and the dog, where she hands him over to the man in the dead boat; and he takes the wicked spirit across the river and leaves him to wail in the wilderness of anguish until the judgement day.

When that woman died they did not take her through the door, but made an opening in the wall on the lefthand side of the door as one stands on the inside of the house facing the door. From this time on, they have never taken a dead body through the door, but always make an opening in the side of the house on the left hand side, through which they take the body. The Indians teach their children never to stop or stand in the doorway, in going or coming in. One will never see anyone, old or young, stop, stand or sit in the door of an Indian house. Since the death of this woman they always burn the basket material of the deceased, or any unfinished work that belongs to the one that has just died.

There is a course grass, a sort of saw-grass, that grows on the ridges and under the tanoaks and fir timber which they use in nearly all their baskets, and this grass we call ham-mo. When one dies and the body is taken out of the house, they place some of this woven grass over the door on the inside, in a manner that one would not notice it unless it was shown to them. The family will wear strands around their necks, and this is done to prevent them from seeing or meeting the spirit which hovers around and near the body for five days before departing for the unknown realms beyond.

The custom of cutting the hair on the death of a near kindred extends back to the time when they were in the old land, Cheek-cheek-alth.

Hoopa Valley School, c. 1895-1905. Drawing youngsters away from their families and villages and "educating" them out of their traditions—often under the guidance of missionaries—was a well-established practice of the times. Photo by A.W. Ericson.

Chapter IX
The Indian Devil

The Klamath Indians, in bringing down their legends from the creation of man until the present day, say that some were made to be good and honorable, some bad; and some were real bad and mean, which they termed devils, or Oh-ma-ha. We have the conception of the invisible Satan (Sye-elth, or wicked old woman) and a real living devil such as walks the earth, and we fear them, as they will harm us if they get the opportunity. We have had these living Indian devils (living human beings) all through the long and weary centuries, ever since the creation of mankind—such devils as we find in every race and nation of the earth. Our Indian devils are Indians who for some reason or cause leave the tribe and go far away into the lonely mountains and into the depths of the forests, where they live near the streams and places almost inaccessible. In their loneliness they roam through the forests and over the mountains like some wild animals of prey. They forget the language of their mothers and become something like wild beasts, fleeing from the sight of human beings.

In olden times, the women especially were always careful to keep together on their camping trips when they were gathering the acorn crop, grass seeds, pine nuts, etc., for fear of these Indian devils. These Indian devils would sometimes watch the camps of the Indians very closely and follow them about as they moved from place to place, watching for an opportunity to seize one of the young women and carry her off to make her his wife. If a young woman strayed away too far by herself, she was often made a captive by one of these devils. The women of the tribe had great fear of them, as they had great horrors of becoming the wife of a wild man.

Sometimes the women would be captured by the Indian devils and would be gone away from their tribe for years, when they would return and tell of their wild life and experiences. They would become the mother of children, and the children would inherit the wild habits of their father, as they would always be whistling, making strange noises, romping wildly about, and always on the go, roaming everywhere in the wilds. These women were never happy when they came back to their people, as after a time they would long to go back to their devil husbands and children. They always managed to get away and return to the old wild life, as it held such a fascination for them, when they once experienced the wilds, that they could not resist the calling of such a life.

When the Indians would go on their hunting and camping trips into the mountains, as soon as they heard an owl screech or hoot, they would stop and listen, and try to distinguish if it was an Indian devil imitating the owl or the cry of a wild animal. The Indians would stop at once, kindle a fire, and hallo; this was given as a warning to the devils that they were awake and ready to fight them if necessary.

When the Indians go camping far back into the mountains, and even if a white man accompanies them, they always insist on making the first campfire when a camping place is selected. In building the fire, the first stick of wood they lay down points directly north and south; on the north end of this stick of wood they place another stick some eight or twelve inches back from the north end, placing this branch east and west, thus making a cross. When the cross is made they proceed to kindle the fire, and during the whole time they are offering up a prayer to God in a low tone of voice. This prayer is earnestly offered up to the Almighty, asking Him to protect them from the Indian devils and wild animals while they are in the wilds and to keep them from accidents. After the first worship has been offered up, anyone can build the campfire as long as they camp in the same place, and the Indians do not repeat this form of worship until they move away to a different camping place. The Indian places his soul in the care of God, and worships at his shrine under the open Heavens and boundless skies, and not at the religion and traditions of another race that has a tradition from the beginning of the creation of a living man, and down through the long centuries of thousands of years. If this is true, let me quote from the so-called civilized races. For instance, Rome had its Caesar, oft writ in history, "Great and brave," but all the world knows that he lived the heartless conqueror, crushing out the lives of men; his hands were dipped in human blood, and he died the tyrant's death. All the world knows that France had its monarch; his name is writ on Fame's record as the mighty conqueror of Europe. The winding rivers of Europe were once red with the blood it shed; there were gory battlefields left in his wake, to say nothing of broken-hearted mothers and children who went weeping under cheerless skies without a home to shelter them. For example, [in] our own United States, in 1861-65, cities went down in ruins, homes were destroyed, human blood flowed like wine. Thousands sleep in unknown graves; they died martyrs for a great cause. And the Redman was just as much of a martyr for his cause as they.

Truly our tribes were not bloodthirsty, for the love of blood or the lust of glory, but instead were compelled to yield to a superior race; and our noblest men sleep in narrow graves with the best, the proudest of the race, dead around them: exterminated rather than educated, until the noblest of our race are gone. And out of the miserable remnant comes a feeble cry today that for nearly four centuries the Redman has merely existed, without a country. Love for the child-race of a bygone age, tears for the infant race, in all its infancy a type of primitive manhood, reserved and poised, courageous, enduring, master of self and above all self-controlled, a proud, vanishing figure in a nation of unrest. Love for the adult race saddened with regrets hanging heavy and the stain of blood on their hands from the infant tears for the superior race, for who can tell what this child race might have been when they were full grown and educated. Tears and love, love and tears, sweetly mingled when infant and adult meet in one great brotherhood of forgiveness. Always thus, since time began, someone must die a martyr for the beginning of every cause; and it has ever been thus, since the dawn of history, among all races and nations: the heathen, the barbarian and the civilized nations of the world.

Educated man today, through his long evolution of centuries, knows there is only one God, and all are seeking one goal; and the soul of man cannot be lost just because he worships a little different from his fellow man. Every race has its own creed, and one race has no more of a right to say another race is lost forever and eternally just because they differ in their form of worship; and the rising generation of the present century knows better. So at least let the tradition of the noble type be just, as he is being fast absorbed into another race; and even at this day, all that remains of him is tradition of his past existence, and usually that tradition is of a mongrel type, rather than the true.

We are always afraid of the visible devil (Oh-ma-ha)—that is, the living devil here on this earth, as we are compelled to guard continually against these monsters in keeping ourselves from being harmed. We are at all times at peace with God; we love Him as the Great Ruler and we are always ready to offer a prayer and to worship Him.

When an Indian sits down to smoke, he fills his pipe, lights it and takes a deep breath, filling his lungs with smoke, and then expels it slowly through his nostrils and mouth with a low grunt. Then in a low and solemn voice he offers up a prayer to God, asking Him for good health, long life and good luck. This good luck is in earning money, accumulating vast riches, success in fishing and securing wild game, and in fact all the success in the pursuit of an Indian life.

The devil is termed as key-mol-len, which means a low, miserable person or animal. And God is in the Heavens as invisible Being to living man; He is everywhere, and He rules over all.

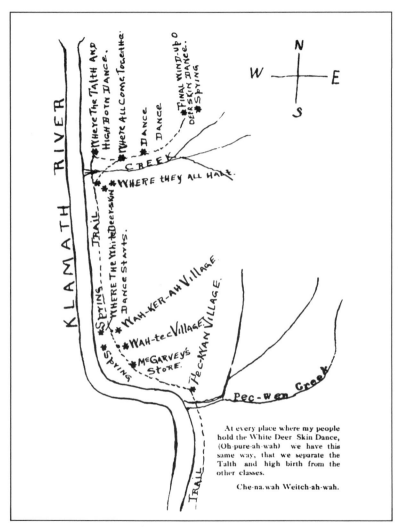

Lucy's map of the region. (Illustration from the original edition of *To the American Indian*.)

Chapter X
The White Deerskin Dance

The fish dam being completed, all except the ones that are to stay there, Lock-nee, Nor-mer, the Wah-clures and the Char-rahs, now move down the river and go to their different homes to prepare for the White Deerskin Dance. This dance is held about ten miles down the river from where the fish dam is put in, and this place they call Wah-tec, a pretty place containing about fifty acres, a nearly level place, being a high bar or flat so that no water ever gets over it, and situated on the north side of the river, just down under the village on a gentle sloping place. There is a large spring of cold water flowing from under the upper flat or high bar, while some forty steps below the danceground there is another spring, larger than the other, clear and cold, which is used for part of them that camp, all being some three hundred yards down the river below the old Klamath Bluffs or Johnson's Store that was put there in the year 1855 or 1856 by a man named Snider, and owned so long by Bill McGarvey.

Before the dance starts, two that are of high birth, one girl and one man (the man can be young or old, but they [both] must be of high birth, and sometimes one of them is a Talth), go first and clean off the ground (all of which parts I have taken) by taking the grass off, then sweep it clean; then three smooth stones are set well down in the ground, but extending above the ground some eight or ten inches. These stones have been [used] for a long time and are for the three in the center of the row of dancers, which are fifteen and seventeen in number. The girl makes a small fire and then places her incense roots on it to burn so as to please Wah-pec-wah-mow; she remains there to keep up the fire while the dance is in progress. This man and girl are called May-wa-lep, and eat their regular meals each day. When all is in readiness for the dance to start in the evening of the first day, the two first villages up the river from the dancing place, all dressed in their robes and regalia, go down to the riverbank and get into a large boat or canoe; one sits in the stern to paddle and keep it pointed down the river until they come to where they have prepared their camping place for the dance. The first village up is called Cor-tep, and the next one above it is Pec-wan. Pec-wan is where the big Talth Lodge is situated for the Po-lick-las division, and is very wealthy. This village is my birthplace, and always comes in strong with the finest of regalia and the most beautiful display of deerskins. Now each village dances separate and one at a time. As the Cor-tep village dancers come up and form themselves into line, the three in the center are the leaders and the middle one of the three is the one that lowers the pole that had the deerskin on it. He raises his right foot and starts to sing, letting his foot down at the same time, and the rest all follow. Now there stands at each end of the row of dancers those who in their right hand hold a large flint which they call Ne-gam. This has a strong buckskin string tied tightly around it and then looped around the wrist so as to keep it from slipping off the hand. And as the dancing starts, they go back and forth in front of the row of dancers, passing each other at the middle of the row of dancers, and they have a whistle in progress. After dancing until they are all tired out, they stop, and the three in the middle of the row sit down on the stones while the rest stand, all raising the pole on which the deerskins are held, letting the butt end of the pole rest on the ground. After the Cor-tep village has danced out, they retire to their camp, and in from fifteen to thirty minutes the Pec-wan village dancers come up and go through the same performance.

The regalia and deerskins are the common kind, and the count of the days that the dance is to run has not yet commenced, as these two villages may dance two dances for each day, after the first evening, for three or four days before the rest of them can get ready to come. There are five of them in all: next above Pec-wan to come is Ser-e-goin, then Mo-reck, and the next is Cap-pell where the fish dam is. When they all get to the dancing place, they dance ten days, and each village dances in its turn. They start the first dance about nine o'clock in the morning, and it is fully twelve o'clock, mid-day, before the last one has finished. Now bear in mind that there are two or three men all the time in the different camps asking the men, one and all, to come in and dance. It does not matter from where they come or to what tribe they belong, they are asked to come in and take a part in this great festival, so that the dancers are changing all the time, and from one village to the other; and whichever village they dance in, they are invited to eat at their camp. All is free, and no one is allowed to go hungry. And there would be some from far off that could not speak a word of the Klamath tongue, only by signs with the hands; yet they were carefully looked after, shown around, fed and asked to get in and dance, the others carefully guiding them through so they would make no mistake; and it was considered the worst of ill manners to make light of their mistakes anywhere in their presence. They were guaranteed protection and courtesy, and seen to get home without being harmed or molested.

The different dance camps have a number of women, sometimes eight, ten or twelve, and they work like beavers, cooking and preparing the food. These women are the sisters, aunts and other relatives. Some of them may own one-half of all the valuable parts of what they are dancing with, and all may own some part. As with the Klamath Indians, the women own by inheritance or accumulation all of their own wealth, just the same as the men do; and a wealthy woman is just as much sought for a wife by the Klamath Indians as they are by the whites, and just the same a wealthy man is sought for by the women as they are by the whites.

The girl keeps her fire burning while the dance is going on, and the man assists her at all times. Now the village to which the dance belongs starts about dark in the evening and goes through the same performance, each giving a dance, keeping it up till about nine o'clock at night, when they retire to their different camps, [where] they all take their evening meal. After this they all prepare to sleep for the night, and the most of them sleep until full daylight in the morning, when they rise to go through the same routine. On the last day at this place, or the tenth day of the dance (Oh-pure-ah-wah), this being the great day, all that are to be there have come, and this day they bring out the white deerskins and the longest of the flints, some of which were red, while others were streaked with red and white, the white being the most valuable; some of them are twenty and twenty-two inches in length and from four to five inches wide in the center of the blade and quite heavy to handle. The Pec-wan village leads all others in white deer-skins, they having five that are white and many that are light or nearly white, all being dressed softly and nicely with the whole skin, nose, ears and the hair left on; even the hoofs are white, and the nose and ears are decorated with the red feathers of the woodcock or Indian hen taken from the scalp of the bird and put on strips of buckskin with small pieces of the abalone shell hanging down in front of the nose of the deer some four inches long. Ser-e-goin comes next with the longest flints, the most valuable belonging to a family of sisters, and the other villages that make up the five come in [according] to riches in valuable articles for the dance. Now [Next?] the upper river or Pech-ic-las come into the different dances with their valuables as to the line of relationship or old-time friend-ship, and the women put in their wealth and take their places and help to cook and wait on all just the same as the Po-lick-las, yet they speak a different language. But they are so closely mixed in marriage and so many of them speak both tongues, and the whole meaning of the big dance being just the same to both, that there is no mistake between them in any part of the management of the dance.

The men all wear a buckskin blanket made of two and three deerskins, dressed with the hair on and made very soft; these are sewed together with a bone needle, with the sinews of the deer used for thread, and to the lower part of the blanket they sew the tails of the civit or ringtail cat. This blanket is fixed so as to be tied around the waist, and hangs down below the knees with the cat tails dangling at the bottom. If clear dry weather, they wear these blankets with the hair side next to their skin, which leaves them looking very white, but if it turns damp or commences to rain, the blankets are turned with the hair side out so as not to get the flesh side wet and soiled. All of the dancers have great rolls of shell beads, called turk-tum, strung around the neck, hanging down over the breast and reaching to the waist. These shells are the same species of shells as the cheek, only they are shorter and do not have the value, by from fifty to one hundred times as much; and all [the dancers] have headdresses, but no feathers—only the one bald eagle or other eagle feather that is stuck in the back of the hair and stands up perpendicular. The four men that stand at the end of the row of dancers and which carry the large flints and whistles in their mouths have for a headdress a close-woven cloth which we make ourselves from the small thread fibers of the flag. These are twisted into strands and woven into a thick, heavy cloth; these are some eight inches wide by three feet in length, or more, and are ornamented with the tusks or teeth of the sea lion fastened at the upper edge of the piece. And this cloth is placed center of forehead, then back to the back of the head and tied, leaving the ends floating with the tusks sticking out in front. This headgear is called cher-wer-ner, and the blankets are called cah-ane.

This white deerskin place is called Wah-tec, and the village that sits just back of the dance place at the brow of the high flat, or bar, is of the same name. The Wah-tec village is north of the dancing place, and just north of the village is the level flat where they play their stick game, which is as rough as the white man's football game. This game is called werlth-per, and I have seen them pile in heaps at this game and many get hurt. There must be no fighting, yet they take a deceptive way of hurting one another if there is a dislike between them, just like the whites do. The White Deerskin Dance at the end of ten days comes to an end at this place, and the whole place is alive with Indians from all parts. Now the whole thing comes to a halt, and all that are managing the dance return to their villages for more supplies. This stop is for one day only. And now the stick game starts, and they may have several games between the upriver and lower rivers during the next few days. After the one-day stop, so as to replenish provisions, they all start very early on the morning following and first go down the river from Wah-ker-rah about one mile to where a small creek enters into the river. This creek is known as Bloxer Creek, but we call it Hel-le-gay-ow. This is on the north side of the river, where this creek comes into the river. Now when they get to the creek, they being on the south side and close to the entrance of the creek to the river, here all halt, this being where there are two trails. One goes down next to the river, crossing the creek, and up to a small flat just at the foot of the hill, with the large pepperwood trees hanging is a place where the dance starts, and on this trail and to this place, none can go unless they are born of the highest marriage.

The girl and man that are of high birth have already gone and cleaned off the grounds, made the fire, and are burning the incense. When the host arrives here, they must give all their valuable articles that are to be used at this place over to the poorest and shabby-looking ones, if they have the right birth to take them over this piece of road or trail to this place, Hel-le-gay-ow; and all from all parts know whether they have the birth, as this is kept close track of by the full-blooded Klamath Indians. And if any persists or offers to go over this trail, to this place, they will be told very firmly to keep back, and if needs be they will tell them that they are not born good enough to pass this way, but wait and go the other way. There has never been one of mixed blood, of any part with the white man's or any other mixture of blood, that they would let go this way. Only pure Klamath Indians are allowed. There was never a white man (Ken-e-ah) that they would consent to let pass this way, for they did not know what kind of people the whites were and that the white marriages were not such as to give them the birth.

I can pass and have passed many times, and have the training to know which can and those that are not allowed; and the powerful in riches have to stop and take the upper trail, such as Pec-wan Colonel and Captain Ser-e-goin Jim and others whose wealth and influence that the white man thought would allow him to any part or place. I am one that knows that the birth is the one great event that gave to my people more honor, more power and more of everything in this life than all the riches in the whole world could buy.

My people do not talk and tell of this for many reasons. They do not tell the white man, thinking that they might wish to disobey the rule or right to stop them. And of all the white men that have married the Indian women, we do not think that a single one of them ever told their husbands of this for the reason that they themselves did not have the birth to pass over this part of the trail, and was therefore ashamed to let their men know that such was the case. And the white men, thinking nothing of it, stopped and did not notice that such was the case. It is kept from the mixed-bloods, where their [non-Indian] fathers raised them, in the same way, not even their own mothers telling them, ashamed for her children to know of her birth; and the mixed-bloods that are raised among the Indians know that their birth does not admit them, so keep in their right place and are also ashamed to say anything about it. And so it has been kept until I told my husband how it was, we being duly and truly married in the high marriage of my law and married in his law, my husband being a Free and Accepted Mason, and for him to look and see for himself, but to stay back; and that we would take the upper trail and go with the rich, the warrior and the throng that could not go the lower trail, where my father (a Talth) and sisters could and did go, yet they were poor, and others could go, there being few that could go, while many went the way we did. This I never could have, which was very easy to see when once told and shown.

Now after the Talth and them that have the birth have done their dancing at this Hel-la-gay-ow, the girl and man slip out and go on up the hill through the timber into the other trail for a short distance, and there clean off another place, make a small fire, and place on it the incense to burn, and the girl sits down in front when the dancers come following up as they come into the trail.

Now all the rich, the proud of all but their birth, come in behind, and as they come up to the next dance-place and form into line to dance, all can look on and see. Soon this is done, and the same is done in two more places until the whole of them finally arrive at a large prairie that they call Bloxer, meaning wide in shape. As they come to the opening they cross a small branch and turn to a flat between two small branches or creeks that contains about two acres. At the foot of the rise from the flat is a large spring of cold, clear water flowing; here they halt for the final wind-up. They have been at this all day, and the girl and the man (May-wa-lep) have the fires burning the incense. In the evening they dance; each one dances their turn, using here the white deerskins and all of the finest of their regalia and valuables. After the dance is over they have their supper and retire, tired out. Early the next morning all is astir, and they dance the five dances in the forenoon and eat dinner in the after-part of the day. The last and final dance is to come. When this is finished late in the night, about nine o'clock, then all take their meal, when many of them depart; and the great White Deerskin Dance is closed for two years at least, or maybe more, and all go home. Now when we speak of the dance being closed for two years or more, we mean by this of the old and ancient laws, by which it was conducted, for it has already been carried through in a spurious or farcical way by them that are of low birth, not having a single one that was a Talth to take the lead and carry it through in proper form; but the white man sees it and does not know the difference.

Those of high birth come to the remaining Talth to ask a few questions, while the Talth answers them in a smooth tone of voice, which is their gift, and lets it pass on in quiet, knowing that it is forever done. The Talth that now live make only one last request of the living: that is that when they come to give up this life, that before they are laid away, when being prepared for burial, that the emblem or mark of the Talth be placed on them. This is four black stripes placed on the breast eight inches in length, one-half inch wide and one inch apart; and on each arm between the shoulders and elbow there is to be three stripes four inches long, same width and one inch apart, which are the marks or emblem of the Talth.

Then they are prepared for the last resting place, the grave, and these emblems or marks are never put on any of them unless they have been put through the secrets of the Lodge, and carry in their breast that true name of Wah-pec-wah-mow (God). There are only two of these left; one is myself and the other my father. This chapter now closes, and we take up the greatest of all, the Lodge Dance (Wah-neck-wel-la-gaw), called by the whites by many different names.

144

Chapter XI
The Lodge Dance

The white man calls this dance the jump dance, and this has caused the Indians to call it thus when they speak of it in the white man's tongue, but we call it in our language Wah-neck-wel-la-gaw, which has no meaning as to a dance. This dance is held at the Pec-wan village, and it is about one mile up the river from where the White Deerskin Dance is held. This festival is held one year after the White Deerskin Dance, or is held alternately. This is the most sacred festival that we have, and like the fish dam, we start preparations for the festival some two months ahead, and all differences and disputes are settled before this starts. If there are any who cannot or will not settle, they must not come to see or take part in the festival.

By this, the reader can see that this once powerful and numerous tribe of Indians, by making these complete settlements among all of their people once a year, one year for the fish dam and the next year the Lodge Dance, could be managed by the High Priests and be well governed without the aid of a chief, as they never had a chief.

The Pec-wan village was in olden times a very large and wealthy village. This is where the lodge of the lower Klamaths is situated, and this lodge and the house where all the tools of the Talth are kept is the only one now, at this writing, left of the whole tribe. In the times when the white man first came, there was one of these lodges at Big Lagoon which we call Ah-ca-tah, and one at the mouth of Redwood Creek which we call Orick; one at the mouth of Klamath River which we call Reck-woy; and one at Pec-wan. These four lodges belonged to the lower division of the Klamath River, and the upper rivers had a number of lodges, but there is not one of them left. There are no Indians left to tell of them, or how and what they were used for, so making it at our time, only one is left, and only two of the Talth are left to tell of the use and meaning of the grand good that come from them to the proud people.

When all is ready the three Talth start very early in the morning and select the timbers for putting up a complete new frame of the lodge, not leaving a single piece of the woodwork of the old lodge, but replacing it with new. Upon their return from selecting the timbers, the Talth then go into the house, where the tools are kept, and take them out. Those that are used for getting the post and the frame with all the sidings, they put these in a very nicely knit sack which is made of good and lasting material and kept for this purpose; then they take it on the outside of the house and leave it there for the night.

Now the Talth return to their homes and family, always bathing themselves, for they are as near perfect in their cleanliness as it is given human beings to be. They go into their homes with smiles for their wives and children, and all others that they may come in touch with. These Talth are very firm in their manners, very witty in jokes, but slow to speak in matters of decision. After supper they retire to their sweathouse to sleep. There they first take a smoke and then go to sleep. Now the ones that are the workers have already been selected for getting out the material to put up the wood part of the lodge, and the whole of the work must be done in one day. Every piece is made to fit in its place, where it is gotten out in the woods, so that when it is brought in, which is done the same day, all fits into its place. The whole structure is set up without the use of tools; no noise and no words are spoken, only by the three Talth, and by them only in a low voice.

Those that work to get out these timbers must all be of good birth—not necessarily of the highest birth, but of good birth, of the wealthy and well-to-do class. Some of the ones of the highest births are not considered to be of the right minds, with good behavior to be made a Talth. No one of the low births or slaves are allowed to take part in the making of the old lodge, Talth-ur-girk. We have degrees in this lodge work; some are allowed to go in and learn a small part of it and are never given any more, while others are allowed to learn a greater part, and they are never given the true name of God.

This highest marriage takes twelve strings of cheek, twelve pieces to each string, and out of the few marriages there was very few that was good to be made a Talth; and by this they were compelled to choose from the girls as well as the boys the ones that were right for the Talth, to keep from losing the workings of the order, as well as to keep the sacred name of God from being lost. If through famine or epidemic it would be lost in some of the places or lodges, they could get some that were Talth to come from Ah-ca-tah, Orick, Reck-woy or from some of the lodges from the Pech-ic-las, so that they could fix up the lodges and take some of the ones of the right birth and initiate [then] into the secret workings of the order, and make them Talth, and build the order up again. These things have happened many times in their long history and occupation of this land. Now all the old lumber that is taken from the lodge when it is to be made anew is taken to the house which the Talth use for their preparations, and to keep the working tools in, and there it is used to renew the weak parts; and the rest is used for firewood in this house, so that none of it is wasted.

The dance, after everything is fixed and all in readiness, will last for ten days, and when all is ready the Talth and all the workers, which are called Wer-ner-ger-ee, go to their different homes or friends and eat their supper. And after this is finished, all the workers, with two of the Talth, go out and gather wood, which is the small limbs and twigs of the huckleberry, which we make use of by keeping a small fire through the night in the lodge; and on the fire we burn incense roots which give off a pleasant odor. Now the other Talth, who is the Master of the ceremonies, goes straight from the house to the lodge, and with him the one, or the two, girls. These girls are not always a Talth, but sometimes one of them is, and has the whole secrets of the order, even to the real name of God. These girls must be born of the highest birth to even help. The Master, when he goes in, talks or prays, while the girl or girls sweep it and place things in shape, which keeps them busy; if there is only one girl, she does not have time to leave the lodge.

Jump Dance, involving old and young in the ageless responsibility to "fix the world." Many of the baskets and other regalia are still being used today. Photo by Ruth K. Roberts. *(Courtesy Humboldt State University)*

Woman with pet deer and cat. Photo by Ruth K. Roberts. *(Courtesy Humboldt State University)*

About nine o'clock the Talth with all the workers come out in line, single file, with a bunch of wood, each one with his bundle on his shoulder, all singing; and this in the night or evening sounds most beautiful, as it is most perfect in time and tune and makes one feel the love for the great Creator of all things.

When they arrive with the wood, all lay in around the top of the house or lodge, then either one of the two Talth takes some inside of the lodge and makes a small fire inside. The floor of the lodge is made of marble, and they have a large bowl made of marble in which is placed clean, pure water, and in this water is placed the roots of walth-pay. Now when the time is ready, all will come inside of the lodge and bathe in the marble bowl with the walth-pay in it. This bowl is kept secreted and only the Talth knows where it is. The Master of the lodge has taken the bowl out from its hiding place and puts it in its proper place, and puts the water and walth-pay roots in it. Now when the workers and the two Talth come with the wood, and after the fire is started, the two Talth remain and all the others go outside, and the three Talth bathe themselves, also the one or two girls, as the case may be. If one of them is not a Talth, then she too has to go outside. Then the Talth go through all the secret parts of the work in the lodge, while the girl that is a Talth remains inside of the lodge and takes part in the secret workings. The lodge is now opened, and all the workers are invited to come inside. Some of the workers are Talth, sometimes nearly all of them; if not, they are high born. They all wash themselves in the marble bowl and all have the Indian comb, the men's being longer than the ones the girls have. After washing, each one washes and combs their hair until it is clean and glossy, leaving the hair hang down loosely, using the combs to stroke the hair back, and [being] careful not to touch it with their hands.

The men are perfectly naked, while the girls have a maple bark dress fastened around the waist, hanging down to the knees; otherwise they [are] nude. Now the Master takes his place in the southeast corner of the lodge, sitting on his Indian chair, and in his hand he holds his staff, or rod, which is the stalk of the walth-pay. This staff is the stalk which grows from the herb or root that God made women from in the first creation, and the staff is so old that it is black with age. The next one in authority sits in the northeast corner of the lodge, while the third one sits in the northwest corner of the lodge. The lodge sits north and south; the entrance is at the south end, the west side being left dark. The Master in managing the ceremonies has a helper (this was my part, and the emblem I wear is the Dove) who sits on the righthand side of the Master. And if there is no girl that is a Talth, then a man that is a Talth has to fill the place, and this one has to place and move the chair of the Master as he rises and sits down. And if there is only one girl, then she has to perform a double duty of removing and placing the chairs of all three officers of the lodge, and when this happens she is kept on the move all night until five o'clock in the morning, when she comes out very tired, yet lighthearted and very proud of her birth, her standing and the great knowledge she has of the secret history of her people. Very few there be that has ever been admitted to her high plane, and none has ever excelled her. She knows that she and all the other Talth are full-blooded Klamath, and [have] no mixture of any other blood in their veins. This secret organization dates back to the very beginning of God's creation of man and woman, as this staff of the walth-pay is what God made woman out of. This walth-pay they have preserved in this land in selected places, and it still grows here; and we still use it in all of our secret work. It only grows in a few places, and all of us know where to find it. They brought this with them, from the old land, and on down through the ages to commemorate the first creation of woman.

I have offered to go to the lodge and teach one or more when there was enough of the Talth left to do so; but now there are none left, and they could not pick out one girl that was eligible to give it to, until now there is no chance left, and whatever is done towards the meeting of this old and ancient order is only a farce, and done by the low births, the low class and the slave class. When I first told my father that I was going to marry a white man, my people objected, saying that if I had children they could not be admitted to the order. It was then I told them to select one that I might teach the secret part of the lodge to. It is sad for me to write of the inside working of the lodge, and who can blame me. My people are passing away, being absorbed by the white race.

Now all are inside of the lodge, and they give the whole night to chanting and praying to God, to please the Creator, to give them health, wealth and to watch over them, keeping them safe from disease. They keep this up until about five o'clock in the morning, and then they all go down to the house where the dance is to be held, and this house is called Ah-pure-way. They build a small fire and place some roots on it. Now during this time the wealthy families have moved from their homes, bringing their wives, sisters and daughters to cook and prepare food.

The first dance is hurriedly gotten ready, and then the dancers come up to the house, going in and taking their places. The dance starts and will last for ten days. As soon as the first dance is over the Talth go to their homes to eat and rest, and the tired but proud little girl goes to her home and eats, after which she takes a much needed sleep. All have bathed, which they never fail to do, and dressed their hair and combed it cleanly. There are five villages that take part in the Po-lick-las dance, being the same ones that took part in the White Deerskin Dance. All Indians are invited to come, rich or poor, from any and all tribes, from far off and near by. Far away tribes are looked after, fed and asked to take part in the dance, even if they cannot speak the language. They will motion to them and show them how and give them full protection at all times and under any circumstances, so that they may enjoy it to the fullest. This is the time the very poor and slave class of our own people are made jolly and contented, proud to be known and called a Klamath Indian. They are here allowed, both men and women, to put in whatever they may possess that is of value, that is used to dance with. The wealthy ones that own lands, hunting territory, fishing places, slaves, flints, white deerskins, fisher skins, otter skins, silver gray fox skins and fine dresses made of dressed deerskins, with fringes or shells knotted and worked in the most beautiful styles, that clink and jingle as they walk and makes one have a feeling of respect and admiration for them. The eyes will strain to look on this most pleasant sight, which can never leave one's memory that has seen it in its flowery days.

They take the scalp of the woodpecker, which they sew together from sixty to one hundred in number on a piece of nicely-dressed buckskin, the edges also being buckskin; it looks like a plug hat. They let the ends hang as streamers at the back of the head. These are valued at from one to two hundred dollars, having red and white fringes, which makes them look very pretty. These headdresses are called Rah-gay, and the scalps are called cheese, whether one or many of them. They have great strings of the long hollow shells, called cheek and turk-tum, around their necks, hanging down over the breasts to the waist. This, the most sacred of all their festivals, is held in a house, and more of their wealth is displayed at this time than on any other occasion. The wealth of the whole tribe of the Klamath Indians, even the Hoopas and Smith River, and any other tribe, can put in and help in this dance. Here in this dance the rich ones will turn over to the poorest of them their display of wealth and go away, leaving it in their care. Our people use feathers but very little, less than the white people.

In the evening of the second day's dancing, the Talth go back to the lodge, and the Master with the girl who is a Talth go into the lodge; and the Master puts fresh clean water into the bowl, pounds and places the walth-pay roots into it, and it is ready for use. The other girls remain in the preparation house or go to other parts to perform when they have things fixed for them. The Master gives prayers to God while the other two Talth in authority will take the same ones, the workers, and go out for more wood the same as the first time, coming in about nine o'clock, all in single file, led by the two Talth singing the song as they come, and place the wood the same as before. Now the two Talth go inside and the lodge is opened, the Talth girl helping until all is in readiness. Then the workers are called in and the Talth each take their place, the Master with his staff of the walth-pay, and the girl in her place by the Master; and the workings of the lodge are gone through with as before, and kept up all night until five o'clock in the morning, when they come out and go to their homes and camps to eat. Now the dancers take up the dancing, and the whole thing moves along smoothly, without a thing to mar the good times. The Talth do not take any part in the dancing, and are but seldom seen to take a look at it, and the Master does not come to see any part of it; but if he does, he just passes on, laughing, joking and jesting with all the men and women, and they are more than glad to see him.

The Talth call each other brothers, and the girls sisters, and the word brother and sister is used a great deal among these people.

When the lodge is working in its secret part of the order, there is a guard stationed at the door on the outside to keep others from hearing or entering. In the evening of every second day they open the lodge until the dance has run for eight days, when they open the lodge in the same way, in the evening, for the fifth and last time. The Master and the girl go into the lodge, while the two Talth and the workers go and get the wood, coming back at nine o'clock. Then the same performance is gone through with, ending about five o'clock in the morning; then all the workers are expelled from the lodge, and go to the dance house and make the fire, burn the incense roots, sweep and clean the house for the last two days of the festival. The three Talth and the girl remain in the lodge and finish the winding-up ceremonies of the lodge for the dance, after which the bowl, staff and other emblems and tools are placed in their secret hiding places so that them who are Talth know where to find them; then they come out and go to their homes to eat, sleep and rest. Now the last two days of the dance commences, and the finest of dresses and the most valuable of articles are used. All the riches are brought out, showing which are the most wealthy of family, some of which have long records dating back for generations, telling how the family first started in prominence, and up to the present time. This festival is held for the purpose and equality of the whole people together: [to help] the rich, the poor and the slave make themselves come together in peace and harmony as one family; and to make the poor and the slave feel that there is some good to live for; and more and above all, to make them warriors, that none dare scorn; [and so] that if any other tribe dare to violate the laws of humanity, such as to mutilate the dead by scalping and other ways, the Klamaths would not tolerate [it] for a moment. And [the festival is held] by the Talth to keep and preserve their old and ancient teachings of the sacred order which has been handed down to them through the ages, which they say after has never been [lost], through it all, down to where it is now. They say that a number of times it has been low, yet there was enough to revive and bring it back to its proper place, so as not to lose it in its secret parts and keep it up. At the end of ten days the dance, late in the evening, closes, and the people scatter in all directions, while the rich families, that have so many women to help in preparing the food, and some with children, and so much wealth to move, will keep their camp open until the next day, and some for two days longer, until they can get everything ready for moving home.

Baskets and other articles collected at Brizard's Store on the Klamath River. Baskets and other goods were often used as currency to buy food and pay bills, and stores often had extensive collections of Indian wealth. Basketry caps are on the floor, a woman's ceremonial dress is to the right. Also visible are pipes, ceremonial obsidian blades, dentalia, etc. Photo by A.W. Ericson.

Chapter XII
Our Christ

A young woman of the Pech-ic-las, the upper division of the Klamath tribe, lived at Cah-ah-man, now known as Orleans Bar. She was the mother of Po-lick-o-quare-ick, our Christ, and never married after the birth of her son, and lived single all her life, residing with her folks at Orleans Bar. Caw-ah-mis-o-ma, the mother of our Christ, during the years of her womanhood, would go alone daily to a high rock, not heeding the remonstrances of her parents and kindred, and would ascend the sides of this rock to its top, where she would seat herself and weave baskets every day. She went alone every day for nearly three years to this rock and made baskets, and one day Wah-pec-wah-mow (God) appeared to her and said that she would bear him a male child, which would be His Son, and this Son would be our Christ, or Savior, who would be a very wise and talented man of the two tribes and would rule our people.

Upon reaching her home that evening, she told her parents and the people of the tribes that she soon would give birth to the Son of God, that God himself, having appeared before her, made facts known to her, and that she should not be looked upon in disgrace by her people. Her parents and a great many of the people of the Klamath tribes believed her story to be true, and they made ready to receive the Child.

Caw-ah-mis-o-ma gave birth to a son as she had said, and
cared for the infant in her father's home, giving it the name of
Po-lick-o-quare-ick, proclaiming the child to the tribes as the
Son of God. Her parents and a great many of the people of the
tribe believed in the infallibility of the child, while a number
of the people did not believe in him as infallible, and regarded
him as a bastard child. Some of our Talth, or High Priests, did
not believe in his divine birth and considered him as the
bastard son of man; however, they recognized his great
powers and wisdom as an ordinary man. Most of my people
worshiped the child as divine.

During the childhood and boyhood years of Po-lick-o-quare-
ick he sought the solitudes of a great creation, as he never
played with other children, and never mingled in the social
gatherings of his people. As a little child he played alone, and
when he had reached the age of about two years, he had a little
canoe that he would play with and sail it in the waters at
Orleans Bar. This little toy boat was one of his earliest play-
things, and when he left his early childhood scenes, he left this
boat at Orleans Bar on the south bank of the river in a rift or
crevice of a large rock. There, to this day the Indians say you
can see the little boat that he played with and which has
turned into a solid stone, and is still the perfect shape of a small
boat. (This I have not seen.)

While yet a small boy of tender years, Po-lick-o-quare-ick
came down to the river to Ca-neck, alone, where he spent a
great deal of his early boyhood years in restless wandering, as
he was never still. He would never go with his mother, or with
anyone else, as he went from place to place alone. On the south
side of the river at Ca-neck is a small lake at the foot of the hill
back from the river, and [it] is surrounded on the outer banks

by marshy lands. This lake cannot be observed from the river or village, and its existence might never be known except by coming upon its very banks. He spent a great deal of his time playing in his solitary ways about the lake. Just back of this lake is a rock that our Christ used as a place where he would continually be sliding down its side. He wore away one large and some small grooves with his heels, in this solid stone, which can be seen to this day. (This I have seen many times, and my people rub their fingers on these grooves and then rub the fingers on their eyes, to cure weak or sore eyes.) About half a mile below the lake, located on the same side of the river, is another rock, where the young man went for prayers which he offered up to his father (God), to bless him with great powers and wisdom. As he knelt at the top of this rock in prayer, he left the sunken imprint of his knees and feet in the rock, which is still visible.

Another rock concerning our Christ is located a short distance above the lake on the bank of river, which was his special fishing place, where he would sit on the rock and fish. Here also in the solid stone is the sunken imprint of his bare feet and knees, and also the pool of water, close by, that he cast his fish in, all of which are left as his written memoirs of his past existence. These are his written annals left upon the rocks: the traditions handed down through the long centuries when the Christ himself had passed away, far out on the ocean waves, perchance to a better land than that which had given him birth. (This place I have been close to many times, yet I never went to see it.) He could speak the language of any tribe or nation without teaching, and could peer into the darkness of the past, telling the events of bygone times. He could gaze into the future and tell of the events to be, so great was his wisdom;

he could also command anything he wanted, and his commands would be answered, to his every wish.

When he was in the prime of his years, he took a lot of valuable things, such as cheek, cheese (the scalp of the woodcock) and other things, got into his canoe and started down the river, and when he arrived where Bill McGarvey's Store afterwards was built, he stopped and took a rest in the early morning sunshine. This is the reason this place is the warmest and most sunny the year round that is to be found in any part of our whole territory. After resting as long as he wished, he started on down the river. Many of the Indians followed after him, and as they were crowding quite close, he commanded that an opening be made through the rock bluff at Reck-woy, which was done, and this turned the Klamath River into the ocean at that place, some six miles south of where it went into the sea before, at Ah-man (Wilson Creek). Thus they never caught up to him but could see [him] out in the ocean, gliding gently on towards the west. He had previously told them that he was ready to go and was going, that in some future time he would come back. He was the wisest man that we have ever had among our people; he knew all things, and could do all things and we hold his name with great reverence. It is the custom of our young women to use the expression: "When we get married and if we have children, we wish they can talk all languages like Po-lick-o-quare-ick." My people for many generations look for him to come back, but since the coming of the Ken-e-ahs, the white people, they are losing trace of his name and the things that he did, and it will soon be lost. It is now my desire, after many years of thinking, to write it all out so it may be preserved for the American Indians, that they may know something of the religion and teachings of our forefathers.

Chapter XIII
The Sampson of the
Klamath Indians

Kay-kay-my-alth-may, the Sampson of the Po-lick-la's (the lower Klamath Indians) and the Pech-ic-las (upper Klamath Indians), was born at the village of Auh-leek-kin on the river. This village is about twelve miles down the river from the old Klamath Bluffs Store, and about the same distance from the mouth of the river at Requa. It was once a large and flourishing village a long time ago, at the time of Sampson's birth and long after he was dead.

This Indian Sampson was a tall and handsome fellow, with sinewy arms and a body of muscle. His hair was extremely long, such flowing tresses of beauty and strength, wherein his wonderful physical powers lay. This man of wonderful physique was a Klamath Indian, a lone and mighty warrior for all who opposed him; and it mattered little how many in number were against him, they were always defeated. This warrior did not use bow and arrows, spears or shields to defend himself in his conquests, but used instead the sling and pebbles. He would raid whole villages in the quest of wealth, and none dared combat him but what were defeated. The tribes feared him for his great strength, as they knew not where he got his supernatural power.

The tribes of the Smith River, Hoopa and Klamath feared him greatly as he reached the dizzy heights of his powers and massacres. He refused to pay tribute to any of the tribes.

One day this warrior bold, emboldened by his triumphs, met a beautiful and shy maiden of another tribe with whom he fell desperately in love. Her people were the Smith River tribe, (He-nas), with whom he was fighting at the time. He defeated them and took her captive, and alas, love after a time proved his utter ruin. Ah, what monarch of earth that love will not conquer with her soothing hands! After he captured the maiden he married her so she could hold herself respected before all, and took her to his home at Auh-leek-kin, giving her the name of Auh-leek-kin-on. No children came to bless this union; no childish prattle or laughter to lift the gloom of the coming years.

This Sampson's dwelling place was in a house where he had made a cellar in the clay, and in this cellar he always retreated at night that he might not be suddenly surprised and taken by his enemies. His wife yielded to his love, seeking the secret of his great strength, and alas, mighty man and warrior, the conqueror of tribes fell before the weak hands of the woman he loved. Day by day, so gentle and sweet her endearing words of affection fell like balm on his troubled soul, soothing the afflictions of a dark and turbulent career. Patiently as the months passed by, she gained his confidence. Ah, 'tis sweet to yield to woman's wiles, though she leads you to the grave, yawning with the grim jaws of death. In this woman's feeble arms, this powerful man revealed his secret, that his mighty strength was in his long and flowing hair, the beauty of night and the strength of nations.

False woman came to dwell in his life as she gained the

secrets of his mighty powers; siren-like was the touch of her fingers upon his troubled forehead. Fascinated in the comfort of one he loved so passionately, he fell asleep; and one fatal day with his head laid lovingly upon her lap, the cruel woman of destiny arose stealthily and stole from the fire embers a flaming torch, and burnt the raven locks off closely to his head, as he slept soundly on.

Upon awakening, to his great alarm and grief, he found that his superhuman strength had left him. The pride of his life, his long and flowing locks, were gone, and with it his fate was sealed. The powerful warrior lay vanquished at the feet of his enemies, to grieve his loss as only great men can grieve.

After his enemies had captured him, they decided to put out his eyes that he might nevermore be able to fight them. Thus, at last, the great and strong Kay-kay-my-alth-may was defeated by the weak hands of a woman he had loved and trusted so much.

After he had been captured and tortured, his proud spirit gave grief so intense that only a great physical strength could long endure. He lived a few short years, in his native village, but the time seemed long in his blindness. He could no longer behold the splendors of the sunrise on the mountaintops or the splendors of the sunset on yon Pacific Ocean. The wonderlust of his life had set in dismal gloom, as he pined away and died of a broken heart. His faithless wife returned to her people, where she also died, leaving no one to mourn her and only the memory of his great strength.

(Top) Sandy Bar Bob (a Karuk), playing a square drum typical of the area. (Bottom) A gambling game at Blue Lake, on the Mad River. Gambling, a pastime for both men and women, was a great sport and a highly developed art along the Klamath River.

Chapter XIV
The Deluge of the
Klamath Indians

It has been handed down from long ago that the people became so wicked, no good was found in anything, and human progress retrograded into destruction. Unwedded women became the mothers of a host of bastard children as the men led a life of debauchery and the women a life of shame. Crimes and murders lurked in every corner; plunder and the greed for riches followed each other in a terrible way. Men sought not honest lives, but sought the greed and plunder of riches. Those who commanded their self-respect and cherished their family pride became few and far between. Profane language became the rule, laws became corrupt and unheeded, and whole communities swerved downward in utter ruination.

God became angry upon looking down. He saw the people growing more corrupt, year by year, where human beings eked out a miserable existence in their greed. God appeared to one of the good men (a Talth), a man who had always lived an honest and upright life, respecting his fellowmen, and observed above all God's moral laws. He appeared to this man,

Gus-so-me, who possessed in his secret breast the true name of God, and God said unto him that He was going to destroy everything on earth with a great flood, as the people had become so wicked that He would no longer endure the sights of such wickedness. Gus-so-me pleaded with God not to destroy the people by flooding the world, and God then told him to go forth among the people and see how many good ones he could find. He could find but one more, so God told him to prepare a raft, as He was going to destroy the world with a flood. This one man that had the abiding faith of an honorable man was Haw-gon-ow, also a Talth. God now appeared before these two High Priests and bid them prepare for the final deluge, as there was no good people to be found on earth, except the two Talth and their wives. He bid them to build a large raft upon which they would float, while the rest of the creation would sink beneath the rising waters and perish.

Gus-so-me and Haw-gon-ow began at once to build the raft (men-up), while the people continued in their wild revelries, jeering in contempt at the two builders; but they heeded them not and worked steadily on. When the two Talth completed the raft, He caused it to begin raining, and it rained steadily, causing the waters to rise higher and higher, until the o-plah-peck (flood) waters covered the entire world. When the waters came up around the raft, the two Talth took their wives, Ger-ke-er and Ca-wa-mer, onto the raft, where they remained and floated upward as the water rose. These two wives were also Talth, and our holy order was kept intact over the great deluge. They carried with them upon the raft, the herb, or walth-pay, which as before kept perfectly green and bloomed. They also took with them the raven and the dove, but all the other species of the earth were left, and they were destroyed in the great flood. It rained steadily for many days and nights upon a terror-stricken world, until all the valleys and lowlands were one continuous sea, and only tops of the highest hills and mountains remained uncovered, where the people stood huddled together, as they had been steadily driven up the mountainsides by the water. And still it continued to rain, the people running hither and thither. Piercing wails went up as the terrible apprehension of destruction was upon them; their piteous cries were only answered by the rising waters, as their bodies were tossed a moment upon the angry waves and then sank to their graves in the unknown depths. Soon all the highest mountain peaks were covered with water and the world was one continuous sea. All living creatures had perished from the earth, as they had sank beneath the waves to live no more.

When the rain stopped, Gus-so-me sent the raven (bua-gawk) forth from the raft to see if it could bring any tidings of dry land. He flew away over the waters until he found some dead fish and never returned. This is the reason the raven ever since has lived on carrion and always remained so wild, inhabiting the far-off crags of the mountains that command a view of the surrounding country so they can see anyone approaching and fly away. After a few days had passed and no tidings of the raven came, Gus-so-me sent forth the dove (aw-rah-way), and after it was gone a short time, it returned to the raft with a twig of the pepperwood. Gus-so-me now knew that the waters on which he floated were going back, and soon there would be dry land, and from that time on, the Indians have had a great reverence for the dove. We carry the symbol of the dove in our sacred lodge, and teach the children from childhood never to harm the dove; and we never harm it in any way.

After the return of the dove, the raft floated on the waters for a few days longer and finally rested on the top of a very high mountain, known as Ne-gam-alth, which is located in the far northeast on this continent and not across the ocean. This lofty peak glistens in the sunlight and can be seen from a great distance. The raft as it rested on this mountain turned to white flint, and when the sun shines this flint glistens brightly. In our traditions only one man has ever climbed this mountain and returned to our people since the flood, bringing with him a piece of the flint, and since this time we have used the white flint at our festivals, it being the most valuable of all other kinds.

When the waters went down sufficiently, God commanded Gus-so-me and Haw-gon-ow, with their wives, to go down from the mountain and repopulate the earth. From these two Talth and their wives came our present people, and they again scattered over the continent. In coming down from the mountaintop, the Talth carried with them the walth-pay, the same as they did when they first made their long journey from the land of Cheek-cheek-alth. This divine herb bloomed perpetually again, and Gus-so-me, with the assistance of Haw-gon-ow, in using the correct words of their prayer to God, could command with the herb anything they needed for human existence, as their prayers would be granted by God.

God now created the animal and plant life that was destroyed during the flood, with the exception of the raven and the dove, which the High Priests carried with them upon the raft. When the re-creation was made, God first made the white deer, then the red eagle, the same as in the first creation. He also placed the rainbow in the heavens as a promise to Gus-

so-me and Haw-gon-ow that He would never again destroy the
people by flood, but if the people ever become so corrupt again
He would destroy them with a great fire burning the world.
When the Indians see the rainbow in the heavens, they always
look upon it with the assurance that it is the promise of God,
that He will destroy the world no more with rain. When the
heavy rains fall, they always say that it will not continue to
rain very long, for the next time all the world will pass away in
flames.

The Talth bring down the traditions that when they first
arrived in this land, the white race which they found here
were a highly moral race. They lived in peace and happiness,
and crimes were things unknown. With the passing of this
white race passed the age of innocence and peace.

Upon the arrival of the present white race, the Indians first
believed that it was the ancient white people returning. The
tribes rejoiced, as they thought peace and happiness would
reign again, for the Wa-gas had given them their faithful
promise that they would someday return. Alas, the sad mistake and identity of these people, for they were foreigners who
took advantage of our hospitality, and soon wanted to claim
the land of our forefathers. Crimes followed in their footsteps
of extermination, together with race hatred has covered
nearly sixty-five years of their annals. Worse than the shot and
shell, it brought the pride of our race to their graves long ago.
The introduction of whiskey brought desolution and ruin upon
us, without an example story to tell. They ruined the splendid
morals of our women, and led them to prostitution, which they
had never known since the re-creation of our kingdom. They
filled their bodies with loathsome disease that we had never
known since the world began, and our Indian doctors gave up

171

in despair for they could not find any cure for these diseases.

When our loyal good men rose up and remonstrated against these outrages, these foreign white men were wont to abuse us and call us savages, and sent some of the tribes away to distant reservations to starve and die. They called our women "Squaws," and our men "Bucks." It seems they had an idea that we did not possess human souls, cherished with the human love of devotion. They claimed our lands, and their historians termed us as "the wild denizens of the forest," as if we were foreigners in the remote ages of a vast antiquity. Fortune seekers, gamblers and cut-throats lived with our women in adultery until they grew weary of them and left them with children: poor little children of their own flesh and blood, children without a birth and without a parent to legalize them as his own. The fathers of the animal kingdom are proud to fight for their young and will not abandon them, even in the jaws of death. Can such a class of people as this have a soul when they have committed such outrages upon my people and have disgraced the living by their deeds? The origin of our race was proud, the proudest that ever walked the earth, and when these children find their pride forever robbed by no fault of their own, their proud hearts break down in the sorrowful years that follow, as their fallen parentage leads them to unhonored graves. Such sorrowful processions as these follow each other under the gloom of oppression. I have today looked among my tribe of the Po-lick-la's and the Pech-ic-las and am deeply grieved to find but very few babies born of good pure blood that is not tainted with the virus of venereal diseases.

Where do these pathetic conditions arise? We are reluctant to point again to the white man. In some instances a large family of brothers and sisters do not know their true relationship. I dare say, perhaps each one came from a different father, and the father comes from God knows where, and has gone they know not where; but such a father will undoubtly answer at the Throne of the Almighty God. I pray that God may have mercy upon such children who are left to suffer the disgrace of an unworthy parent. Today where the Klamath rears its regal monarchs of the forests, where it rears its lofty mountain peaks from its rugged shores, and mingles its waters with the Pacific Ocean, this glorious country once in its beauty and pride, I have scanned its hostage and find not one whose birth will admit them to that Holy Lodge, not one who can burn its sacred fires at the sacred altar. The Talth are waiting ever, for no more will answer their piteous pleadings to save and cherish a sublime religion. A precious few of the middle-aged have the birth, but their morals in a larger sense have been corrupted, their integrity has been undermined until they think a promise broken is better than a promise kept; therefore, while the world lasts they can never be admitted to this sacred lodge. Some of the Ken-e-ah men have been honest enough to wed our women under their laws, and some of them have married under both the white man's and the Indian's marriage laws. Most of these men have brought up large families, and the children from these unions, on an average, make men and women that the American nation might well be proud of.

The High Priests say today that from their ancient teachings and their ancient religion, that [with] the corruption of the ken-ne-ahs (whites) among themselves, and the demoralization of their own race, that the two races are becoming very wicked. Men and women alike use profane languages, men debauch their women into prostitution; the whiskey and wine from the saloons pierce the hearts of young men and women alike, breaking up the ties of peaceful homes, and tearing asunder the love of human hearts, thus leaving desolation as it goes on. The greed for riches by trickery and dissention in general leads the Talth to believe very strongly that ere long God will send the great conflagration that will consume all the world in flames, and that its people will pass away. Over their ashes God will create another people, where they will build their stately mansions of the soul unto God. Over the ashes of the obliterated ages will prosper a new people with new governments and new laws, and the ages of peace and happiness will dawn again, shedding its radiance of glory over the entire world. Thus have prophesied our High Priests.

Chapter XV
The High Priests

The Talth are born under the highest marriages, and there has been at no time but very few of them on account of the scarcity of cheek (money) to make the marriage. There had to be twelve pieces to make one string (caw-ton-a). They count them only as ten pieces, and it makes twelve strings, so that when it is counted there will be one hundred and forty-four pieces. The woman that a Talth may marry does not have to be of a Talth family, but can be born of the middle or wealthy class. Her people can match back, or nearly so, in valuable articles for the twelve strings of cheek that he gives.

Under such a marriage as this there may be several children. Now if the mother and father are full-blooded Klamath Indians, then their children are of the right birth. Yet there may be one, and perhaps two of them, which is not often the case, that might be of the right disposition, close of tongue and bright of mind, so as to weigh all matters of whatsoever kind intelligently, giving a broad-minded and liberal decision in any case. This applies the same both to man and woman; and if all is satisfactory, either he or she, under the birth, can be admitted to the Talth Lodge. And sometimes they are taken through only one part and cannot go further; and sometimes they are taken through two parts and are not taken any further; and but few are taken through the whole and become a Talth. And no less a number than three can act in the lodge, and make a fourth to be a Talth.

Now all these other children are of the high birth, and are put to act in many important places to fill at the festivals and in other ways. Many of them never make an application to become a Talth, and many of them are rejected, and not allowed to even make a start if their conduct is not proper. There never has been one born that is half white, or any part of any other tribe, that was ever admitted to the lodge. They must be full-blooded Klamath, of the upper or lower division of the tribe, and down the coast from Ah-man to Trinidad. The upper rivers from the junction of the Trinity speak a different language and intermarry very freely, and have the Talth Lodge in which they work together. Up the river they have entirely lost it all now, and have not one lodge left. At the mouth of the Klamath the old lodge has tumbled down, but not one of the Talth is left. At Pec-wan, twenty-five miles from the mouth of the river, is the Talth House, where all of their working tools are kept, and it is yet in a good state of preservation; the lodge is left, but it is old and dilapidated.

We have in our breast the feeling of love for the present white race, which love was instilled in us by the cherished remembrance of our Wa-gas. We loved this race, and this is the reason our women are so willing to marry the white man, and so easy to be deceived by them.

Chapter XVI
Laws of the Fish Dam

When the fish dam is put in, they have very strict laws governing it. There are nine traps which can be used: one belongs to Lock and his relatives, one to Lock-nee and his relatives, one to Nor-mer and her relatives, and so on down the line. These families come in the morning, and each one takes from the trap that which belongs to them, as many salmon as they need, by dipping them out with a net that is made and used for this purpose; and they must not let a single one go to waste, but must care for all they take or suffer the penalty of the law, which was strictly enforced. After all these get their salmon, then comes the poor class, which take what they can use, some of which they use fresh and the rest they cut up, smoke them lightly, then they are dried. When they are dried, they are taken down and packed in large baskets with pepperwood leaves between each layer so as to keep the moths out of them, and then they are put away for the winter. The Indians from up the river, as far as they are able to come, can get salmon, and down the river the same.

In these traps there gets to be a mass of salmon, so full that they make the whole structure of the fish dam quiver and tremble with their weight, by holding the water from passing through the lattice-work freely. After all have taken what they want of the salmon, which must be done in the early part of the day, Lock or Lock-nee opens the upper gates of the traps and lets the salmon pass on up the river, and at the same time great numbers are passing through the open gap left on the south side of the river. This is done so that the Hoopas on up the Trinity river have a chance at the salmon catching. But they keep a close watch to see that there are enough left to effect the spawning, by which the supply is kept up for the following year. The whites have often said that the Indians ought not to be allowed to put in the fish dam and thereby obstruct the run of salmon to their spawning ground, and it has been published in the papers that the fish dam ought to be torn out. One year it was published in the county papers that it had been torn out by the wardens. This was a false publication, as it was never torn out by Indians or whites. On the other hand, after the salmon cannery was established at Reck-woy, which is at the mouth of the river, the whites and the mixed-bloods commenced to fish for the cannery; the whites have laws that no one is allowed to let a net extend more than two-thirds the distance across the river, and wardens are paid to see that the law is obeyed. Yet the whites set one net from one side two-thirds across, and then just a few steps up another net from the other side, and which extends two-thirds across in distance. And in a distance of sixty yards, there will be from eight to ten nets, making so complete a network that hardly a salmon can pass. Will the whites preserve the salmon through all the ages, as the Klamath Indians have done, if they should survive so long? Not unless they enforce the laws more strictly.

While the fish dam stands against the strain of the pressure of the water and salmon, Lock, Lock-nee, Nor-mer, all the girls (Wah-clures) and the boys (char-rah) remain and watch things until the water rises and washes the dam out, which often takes two and three months, and then they all go to their homes, glad that the dam is washed away. Lock and Lock-nee, during all this time at the fish dam, use the utmost care and precaution to see that they are all kept in good health, bathing daily and keeping clean, so as not to soil their beautiful buckskin dresses that has taken the most skillful and patient work to make, and the most patient and skillful work to clean if soiled. All this whole ceremony of putting in the fish dam has been carried through so precisely with the teachings that have been handed down to them through many generations as God's laws, that a white man, to see it and understand the meaning of the different parts, and then not have a decent respect for it and carry himself accordingly, has not been born of a God-loving mother. The writer has helped as a Nor-mer in putting in the fish dam and knows the meaning of every move that is made.

These sacred laws were given to us by the white race of people that inhabited this country when my people first came to this land. The Wa-gas in ancient times first put in the fish dam some twenty-four miles farther down the river, at a place called by the Indians as Tu-rep, which is a flat bar containing some eighty or a hundred acres, and is located on the south side of the river, the north side [of] which is steep, being nearly a bluff, the same as it is at Cap-pell. The Wa-gas changed it from Tu-rep to Cap-pell, saying that Tu-rep was too close to the ocean. At that time the river went into the sea at Ah-man, six miles north of the present mouth of the river at Reck-woy. Cap-pell gave more of a chance for the people to get to the fish dam, and therefore benefit a greater number of them. They taught my people to put in the fish dam, and gave them all the secret and sacred teachings of the laws governing it. This was done before the great deluge that covered the world, and drowned all but the two Talth and their wives, who went through it all. The present site where the fish dam is built has been there for long ages, and the laws governing the fish dam are very ancient, and are now lost forever. They may put it in, but not by the sacred laws and regulations that was used so many generations, as they are lost, and no one can get them.

Chapter XVII
The Ancient Houses

Many of the houses of the Klamath River Indians date back to the prehistoric centuries of the long, long ago, and have been repaired and rebuilt many generations. Some of them are hallowed with alluring traditions and inspiring history, when our people were powerful and ruled a mighty nation. The Indian name of these houses is Oc-lo-melth. One of these houses is situated at Wah-tec, less than two hundred yards from where the White Deerskin Dance is held, and is my mother's house, where she was born and where she first looked out upon the light of a strange world. The surroundings of this house are filled with the romance of centuries, together with the wonderful history of the passing ages, as it dates back before the Indians came to this land from Cheek-cheek-alth. They say the house first belonged to the Wa-gas, the white people that were here when they first arrived. The Wa-gas were very fond of pets, and while they lived in this house they kept a number of deer as pets.

When the Wa-gas left this land, they left behind at this place a young man that was half-Indian and half-white. He remained for some time and cared for the pets, as the Wa-gas cherished them. The young man became lonesome for his people, in spite of the fact that he was very devoted to the deer, and one day he answered the call of the Wa-gas and followed in their footsteps, to join them in the far north. As he was leaving, he asked the Indians of my ancient blood to care for his pets, as he would be absent and never return. This my people have done according to the request of the young man and out of their great friendship between the two races. This ancient house became a hallowed spot where sacred memories of a people that have passed away in silence long ago fill its every surroundings.

In one corner of this dwelling, within its walls, is a large stone trough which was made and placed there by the Wa-gas untold centuries ago, so they could feed their deer. The deer were fed upon the stalks of tobacco and the walth-pay, the stalks being pounded into fine meal, mixed together, and then placed in the stone trough for the deer to eat. It was said for ages, and up to the advent of the present white race, that the spirits of the departed Wa-gas would come earthward in the deep shadows of the evening-time and open a door, which was made in the corner of the house for that purpose, so the deer could come in at night and feed upon the meal. The deer would stealthily emerge from their forest homes at night and upon finding the door open would enter the house and eat the meal; then just before the break of day they would silently vanish into the forests, and the door would be closed when morning came. My mother has seen the deer coming toward the house in the dark shadows of evening, but she has not seen them for a good many years, as they have become hunted beasts of prey.

Through the memory of the passing ages the Wa-gas left this land before the world was covered with water, and according to these traditions this house goes back for hundreds of centuries. This house has survived, with its long line of descendents, but it is now fading in the storm of years that are passing, and the place of its ruins will soon be forgotten.

There are a number of these old houses in the different villages along the Klamath River, from its source to its mouth, and on the coast from Ah-man to Trinidad. At the present day most of them are deserted, and are left to sink into ruins and oblivion.

The rattlesnake is called May-yep-pere, and they make their dwelling places under the ground and in the dark recesses. The children born in this house are not afraid of these snakes, as they never harm them. The snakes crawl out and over the house without restraint. I had no thought of fear, as the blood of ages had made me a kin to these fierce reptiles, where my people had sheltered them and fed them for thousands of years. In olden times the whole family would go away and leave the house alone for several days, sometimes for two or three weeks, and during their absence the snakes would creep out over the house and lie about in numerous places. If a stranger tried to approach the house, they gave him warning, and if he attempted to enter, they would at once be aroused into a fury and would attack him. My mother says that strangers have attempted to enter the house while the family was away and have been severely bitten by the rattlers. Therefore, the door of this house was always left unlocked, as no one would ever attempt to enter it that knew its strange history. If the family was at home, strangers could come and go at their will, as it was never known that the snakes ever attempted to harm anyone while some member of the family was present.

When the family would return from their sojourn, the head of the household, or someone who was born in this house, would precede the rest. I remember it was always my mother's duty upon reaching the door of the house, and she would begin talking in a low tone of voice, saying: "We are coming home; we are here now, and you must all go out of the way." Upon hearing her voice, the snakes would immediately begin to creep away to their hiding places. Upon entering, she would begin to tap lightly upon the floor with her cane and would keep talking until all the snakes would disappear, after which the rest of the family would enter the house, talking, laughing and playing without any thought of the snakes ever harming them.

This historical house is now owned by my mother, and in which she has not lived for fifteen years, but up until about five years ago she would go almost everyday and build a fire in it and sit around the house and weave baskets. In the past five years it has not been repaired and has racked into ruins, so bad that she does not care to enter it anymore, except on special occasions when she wants to break up something. For the past twenty years she has been breaking and pounding to pieces the stone bowls, trays and all the ancient implements that were left by the Wa-gas. She is endeavoring to destroy all these sacred reminiscences of the prehistoric days that they may never be ruthlessly handled and curiously gazed upon by the present white race. The stone trough that the deer fed out of is so large and heavy that she cannot break it to pieces, but is letting it sink into the ground; and it is being covered with rubbish, together with its strange charm and fascinating history, where my pen has failed to impress, this deep sentiment, therefore its wonderful tradition has faded with the closing of this chapter where a new era has dawned. My mother gave my husband two of the small stone bowls as relics of the days that are gone forever, and he keeps them as cherished memories.

Chapter XVIII
The Wars of Klamath Indians

The Klamath Indians as a tribe are like all other people that have a history dating back long before the great flood, as their legends plainly tell. They have had wars and plenty of them, through all the ages, and never have laid down their bows and spears at any time to any other tribe or tribes, and have at different times had to fight every tribe, and sometimes combinations of tribes. They have many times been nearly exterminated at different places of habitation. It was at the junction of the Trinity River that the Hoopas (Ar-me-musees) would come down the Trinity River and strike them in the center of the tribe, and kill, burn and scatter them before they could gather; and at times they would patch up the differences with the Hoopas, and let it go by without war. Thus the Hoopas became more bold and cruel, and began the tactics of mutilating the bodies of the slain, or cutting off the hair of the dead and wearing it when dancing their war dance. These things when carried to a certain point would not be tolerated, so the Klamaths would gather in great numbers, strong enough to throw a force against them that they could not resist, and burn their villages and drive them back, taking both men and women as prisoners, until they would beg for peace and things would be settled, sometimes for a long period. In these settlements they gave women for marriage on both sides, so as to make relationship between them, which would keep long and everlasting peace periods. The Klamath Indians would take Hoopa men for slaves and give their own men for slaves, but at all times these were of the low birth and slave class that was given in this manner, and never of the wealthy class.

Our tribe extended to the mouth of the Klamath and six miles north to Ah-man, and here they had to fight back the treacherous Crescent City and Smith River Indians. These He-nas were hard fighters, brutal in every way, killing women and children; and when they took a fancy to a fine-looking young woman, they would exterminate her people, and take her and try to kill her by being abusive and starving her. The Klamaths would fight the tribe for such deeds, and they would fight on and on for many years, and settle and patch up until the He-nas would do some unbearable act, when the Klamaths would gather a strong force and go after them. On several occasions they nearly exterminated the whole tribe of the He-nas. They were married and mixed in relationship with the Klamaths for over one hundred miles up the river, but the Klamath women dislike to marry among them on account of their cruelty. On the other hand, the He-na women were pleased to get the opportunity to marry Klamath men. Our tribe extended down the coast as far as Trinidad, a distance of over fifty miles, and here they had to fight back the Mad River and Humboldt Bay Indians, which we call the Way-yets. The Way-yets were a large tribe, fat and lazy, living mostly on clams, shellfish, mussels and other fish. They were not good warriors, but strong in numbers, and the Klamaths easily held them to the line of their own territory; and with the Way-yets they would not mix in marriage, claiming that they were too low in morals and did not make and live in permanent homes, all the time moving and camping here and there.

The Klamaths had some wars with the Redwood Creek Indians and some with other small tribes, and held themselves all through the ages so as to have many that could call themselves pure-blooded Klamath Indians.

The worst of all the wars was that the Klamath Indians were almost continually fighting among themselves, village against village, sometimes close together and sometimes far apart, one rich family and their slaves against another rich family and their slaves. The great festival, one of which was held each year unless prevented by some great calamity, would bring about an almost complete settlement of their differences, and bring them together on as near-friendly terms as could be had, and caused the fighting to be stopped for nearly half the time, in many cases stopping it for all the time. In this way the Klamath Indians were kept from exterminating themselves, and were held together as a powerful tribe, there being several thousand of them when the first white men came. Our tribe was governed by the Talth, and without ever having a chief.

My people wore hats or caps that we made with our own hands by weaving them out of our basket material, with the different marks or designs woven into them, for many generations before the coming of the present white people. No woman would wear a hat that she would make herself, believing that it was unlucky for her to do so.

It is a pleasure for me to say that my people never had a war with the present white people, for in the first coming of Ken-e-ahs we took up all differences of a serious nature between us and settled it ourselves, so as to make it satisfactory with them, and forced it to be satisfactory with my people. Thus we kept down those of our people that were disposed to go to bloody wars, and only for this we might have held the whites back for a long time on account of the roughness of the country. It is only about seventy years since we first knew of the white people that are here now.

Chapter XIX
The Marriage Laws

The Klamath Indians intermarry to some extent with the surrounding tribes. The upper and lower divisions of the Klamath tribes marry very freely, being the same tribe, with the exception that their language is different. The two divisions are so closely associated with each other that many of our people speak both languages fluently. It was always considered a good marriage for a man of the lower division to marry a woman of the upper division, or a man of the upper division to marry a woman of the lower division; but they always preferred to marry outside their own division if possible, as they were not so liable to marry relations. It was not considered good to marry relations, even to fifth and sixth cousins, as their law taught them that marrying blood relations was a crime against posterity. It was considered a crime for parents to bring demented or deformed children into the world.

By marriage they keep a close trace of their relationship. The woman never loses her identity by marrying, as she takes the name of her husband and the husband takes the name of his wife, as the following will illustrate. A Trinidad woman marries a man of the Pec-wan village, the Indian name of which is Cho-ri; therefore the woman is Cho-ri woman, and they call her husband after marriage Cho-rosh. The husband is a Pec-wan man; therefore they call the wife after him and call her Pec-wish-on. The children are called Pec-wan-alth, and are always addressed by these names, which remind them that their mother is a Cho-ri woman and their father a Pec-wan. This custom is followed so that they can trace out their relationship exactly for generations.

Occasionally a Talth will marry the daughter of a wealthy family; however, they are very careful in selecting their wives, as they usually marry into the Talth families, if they can marry where there is no relationship. Some of the very rich men had plural wives, or as many wives as they cared to support, but the average Indian had but one wife. There has been some instances of plural marriages since the white man made his appearance on the Klamath River, one of which I will make special mention of.

This Indian who had made eleven women his wives was born under the very lowest marriage laws at the Wah-tec village, and was known as Ca-wah-ter; his parents were extremely poor, living in poverty and squalor at the Wah-tec village, where they raised a large family of children. The romance of his parents was very pathetic, as they had nothing to give in exchange of the marriage vows except some manzanita berries. The exchange of foodstuffs in the marriage ceremony is considered the very lowest of marriages that could be called a marriage. From this lowly marriage were born several brothers and one sister. Ga-wah-ter and his brothers, when they had grown into manhood, were all industrious and became good managers in securing wealth, as the bitter taunts of the poverty of their parents urged them on to greater ambitions. While they were children, the children of the middle and wealthy class would not associate with or play with them; they were always being coldly shunned by the other children and looked down upon as unworthy of respect. Children of the wealthier class would always make insinuations that the brothers and sister of this family were born under the very lowest of marriage, that their parents were nothing, hardly worthy of notice. These children grew up almost in desperation, being despised so much for their poverty, and the storms of insinuations were continually hurled at them in defiance: to become anything better, where their birth was so lowly. When they reached manhood, they were stricken with remorse because of their lowly birthright. Their parents were both born of good birth, their families having at one time a good deal of wealth before they were married so unfortunately. With that remorse of poverty sunken deep into their hearts, these young men started out in the pursuit of the Indian life to hunt, trap, fish and accumulate all the wealth they could possibly get. Early and late, the brothers were always at work, as great ambitions spurred them on to accumulate vast riches and rise up from the lowly depths, where they had been so despised. They worked and banked their wealth together until they became very rich; then they separated and married, each taking his portion of the wealth as they went to different places to make homes for their families.

Ga-wah-ter, with renewed energies everytime he thought of the bitter stings of his early boyhood years and struggles, determined to become one of the richest men on the lower Klamath River. His prayers were so sincere, his ambitions so great, his toil so earnest, that his reward came after the weary years of struggle, for he was now one of the richest men the Klamath River had known for generations. He rose to power and greatness from a miserable downtrodden child. Now his triumphs were supreme, for he had crowned himself with success and everlasting power, and could now look down upon those who had scorned him so much in his youth, for they could never be so rich as he. When his vast fortune was made, eleven wives shared his home at Ser-e-goin village, where he spent most of his wedded life. His first wife belonged to the upper division of the Klamath Indians, and was the romantic bride of his life, as he had given to her the love of his young manhood, and his tender devotion was hers throughout the years of their wedded life. When the ten other brides had come to dwell in their home, she remained his constant companion and counselor of the household. One to five children were born to all the wives except the first wife. Sometimes the wives would all get to quarreling and become very insolent to one another. Then the husband would appear upon the scene and whip them all, except his first wife; he never punished her, as he loved her more than all the rest.

For many years, with riches, wives and children around him, he was a powerful member of the Klamath Indians. As he grew old, family troubles arose among his relatives and sons, which resulted in bloodshed and loss of lives. One day, under the excitement of all these troubles, he started to swim across the river, as no canoe was at hand, and while swimming across at Ser-e-goin village, severe cramps overtook his already tired body, and he met the tragic death of drowning. A very large family of children were left fatherless, and the wives separated off from the home at Ser-e-goin, each one taking her own children. Some of these children are alive yet and have a great deal of wealth. This closes the summary of one of the plural marriages of the Klamath Indians.

Some of the Talth had plural wives, but they always married the first wife by the highest marriage ceremony so that the children born under this marriage would be eligible to be admitted to the Sacred Lodge. As before, the husband takes the wife's name and is always addressed by her name, while the wife is addressed by the husband's name: an exchange of names as well as the exchange of marriage vows. The other women that may be married to a Talth under the plural marriage are not married by the highest marriage laws; therefore, their children can never be admitted to the Sacred Lodge. Plural marriages among the Talth are very seldom, and a Talth under no circumstances will marry a slave, or anyone of the low class. The Talth usually select their wife or husband with great care from the families of high birth. When they marry, they live very happily and are devoted to their families. They were never known to gamble or drink the white man's whiskey, their soul being free from all temptations.

I will here illustrate the devotion of one of the Talth marriages. This Talth was of a very wealthy family of the Pec-wan village, who married a woman of the Tu-rep village. Under the Indian laws of marriage, the husband took his wife's name and was known as Tur-rep-ah-wah, and the wife was known as Pec-wish-on. After they had been married for two or three years, the wife contracted a chronic illness which made her almost a helpless invalid for a number of years, and the devoted husband would cook, wash, sweep and attend to all the household duties. He remained by the side of his sick wife day and night, administering to her every want, leading her tenderly about, taking her in his canoe for long boat rides on the river, that she might get the fresh air and grow strong again. He secured the very best Indian doctors for her, and paid all the doctor bills during all these years of her illness. His kind patience and attentions towards her never failed him, as he continued in this way, giving up all his time to his wife for a number of years until, at last, with all his effort, he succeeded in almost making her well, and she is yet alive. He lived for a few years, then died, leaving her a widow.

The Talth marriage is a long ceremony, where a great deal of wealth is exchanged between the two families of the bride and groom. This ceremony is principally performed by the Indian money, cheek, which is a long slender shell, conical in shape and is inclined to be curved. It is about one-and-a-half to two-and-a-quarter inches in length, and is valued according to its length; and the longer the shell the more value it is. This money is measured by the rings of the joints of the middle finger from the inside of the left hand, and it takes twelve pieces of cheek to make one string, which is called caw-ton-a. In stringing the cheek they put the two large ends together and the two small ends together; this is done to prevent the shells from cupping inside. In estimating the value of a string of cheek, we hold one end of the string between the forefinger and thumbnail of the left hand, drawing it tightly up the arm towards the shoulder, keeping the arm extended straight. Ten of the cheek on the string are measured in this way, not measuring the two which makes twelve on the string, as the twelve

Lucy Thompson's father and mother (top) and her mother's house (bottom). [See page 184.] (Illustration from the original edition of *To the American Indian.*)

Salmon was the staple of the Klamath Indians, who prayed for its bounty, feasted on it fresh, and dried it for later use. Their lives revolved around the coming of the salmon; their myths told of its origin.

only make ten according to our numeration; we do not count the extra two cheek on the string, as we wish to give full value so that no one will be able to find any fault as to the value of the string. In measuring the cheek, a tattoo is made on the arm where the end of the string comes, so they can easily detect if any of the cheek has been exchanged, should it happen to be handled by different persons. In marriage the young Talth gives twelve strings of this cheek to the parents of his bride, as it is the real Indian money that we brought from the old land of Cheek-cheek-alth; the parents give in exchange other valuable articles to their son-in-law. The elder Talth always attend these high marriages, bringing with them the herb, walth-pay, with which they give the benediction to the bridal couple, in wishing them peace, love, happiness and success.

The children born under these marriages are selected by the Talth and are given the opportunity to become a Talth. A Talth is very reserved and never advances to meet anyone who is a stranger that is inquiring into our traditions. Our traditions and religion are too sacred to be expounded before strangers of another race; therefore the white man has received most of his allegory from the lower classes of the Indians. This type of Indian readily gives the fairy tales of the tribe, such as mothers and grandmothers tell to the little children for their amusement; and these are the stories that the white man is made to believe as the true traditions and religion of the Indian. These stories are no more like the traditions and religion of the Indian than daylight is like night.

There is another marriage law that is termed among the Indians as "half-married." The prospective husband gives but a small sum of articles, of little value, and receives in return a few articles of little value. In this marriage the husband is taken to the wife's home to live, or in the same house with her parents; and the wife, in this marriage, is the head of the household, and the husband is compelled to obey her in whatever she commands him to do. He is compelled to fish, hunt, work and support her folks just as much as he supports his wife, while the wife teaches the children and rules them absolutely, as the husband has no right to correct his own children or make them mind in any way. When these children become men and women, they must marry according to their mother's wishes, as the husband has nothing to say as to their conduct or pursuits of happiness in life. However unpleasant it may seem to him, he must bear it all with patience and silence. If he refuses to obey his wife and children, she can make his surroundings in home life very unpleasant for him, and if he wishes to dissolve the marriage vows and she is willing, he has nothing to do but to walk out of the house, as his wife guides the children and rules the household, and owns everything that belongs to him, except his own individual life; even his own children acknowledge him as their father in flesh and blood, but no more.

There is a slave marriage where, they being absolute paupers, having no home of their own and no articles to exchange in the marriage ceremony, they are married by the exchange of food-stuffs, and this is considered to be the lowest marriage that could be called a marriage. When they have a divorce they do not have much trouble in separating, as articles are given back by their masters and a settlement is usually made easy.

In some of the Indian marriages, they do not mate happily. After they have been married a short time, or even a number of years, serious trouble arises and results in a final separation, and when such a separation is agreed upon, and there are no children, all the valuables exchanged at the marriage altar are returned accordingly. If there are children and the father wants them to remain legitimate, he must be very careful in counting out the valuables or the wealth that he wants returned from his wife's people. He must divide a portion of the wealth that he gave to his wife's people on his wedding day to each child; the remaining portion is given back to him. If all the valuables of exchange between the contracting parties are returned to him or his people, this leaves the children as bastards, without a law to protect them from slanderous tongues and no rights to a legitimate birth. These children are forever looked down upon by the Indian society as bastards, without a marriage to legalize them as the offspring of respectable parents.

I can truthfully say that in the past twenty-five years and more, since the advent of the white man among the Klamath Indians, that most of the white men have married under the half-married system, until there are no Indian marriage laws. The "squaw" gives her "white buck" her home and supports his low-born half-breed children, while he idles his time away on the Indian ranches or lies about in a drunken stupor. Yet these same white men cry: "Is there no redress for the Indian, has he no soul to save?" Oh, not a soul to save under these conditions. But why do these white men hang around the Indian ranches and reservations, living off the toils of the Indian? There is a pathetic story in this nefarious business of human lives. The Indian himself has followed pursuit after his white brethren in the half-married system, or not marrying at all, until there is no sacred marriage tie. This shows positively that the Indian laws are forever lost. Education is the only way out of these difficulties, for those who have had an opportunity to attend the schools have married under the laws of the United States, and these laws must be enforced, since all the Indian laws have been abolished by the degenerate white men. I trust the day is not far distant when the degenerate white man will no longer be tolerated to camp on the reservations and leave in his path the ruination of human lives.

Before the appearances of the white man, the marriage of the middle and wealthy classes were considered sacred, the most sacred ties that could bind a human being for the cause of the future generation. Divorces were considered a disgrace upon posterity and a shame upon moral society; therefore, divorces were few and far between. When a divorce cause was pleaded, usually trouble ensued that resulted in bloodshed before the case would be settled. These divorces sometimes left the birth of the children for slanderous tongues to assail, and when these children became of age they would resent bitterly the action of their father and mother, and the feud would be renewed, sometimes for several generations before a final settlement would be made. Divorces among the Indians were very difficult to obtain, as it was ruinous to posterity, and a menace upon society. Among the Talth divorces were unknown.

Chapter XX
The Two Famous Athletes

The Indians play a game that is similar to the white man's football game, with the exception that the Indians use sticks and the white man a ball; therefore this game has been termed in English as the "stick game." The Indian name for it is oh-wetlth-per. They select the giants, or the greatest athletes of the tribe, to make up the two teams. In this contest one division of the tribe will offer a challenge to the surrounding tribes, and the challenge is contested by any division who think they are capable and strong enough to make the meet. The [lower] Klamath tribe usually played games with the upper division of the tribe and often plays against the Hoopa Indians, and sometimes the Smith Rivers. Each side would put up large sums of money and valuable articles for their chosen team, which would cause much excitement in betting and gambling upon the games. The side of the victorious team would win large sums of Indian money, which would add to the wealth of their division and make them more powerful. Therefore, each division would be very careful in selecting their giant athletes. The tallest, quickest, strongest and the most splendid physiques of men were chosen.

The Indians selected a level piece of ground upon which to play the game. There is one of these famous playgrounds but a few yards from the Wah-tec village. This game is very ancient, as the Indians say that it goes far back into the ages; and through the memory of evolution they have carried it forward down to the present day, where it will soon be lost forever unless the advent of the new race revives the old spirit of the game again. Upon the playground they draw a very large circle with lines across it; then, stepping to the center of this circle they make a small round hole which is about ten inches across at the surface, and from this hole they draw several other lines out to the larger circle, thus mapping out the different points of the game, as on a tennis court. They take two little sticks about three inches in length and carve out a nob at each end; then they fasten these two sticks together with a strong buckskin string and spread the untied ends apart about two inches; then they place the two tied sticks in the holes in the center of the court. Each team consists of twelve men, and they have an umpire to give the signal to start the game and to see that no foul or unfair means are taken by either side of the team. The men in each team have round sticks about twenty inches in length and that are straight, with the exception that a hook is made or carved on one end which is used for the purpose of hooking the tied sticks and tossing them about. There are twelve points to be played in this game.

When the two teams are lined up on the court, the umpire gives the signal for them to start, and the game is on. The leaders of the teams are watched from both sides, and scramble to see which side hooks the tied stick first from the middle of the court with his stick, and toss it as far as he can over his opponent's side of the court. Both teams now make a wild scramble, and pile up on one another in their effort to hook the sticks again with their sticks, and toss them back into their opponent's territory. If one of the teams can manage to toss the tied sticks out over the large circle of the court, on their opponent's side, they are the ones who win the point in the game. The team that can win the largest score in the number of points played in the game are the winners. The champion team is applauded and praised loudly by the immense crowds that gather to witness these interesting games. The players in their wild enthusiasm for the glorious laurels of victory usually clash together so roughly in their efforts to rescue the sticks from the other players that occasionally some of their members get hurt, and often crippled for life. There are some instances where a player has been killed outright upon the court in his desperate struggle against the onrushing crowd.

In olden-time when this game was played so much, there lived a young Indian by the name of Su-me-ah-chene who became one of the greatest athletes that the tribe ever had. He became so skilled in the game that he would never lose a single point. His dwelling place was on top of a high mountain that rose up in its majestic grandeur from the northeast banks of the Klamath River, and this place was over a distance of five miles from the village of Ca-neck. And this mountain was named in honor of the great champion and still bears his name to this day, being known among the Indians as the mountain of Su-me.

Su-me-ah-chene became very proud of his accomplishments in this favorite game, and issued a challenge to all the young men of the surrounding tribes, as he was anxious to match himself against any of their champions. His challenge was finally taken up by a young man who lived back of Trinidad and whose dwelling-place was also located on a high mountain, east of Trinidad, toward Redwood Creek. The grandeur of this mountain can be seen many miles away, up and down the coast and from many places far back on the surrounding mountains. This mountain is covered with a huge growth of pine and redwood timber, and is known among the Indians as Cay-way-ett Mountain, being named after the famous athlete who lived upon its summit. Su-me-ah-chene, hearing of Cay-way-ett's intentions of taking up the challenge, sent him word that he was ready to play. Cay-way-ett at once accepted the challenge, and they made arrangements to play the game on the Klamath River at the village of Ca-neck. The court was selected at the lower end of the high river bar, which made an ideal place to play the game. The two youthful giants both belonged to the lower divisions of the Klamath tribe. Together, they made arrangements for the day when the big meet should be held. They had now won the distinction of being the two leading athletes of the tribes, and they sent their invitations far and near, to all the people of the tribes to come and witness the great feat for the championship. Inspired with a great enthusiasm, the people assembled around the playground in a vast multitude that was eager, restless and talking, as the two giants appeared upon the court with their teams. Striding upon the court with the spring and step of the greatest of athletes, they represented two handsome figures as were ever seen among the tribes. They proudly met as superb beings in stately birth and tawny muscles, and many a maiden's heart was thrilled with emotion, when they beheld these champions, the handsomest of men. The two champions had as yet been proof against the arrows of matrimony, and all the pretty and wealthy maidens of the tribes had assembled to behold the everlasting courage and endurance of these two strong youths.

As the umpire gave the signal for the game to start, the crowds watched with keen interest. Su-me-ah-chene and his team played hard and furious as their opponents were close upon them, and after a long and desperate struggle he and his team succeeded in tossing the tied sticks over the outer circle of the court, and won the first point amid the applauding and shouting of the spectators. An intermission for rest is always held after each point, and Su-me-ah-chene, glowing in the first triumphs, left the court and walked among the maidens to make their acquaintance and hear their words of praise. As he spoke to many, he lingered in a crowd of upriver girls, where his attention was attracted to three dark-eyed beauties who had come from Cah-ah-man, or known to the white people as Orleans Bar. He at once made their acquaintance and lingered, talking with them until it was time for him to join his team and play for the second point. Renewed with strange emotions, something akin to love, the gallant champion played furious and won point after point, until the game was finished. He had not lost a single point in the game. During the intermission of each point, he would seek out the three pretty maidens, and linger in their company until he fancied himself desperately in love with one of them.

Laureled with fame and wealth at the close of the game, he proceeded at once to the girls, and walked with them as they mingled with the departing crowds. Walking at the side of the maiden, he was loath to part with her at all, as he extended to the three girls a hearty invitation for them to come and visit his home, in the village of Su-me. They eagerly accepted his invitation, as they were highly honored to get the opportunity to visit him, and they inquired of him how they would find his house from the rest of the houses in the village. He assured them that they would make no mistake in finding the house, as he described to them that there was a large pine tree standing just in front of his home. There were no green branches on this tree, as it had died a long time ago, and the small sapsuckers had bored into the trunk of the tree and built their homes there, as they could be seen flying about the tree. He gave them such a vivid description of the tree that he assured them they could not possibly miss his house. The girls were delighted with him and departed with bright anticipations in visiting the champion in his home. Say-gap, or the Coyote who lived in his home at the lower western end of the Su-me village, was near the happy group and overheard Su-me-ah-chene's invitation and description of the dead pine tree, so he planned to entertain the girls himself, that they may not go to visit Su-me-ah-chene in his home.

The day that the girls had planned to visit Su-me-ah-chene, Mr. Coyote moved the pine tree down in front of his house, and when the girls arrived at the village of Su-me, they began at once to look for the tree Su-me-ah-chene had described to them. After they had looked about for a short time, one of them pointed down the hill to the lower western end of the village, to the tree, and said that must be the place they were looking for. Delighted upon seeing the tree, they rushed down the hill to Say-gap's house. Say-gap met them at the door with a cordial welcome, and asked them in. They all entered the house and seated themselves while he was planning how he could best entertain the girls and make himself appear very attractive to them. He summoned his grandmother and asked her to spread a banquet for the young ladies, and told her she must prepare the very best of foodstuffs they had in the house for the evening meal. The grandmother began to move about in the adjoining room in the rear of the house, as if she was preparing the food for supper. She had a large basket of acorn mush already cooked and hid away, so her nephew (he was her nephew instead of her grandchild) would not eat it all himself, as he would always eat up everything that was good and let her go hungry. This acorn mush she kept hid, and did not bring it out for Say-gap and his guests to feast upon. She pretended to look among the shelves for a while and fumbled through them, when she at last brought out a large Indian plate of shrimps, or some sort of worm that looked very much like shrimps. She came into the room where Say-gap was entertaining the girls and began to roast the worms on the coals. The worms would twist about on the coals, pop and fly all over the house. The girls looked at one another in dismay, and wondered if this was the best food that his house could afford. They became very angry and said that they had been deceived. Rising from the seats, they told their host that they now did not believe him to be Su-me-ah-chene, but he was an imposter. They fled from the house in a rage and returned to their homes at Orleans Bar. Say-gap followed them home and kept pleading, saying he was Su-me-ah-chene, their much admired champion of the "stick game." This made the girls more peeved than ever, so they made a resolution among themselves, that they would not accept Su-me-ah-chene's attentions or consider any excuses that he might offer, if they chanced to meet him again.

After a few days the girls received word that Su-me-ah-chene was going to play again at another big meet, so they all agreed to go and see it as before. At the meet, Su-me-ah-chene in his usual good spirits was animated with glory upon winning the first point, so during the intermission he resolved to find the three girls and inquire why they did not keep their promise to visit him, as he felt very much disappointed. Upon finding the girls, he greeted them in his usual good humor, but they drew themselves up haughtily and refused to speak to him, as they believed that he was making light of them and having a lot of amusement among his friends at their expense. As before, he won all the points, and during the intermissions he would return to the girls, thinking perhaps he could find out what was wrong and win their friendship again. The girls as before treated him very coldly, and were so haughty that they would not listen to any of his excuses. Toward the closing of the game the three girls moved over on Cay-way-ett's side of the court, which provoked Su-me-ah-chene. When the crowds started for their homes after the game, Su-me-ah-chene said he would go down to the mouth of the river, at Reck-woy village, to visit for a few days, as he had been turned down by the three girls. Upon reaching the village, a host of pretty girls were glad to meet the much-talked-of champion, and all greeted him with a royal welcome. When his visit ended, he announced to the girls his intentions of playing another game at Ca-neck with the Cay-way-ett team, and gave them all an invitation to come.

Again another game was being held at Ca-neck, for the championship between Su-me-ah-chene and Cay-way-ett. All the Reck-woy girls were to be present, and were highly honored to think that Su-me-ah-chene himself had invited them. Su-me-ah-chene and his team as usual won the first point, and during the intermission for rest, he went among the Reck-woy girls to visit with them. They were all pleased to be honored with his company and marveled over his great athletic feats, and he soon fancied that he was falling in love again, this time with one of the pretty little Reck-woy girls.

Su-me-ah-chene won every point as he had in the previous games, and after receiving the cheering congratulations of the Reck-woy girls, together with the maiden of his choice, he invited some of them to come and visit him at his home. The girls were pleased over the invitation to visit him, and promised to visit him in a few days. He described to them the dead pine tree, where the sapsucker would be flying about, so they could easily find the house, which was located near the center of the village. Four of the girls came to visit the champion as they had promised; they crossed the river and climbed the hill to Su-me village, where, following his directions closely, they easily found the tree and the house. They found him home, and entered, he appearing handsomer than ever as he greeted them with a hearty welcome and said he was glad they had kept their promise. He entertained them so nicely that the time went by quickly, and he was loathe to have them depart so soon. They were having such a splendid time that he suggested they spend the night at his home, to which the girls readily agreed. The next morning the girls returned to their homes at Reck-woy, very tired and happy after being so pleasantly entertained by the young champion. A few days after the departure of the girls, Su-me-ah-chene decided he would go to Reck-woy and return the visit, and during this visit a romance developed into matrimony, as he wooed for his bride the pretty maiden of his choice. After the wedding the proud little bride accompanied her husband to his home, where she began housekeeping in an elegant fashion. Meanwhile his rival Cay-way-ett and the maid of Orleans Bar had married.

After the wedding of the giants, they were very happy with their brides only for a short time, and they challenged each other for another game, to which they both agreed. The multitudes of people had assembled to witness the big meet as usual, to applaud and praise their favorite champion. While the two giants were engaged upon the court with their powerful teams, the wife of Cay-way-ett stole away from the crowd to the home of Su-me-ah-chene. Upon reaching it she entered, and selected one of the beautiful dresses of Mrs. Su-me-ah-chene and gowned herself in it. She dolled herself up very handsomely in the dress and ornaments and seated herself in the seat of honor, as being the lady of the household. Su-me-ah-chene approached Mrs. Cay-way-ett, believing her to be his wife, as she assured him that she was his Reck-woy wife instead of the bride from Orleans. Mrs. Su-me-ah-chene saw her husband, to her great indignation, caress the other woman, and at once believed him to be unfaithful to her. She at once recognized the beautiful dress that Mrs. Cay-way-ett wore to be her own, and all this leading her to believe stronger than ever that this strange woman had stolen the affection of her husband, and that he had allowed her to usurp her of her household. Believing this all to be true, Mrs. Su-me-ah-chene assailed her husband, to his great surprise, with a hot torrent of angry words, and fled from him back to her home in Reck-woy.

The truth dawned upon the broken-hearted champion that Mrs. Cay-way-ett had deceived him in making him believe that she was his wife, and at once sought his girl bride at Reck-woy, and pleaded at her feet to return with him to their home at Su-me. But her pride had been wounded beyond endurance, and she haughtily turned from the greatest of champions, and the greatest of men, and left his stately form bowed down with grief, a sense of a deep loss, and the sorrowing presence of loneliness. Thus the true sweet bride of his affections had been ruthlessly borne by the wings of fate away from the love of his mighty manhood. Grieved and hurt by this great blow, he refused the attentions of Mrs. Cay-way-ett.

This treacherous woman had sought revenge, as she believed that Su-me-ah-chene had deceived her for his own amusement, when she first visited him at Su-me and the Say-gap had followed her to her home at Orleans Bar. As the wife of the other giant, Cay-way-ett, she became enarmored with the mightiest of athletes, Su-me-ah-chene, as she remembered he was once her lover. Having lost his love after he became the champion, she was thrilled with passions for his great victories, and determined to deceive him. She falsely declared to her husband that she was going on a visit to her people at Orleans Bar, and he readily consented to her going. For a time he believed his wife was visiting her people, but to his great disappointment he found her to be unfaithful to the marriage vows, as she was attempting to win the love and admiration of Su-me-ah-chene. Thus the greatest of men were robbed of the affections of their young brides. The cheer and comfort in their homes of fame and wealth, and the love of a glorious womanhood, had faded.

The moral of this story is to impress the fact upon the mind of a young bride: that if she is fickle with the love of a great man, and plans to deceive him in the belief that she will win a greater man, and a greater love, she will most likely to her great sorrow lose them both. Far better to love the truly great, who love you in return, than to lose that love in plotting and planning, for the greatest who love you not.

(Top) Houses along the Trinity River near Fort Gaston and the Indian Agency, Hoopa Valley. (Bottom) Tish Tang Ranch on the Trinity River, upstream from Hoopa Valley. Both photos date from the 1880s.

Chapter XXI
Pec-wan Colonel

Pec-wan Colonel (his Indian name was Me-quin) had been for the last fifty or sixty years the richest Indian among the lower Klamaths. When standing erect he was probably a little over six feet, of medium build, and was very graceful in his movement. He was a fine-looking man, and every inch an aristocrat. He was a descendant of a very wealthy family on both sides of the house, and his mother was born in the Cor-tep village, about one-half mile below Pec-wan village. There was five boys and two girls of his mother's family. His uncles, aunts, and grandmother on his father's side belonged to the upper division of the tribe, and they too were a wealthy family. Pec-wan's mother was from a family of doctors, his mother and her two sisters being doctors. His mother was without question the most noted and prominent woman doctor that the lower rivers had among them, for the past seventy-five years or more. When she married his father, whom they called Cor-tep-pish by his being married to a Cor-tep woman, she married a man of a very wealthy family, and when her mother and father died they cut her off, and did not give her any part of the riches of her own family, but divided it among the four sisters and two brothers.

She had five children, three girls and two boys, the Colonel being the third child, and he followed close to his mother's ways. She would go out and sit on her doorsteps of the front porch, stoop over with her elbows on her knees, and comb her hair over her face with her fingers; then rest her chin on her hands, and sit gazing into the distance; and other ways, thereby causing all to be afraid of her except the Talth and their families, over whom she had no control. All the wealthy and slave classes became sorely afraid of her. Whenever the people would see her sitting thus, they began to murmur among themselves, saying that she was trying to make someone sick, and that somebody would be sick. If someone should become sick anywhere within a distance of a number of miles from her, their first thought was that she had made them sick, and she was the one that could cure them.

These doctors are paid in advance for their services, and when they came after her, instead of accepting what pay they brought and offered to her, she would talk with the greatest of shrewdness, comment on the case, and demand of them the most valuable articles which she knew they had, and would scheme to get all she could. She seemed to have a magic power to cure, and did cure in most cases, as she had perfect confidence in herself and gave perfect confidence to the sick one of her ability to make them well, somewhat on the same principal of the Christian Scientist among the people of today. But for this pay the doctor had to cure the sick person, and if the patient should die within a year from the time the doctor prescribed for them, she is compelled to give back all that was given to her. This doctor seldom had to return her fee, and gathered wealth in abundance and succeeded in her shrewd practice. Taking from her brothers and sisters the entire fortune that her mother and father had left them, she had power and influence among her people. She tried to make doctors of her three daughters, but they became the most commonest kind. She turned nearly all of her fortune's wealth over to her son, the Colonel, and while he did not have the shrewdness of his mother, he managed in the long run, by deaths and otherwise, to get possession of the greater part of the wealth of so many rich relations that he too had power and influence above his people. His walk, manner and very actions were very impressive to anyone that met him. He would never eat in a white man's house; my house was the only white man's house he was ever known to stop in overnight and eat at the table. He was very liberal in his own house, and the white man has had many meals at his table. Pec-wan Colonel was born at Pec-wan village, where the Talth lodge is located.

A full-blooded Klamath Indian, born of wealthy parents but of the middle class, and with all of his wealth and influence he could not become a Talth. Therefore he could at all times and on all occasions keep his place; he knew where he could come in, and where to keep back, with perfect ease. He was closely related to the Talth families, and when it came to festivals, he could and did lead them all with more deerskins, silver-grey fox skins and other kinds, with enough strings of turk-tum and cheek to cover the breast of all who danced, besides long and valuable flints, both red and black, and all kind of dancing fixtures. He always kept a large camp with plenty of provisions, and plenty of women to cook and wait on the crowds; he was very liberal and fed many.

He was mean to his slaves and cared nothing for visiting

Indians of other tribes, only his own Klamath people; and to all of these he was closely related to, far up the river, and he visited them as far up as they lived. In the large festivals he could draw on the Pech-ic-las, his relatives, for whatever he wanted to keep him at all times in the lead. He had but one wife. She was also of a wealthy family, and when he thought at one time to take another wife, she told him plainly that there would be no two wives for her, that she could and would go to her father's home and not return; so he gave up the notion and remained with her.

She was a good woman, very kind of disposition and pleasant of manner. She never had any children, and has been dead now for about twelve years. There is a nephew of his named Pec-wan Harry; he married a woman who lived close to the mouth of the river at Wah-kell village. And he is now called Wah-kell Harry, and they have quite a family of children; and to him went nearly all of the wealth. He too is a fine-looking man of the same build as Pec-wan Colonel.

Chapter XXII
A Narrative of the Humboldt Indians

The following is a true narrative of the way that the Humboldt Indians (Way-yets) have been treated and almost exterminated by the white man. Humboldt Bay, being a harbor where vessels could come in and make a safe landing, was the place where the whites would naturally first make a settlement, and make a base from which to supply the miners and cattle raisers; therefore it soon became a town. First it was called Bucksport, and afterwards named Eureka; and the whole surrounding country was at the first coming of the white man thickly populated with Indians, there being hundreds of them, and even up into the thousands. These Indians, the Klamath River Indians, were called in their language the Way-yets, and the country in which they lived, or around Humboldt Bay, they called We-ott. They also had names for the different places, such as Ar-ca-tah (Arcata), Per-wer (Eureka), and at times they would call the whole of the country Per-wer.

As the whites became more numerous they began to crowd the Indians back more and more, never at anytime willing to concede that the Indians had any right to anything that they wanted, until the Indians began to rebel at being drove from their homes, where they had lived for thousands of years. Whenever they made the least resistence, the whites were up in arms, until finally the Humboldt Indians were moved to a reservation at Smith River and kept there for a time, among the Smith River Indians. The Smith River Indians were not friendly with them, not treating them kindly, and many of them died there for the want of food, as they did not know the country and could not gather food supplies. When some of them would go out to get fish or gather supplies, the Smith River Indians, being jealous of them, would follow and kill them, and the soldiers would never say a word or reprimand them, and only laugh at them. They had no medicine case when sick and had no way of treating the sick ones in their way. They had no sanitary provisions and could not keep themselves clean, which they were strict about in their own homes. The young girls had no rights with the soldiers or white men and were diseased, and if an Indian made any objection to the white man's treatment, they were in return kicked and abused, and often killed; in this way many of them died at Smith River.

The Klamath Indians called Crescent City Caw-pay, and Smith River He-na; and all the Indians are one tribe [in those places], and they call them He-nas, but sometimes designate the certain part in which they live by calling them Caw-pay Indians. So after they had been kept on Smith River reservation for awhile, they were driven like a lot of hogs, only with less care as to whether they lived or died, to the Klamath River Reservation, which extended from the Pacific up the Klamath River for a distance of twenty miles, extending out one mile on either side of the river. When they were driven to the Klamath River Reservation they were treated by the lower Klamath

Indians in a more humane way, as a part of the Klamath Indians were good to them and tried to see them get something to live on, and would doctor the sick ones, helping them as much as they could; that is, a certain part of them would. They kept the ones that were supposed to be unfriendly to the poor Humboldts from doing them harm, yet many of them died while on the Klamath.

After keeping them for a while, the order came to move them to the Hoopa Indian Reservation, which is situated on the Trinity River and comes down the Trinity to its junction with the Klamath River and into Humboldt County; so the Humboldts were gathered together again by the soldiers, and were kicked and clubbed, the children thrown into boats; and when killed they were cast into the river. While this murdering was going on, the head men of the lower Klamath Indians went to the Humboldts and told them to make a break and run and hide in the brush, for they might just as well perish in that way as be all killed by the brutal soldiers. So a good many of them made good their escape, wandering through the woods, and the Klamath Indians picked up many of them and took care of them for a number of years, while many of them died from exposure and starvation. I have seen the bones of quite a number where they had died in the heavy redwood timber, and the soldiers took what Indians were left to the Hoopa Reservation. The Indians here did not like them, and they had no way to gather provisions on which to live and no way to doctor or take care of the sick, no sanitation by which to keep clean. Once a week two or three pounds of flour was given out to each family to live or die on. The Klamath Indians would buy beef from the agent and give it to them to keep them from starving, and when things became more quiet, the Klamath

Indians took most of them that they had picked up and took them to Hoopa, to their own people, and left them there. After this had dwindled down to a mere nothing, by the help of the lower Klamaths a few got back to Humboldt Bay, their ancient home. To finish them up, as they were having a festival on what is now called Gunther Island, just north of Eureka, a crowd of six or eight white men took a canoe and slipped over there in the night with axes, clubs and knives and murdered innocent men, women and children, which nearly exterminated the once great and numerous tribe of Indians known as the Humboldts, and by the lower Klamath Indians as the Way-yets.

One influential Humboldt Indian and his family was kept safely at Pec-wan village by Weitch-ah-wah (my own father), and after everything was quiet on Humboldt Bay, Weitch-ah-wah brought him and his family back to their home, where he lived peaceably for many years, having died only a few years previous to this writing. Today there are not more than twenty or less Indians living, and what are left have lost completely all their old and ancient customs and teachings. They never had only the most spurious ideas of the Talth Order when they were placed here by Wah-pec-wah-mow (God) and given their country and language. Sometimes it seems hard to think of man's inhumanity, but as sure as the sun goes down, the white man will suffer for his wicked treatment of the Humboldt Indians.

Chapter XXIII
The Romance of a Wild Indian

This happened during the early years of my grandmother's life, and concerns principally a family at Reck-woy village, at the mouth of the river. On the south side of the river is a village named Wealth-quow, and at this place the Indians gave a large entertainment, where many guests had assembled to take part in the dance. This dance is commonly known in the English language as the Brush Dance. The Indians always begin dancing these dances after sundown, and sometimes dance until late at night. Large crowds had gathered at this dance, and among the guests were three girl friends from across the river at Reck-woy who joined the dancers in their usual custom of holding a bunch of brush over their faces so no one would know who they were. All the dancers, both men and women, hold the bunch of brush over their faces, after the fashion of a masquerade ball.

While the dancers were making merry, two wild Indians came in and joined them with the brush over their faces, and nobody knew who they were. When the dancers finished for a short intermission, the three Reck-woy girls left the room and went down to the foot of the hill, about thirty yards away where a spring gushed out of the hillside. Laughingly, they had gone to get a drink of nice cold water from the spring, and wash their faces in the cool, refreshing water. As they left the house, the two wild Indians followed them down to the spring, and upon reaching it, they sprang upon one of the girls, named Os-slook-o-may, and captured her, covering her mouth with their hands so she could not scream for help, and the other two girls made their escape back to the house to give the alarm. Everything being favorable for the wild Indians, as the thickets grew high and dense, and the forests being near, they were soon lost in the inky shadows of the big trees, where they carried their captive. The two Indians traveled with the girl all night, going in a southerly direction away from the river, and as they went along through the darkness, she would take small pieces of her buckskin apron and tie them to the bushes, thus making a trail which aided her followers for a long distance. When the alarm was given that Os-slook-o-may had been captured by the wild Indians, the guests did not dance anymore, and all the men who were able went in pursuit of the wild Indians to rescue the girl. They lost her among the dark shadows of the trees, as they could not find any trail to follow that night, and the next morning they all started out in hot pursuit, soon finding the trail she had left. The girl's supply of strings had become exhausted, and therefore she had no means of leaving any further trace of the direction her captors were taking her. However, they searched the hills, creeks and mountains for several days, but never found her trail again, and she was given up to the wilds; and the procession turned homeward, very sad and heart-broken.

Somewhere in the depths of a dark canyon among the redwoods, the wild Indians had carried Os-slook-o-may. When they reached their hiding place, one of the Indians made her his wife, after the fashion of a primeval wedding. The wild Indians are always very rich in all kinds of Indian wealth, and

222

this wild Indian dressed his bride in the most beautiful of Indian dresses, made of buckskin and ornamented with shells, and lavished wealth upon her. A little son came to their home in the wilds of which they were both very proud, and they watched the little baby grow into a robust, handsome little fellow who by nature inherited the ways of his father as soon as he was big enough to walk and talk. He would run away from his mother and skip among the trees, romp among the bushes and seemingly never grow tired of his wild revelry; he would talk and whistle to himself; and this grieved his mother very much, as she had tried every plan to subdue him from his wild romping, but of no avail.

When the boy was about six years of age, his mother became very lonesome for her people and wished very much to see them again, so one day she summoned up the courage to ask her husband to allow her to return to her home on a visit, as she said her folks were mourning for her as lost, having given up hopes of seeing her alive. He consented to let her go home on a visit, and said that she could take her little boy with her, so they began to make ready for the journey, as it was a long distance and the country was very rough. The O-ma-ha (Devil) husband, who was immensely rich, dressed his wife in one of the most beautiful of Indian dresses, and the little boy was also richly clad, and so they started on their journey to Reck-woy. The wild man guided and accompanied them until they neared the village of Wealth-quow, the village from which he had stolen her on the night of the dance, and here as they came into a small open space overlooking the village, he parted from his wife and little son, and they crossed the river and went into her native village. As she entered the village, she was most beautiful to behold, dressed in the most gorgeous Indian dress, with her little son by her side; and startled friends and relatives, who had mourned her as dead, greeted her with much surprise, as they had mourned her loss for nearly nine years.

Her folks were overjoyed to find their long-lost child restored to them, and with hearty greetings and a royal welcome, she found herself back in the village of her birth. With breathless interest they sat listening to her wonderful tales concerning her life in the solemn wilds, how she had been carried over mountain and crag, and through the huge forests, to a strange home in the cave in a cliff of rocks, where one of the wild men had made her his wife. In this strange cave she had enjoyed the comforts of a luxuriant home, for her husband was exceedingly rich and was very kind to her and their child. From her description, it seemed this cave was located at the source of Redwood Creek, which we call Cho-lu-wer-roy, in a dark canyon which is perhaps over a distance of sixty miles from Reck-woy, off in a southerly direction. In a cave of this dark canyon, surrounded on every side by the giant redwoods, she had spent nine years of her life listening to the sigh of the wind among the trees and strange enchantment of the babble of the brooks down the rocky canyon. Safe in her cave and lonely, with nothing but nature and a wild man to comfort her, she had grown more lonely as the years crept by in her desire to see her people once more. How they had traveled on their journey back along the creekbeds for a long distance, over high mountains and around sheer walls of great bluffs, and through the awful calm of dense forests and overhanging thickets. She had at last reached the home of her birth. Parting from her devoted husband for the first and last time, she faithfully promised to meet him again at the close of her visit, and return with him again to the cave in the wilds. During the first days of her visit, she encouraged her boy to associate with the children of the village. But he could not resist the calling of that wild nature he had inherited from his father, and all of his mother's pleadings proved of no avail in changing his character. He would watch his opportunity and run away from the other children and play by himself, among the dense bushes, jumping and whistling as he would go. His mother gave up in despair in her efforts to change his ways.

She remembered the day and place where she had promised to meet her husband and return with him to their home, but she refused to go and meet him at the appointed time and place, as she said she never intended to return, and had merely made him the promise in order to get back to her people; and now that she was with them she would never leave them again.

He waited in vain at the appointed place as she came not to meet him, and after waiting a long time he came to the conclusion that she had made him a false promise, so he crept cautiously down to the river and swam across to Reck-woy village, where he knew his wife was staying. When he reached the other side, he crept up the hillside and concealed himself in a dense clump of bushes, where he could look down upon the house where he knew she was staying, and watched for her. His wife seldom ventured out of the house, as she was afraid that he would get her again, so she kept close indoors that he might not have any chance of getting her away again. One day he managed to attract the attention of his little son, and he came up to his father and they talked together. He directed the son to go and tell his mother to come to him, as he was waiting for her.

When the son delivered the message to his mother, she

replied that she did not believe this to be true, so he returned to his father, telling him what his mother had said. He immediately sent him back to her, imploring that she come to him. The mother looked puzzled at the boy, and said that he must be mistaken, but he said that he knew his father, and pleaded earnestly for her to return to their home in the canyon. Studying the boy's eager face a few moments, she replied by saying that he could choose between her and his father; he could remain with her or go with his father, back into the lonesome wilds. The boy at once preferred his father, and bade his mother farewell. Father and son returned to their hiding place, and the mother, who had once cheered them in the lonesome wilds, never saw them again; they had gone out of her life forever, like a dream that had come and gone, and faded again, with the closing day, back into the primeval redwoods, where you may see father and son staying together among the mystic shadows of dreamland mountains.

When the Indians are dancing for pleasure, such as they did in the Brush Dance, and anyone wants them to dance faster and harder, they shout to the dancers: "hal-o-may-yah," which means dance harder. In this kind of dancing the word "dance" is called "o-may-like." But in the sacred dances, such as the Lodge Dance, it is called, Wah-neck-wel-la-gaw, and has a different meaning altogether.

Chapter XXIV
The Prophet Who Failed

This Indian was a Smith River, and the Klamath Indians in their tongue called him He-na Tom. In the year about Eighteen hundred and sixty-five, this He-na Tom, while living at his home on Smith River, which is north from the Klamath River, his wife became sick and died, and he mourned her loss greatly. In the fall he had a prophetic dream, which caused him to commence a sort of revival among the Smith River Indians, telling them to destroy everything they had ever received from the white people: discard all the clothing, houses, and in fact, burn all and everything, and go back to their old Indian way of living entirely, and in a short time all the dead Indians would come back to life to this world.

As it happened, He-na Tom had a sister that was married to a Klamath River man, and they had a family of grown sons and daughters; and this family lived in a village called Nigalth, which is situated on the west side of the Klamath River, opposite the mouth of Blue Creek, some eight miles down the river from where the Klamaths hold their White Deerskin Dance. So in the fall, after the Klamaths had finished putting in the fish dam and the Indians from all parts of the country had been invited to come and see the ceremony, and the White Deerskin Dance was going on, He-na Tom made his appearance among them with his sayings, telling them to destroy all their white man's goods, burn all the houses that were made in the white man's way, and tear down all their Indian houses; but not to burn the lumber of the Indian houses, thus leaving a clear opening; and for all of them to bring all their Indian money and wealth of all kinds, and hang it up in plain view around him where he was lying, covered with Indian blankets made of deerskin. He told them to go ahead with the White Deerskin Dance, so when the dead ones appeared, they would all dance with them and make a big jubilee, and all of them who failed to comply with his holy orders, and not bring their valuables, that it would all turn into rock or rocks, and those that disbelieved and did not come would themselves turn to rock. He had a great many of the Klamath Indians of the wealthy class, all of the poor class, and a few of the high class that was wild and willing to follow, and there was a lot of valuable property and things destroyed, while the shelves or tables were loaded with provision for the dead when they came, so they could eat, dance and all be joyful, while all the white people were to turn to rocks.

Some of the wise ones of the high class that were versed in the secret mysteries hung back saying no, that they wanted to see. While they were claiming that He-na Tom had gone to meet the dead Indians, and that he would be back with them that night, three or four of the doubtful ones went over to where the large piles of Indian blankets were by a fire, and on lifting up the blankets: behold, there was He-na Tom. They spoke to him, calling him by name, but he did not answer. His followers claimed that his body was there, but that his spirit had gone to meet the dead ones. When the old ones who were so highly versed in the mysteries as not to be hoodwinked had seen enough to convince them that there was no truth in it, they shook their heads, quietly moved back and retired to their camps or homes, saying that He-na's prophesies were a fake and that he was a humbug. As it turned out, that night He-na Tom slipped down the Klamath River to the mouth, and up the coast back to Smith River, his home. So when the Klamaths came to gather back their valuables, there was considerable of it that the rightful owners could not find, and never did get back, which made many of them very angry.

He-na Tom's brother-in-law was afterwards killed, and all of his Klamath relations were compelled to leave the Klamath River and go to Smith River to live for a number of years before they dared to return to the Klamath again. I have long since found that the Klamath Indians are bad fellows for anyone to try to play fake on. They have, or used to have, their wise ones that watched the different positions of the planets at different seasons of the year and tell of hard winters, of cold or warm summers, and of different harvest famines. They sometimes had dreams that they interpreted for good or bad. Other than this I have never heard of them ever having prophets.

Since the white race of people, that they found inhabiting the Klamath when they first arrived there, which we call the Wa-gas, which must have been thousands of years ago, they do not tell of ever having come in contact with any kind of white race, or of any other race ever coming among them until the present white race came, which we call Ken-e-ah. The Klamath River is so inaccessible, winding its way through high mountains, with no valley, that to this day it is a wild country with lots of game and fish. And there never has been a preacher of any kind among us to this day.

A dewy-eyed, romantic view of the Klamath River Indians. Titled "Weaver of Dreams" this image was taken by Emma B. Freeman about 1914.

Chapter XXV
Teachings of the
Klamath Indians of Childbirth

The Klamath Indians say that at the time the sun is at the farthest north and on the point which it is to turn back south, or as the white man counts time, the month of December (and which we count as the tenth month and call Cah-moh) is the worst and most objectionable time we have for a child to be born. Most of them die young or in infancy, and if they live they are of little use to themselves or the tribe. A child born in the time in which the acorns fall, which would be from the tenth of October to the twentieth of November, and which time or month we call Can-na-wal-at-tow, is the best or one of the best times, as these children are nearly all bright, healthy and prosperous, and make the leading ones, while children born in April, May and June, as we count the time, also make good, healthy and bright men and women, and also the leading ones. Children born between the twentieth of July and the first of September, which we call Cher-wer-ser-a, are weak and do not live long, most of them dying young, but if they do live they are foolish and not of any use to their people. Those that are born in the time the white man designates as October, May and June, are the ones that receive the prayers of the mother, grandparent and wise old heads of the tribe, and all look forward to their being useful to the tribe, particularly those that are of the high families. The Klamath Indians are a people that are at any and all times praying to the great father of all, and are pleased when a new baby is born. They take the best of care of the mother in childbirth, but if a woman brings into the world a child that is dead or stillborn, she is looked down upon and is almost cast aside, and has a hard time to pull through. If she dies in the struggle, there is but little sympathy for her loss, and if she lives, she is ever after called Cam-ma-gay so that any and all may know her; and if she is a married woman and has had children and saved them, and afterwards brings one into the world dead, she is always afterwards called Quirk-ker-alth.

In all my life among them I have never seen but few of these women, but do know some that have met with this misfortune. The Klamath Indians are the best in the world at handling their women in childbirth, in the old Indian way.

Chapter XXVI
The Wild Indian of Pec-wan

This happened at my birth place and about one mile up the Klamath River from my mother's birthplace, at Wah-tec village, both places being on the north side of the river. At Pec-wan village, there comes down from the east and north a creek that enters into the Klamath River at or near Pec-wan village, and is called Pec-wan Creek. This creek has three forks, the north, middle and south forks, the south fork being the largest one. The mountain rises to a height of about four or five thousand feet at the head of the south fork, and nearly the whole of the country of Pec-wan is covered with a dense growth of large timber and thick brush. In this vast forest of timber, there are sloping flats on the creek, and up the sides of the mountain there is oak timber, the acorn, from which we make our bread and which we call pop-saw.

In the fall, which is the last part of October, and on through the month of November, sometimes later, there was a family moved back on the south fork to a picking place. At these camps they most always have houses. Sometimes they are made of cedar bark and sometimes of boards, but they are made tight and comfortable, so if there comes a rain they can keep dry and warm, particularly the women and children. After they had been there for sometime and had gathered a quantity of acorns, there came some wild Indians (Oh-ma-ha) around on the outside of the houses, and as there was quite a number of young men in the camps, the girls were closely watched by the men, and were not much afraid of the wild men. The men would go outside and holler at the Oh-ma-has to come into the house, so that they could see them, but they were afraid to come in, only watching a chance to steal one of the girls and take her away for a wife. After the Indians had gathered as many acorns as they thought they wanted, they concluded to go back to their homes, but two of the large, strong and athletic young Pec-wans said they were going to remain in the camp and hide in one of the houses. The rest all got ready and started home, leaving the two young men, who climbed up to the frame where the platform is fixed, that they put the large basket plates on, filled with the acorns that are hulled, so as to dry them, over where they make the fire to cook and warm by, the heat going up through the platform and plates, drying the acorns. So the young men secreted themselves up there, for they could not be seen, and kept very still.

In the evening the wild Indians came, and not seeing or hearing anyone, supposed that all had left the camp, and after spying around awhile, an Oh-ma-ha ventured into the house and sat down by the fireplace and opened a buckskin sack, which we call ac-gure, and which has sticks inside to act as stays to hold it in shape, it being twelve or fourteen inches long and carried it under the arm. Each one of these wild men had one of these sacks, which is a sort of a magic wand, and in this they carry different kinds of herbs. Some of which are very good for a person's health, and some act like magic for poison, and with it they can kill anyone they wish. Now this wild man, after sitting down, opened his sack and took out each kind of herbs or roots, saying as he lifted each one out what it was good for, and after he had taken part of them out and laid them by the side of the ac-gure, he thought he heard a noise, so leaving his ac-gure and the roots, he ran outside. At this the young Pec-wans jumped down from their hiding place and grabbed up the ac-gure and put the roots back into it. Immediately after this, the wild man returned and begged and pleaded with them to give them back, but they refused to do so. He told them they could not use it unless they were taught the art by which to use it. Then they wanted him to teach them, but he said he never would, so they told him they would keep it. After he had begged and talked for awhile, they started home, taking the ac-gure with them, and the wild man following and pleading in every way for them to return the sack to him. As they kept on towards home, the Oh-ma-ha told them if they would return it to him, he would cause anyone that they might wish for to die, and would give them half of all he had, but they refused, and kept on until they reached home. The wild man went with them into the house, and they fed him, and everytime they went out, he went with them. Sometimes they would go for wood for the sweathouse, and he would follow them closely, always pleading for his ac-gure and acting so simple that it seemed this ac-gure was his whole life. They were determined never to give it back to him, and so one morning they concluded to make a big fire in the sweathouse, put him inside, fasten the door, and smoke him to death. They kept the ac-gure, and they say this family was ever after very lucky in getting deer and other game, as they had the wild Indian's devil.

This is the only time where they caused a Oh-ma-ha to die, that I know of. These sweathouses are sure an ideal place to smoke a person to death in.

Indians in Brush Dance regalia, 1923. Photo by William Lange.

Chapter XXVII
How the Rich Tried
to be a Talth

I will give the history of one Indian that was very wealthy, who belonged to the He-nas (Smith Rivers). This Indian, while yet a very young man, had by inheritance been left so much wealth that he felt there was no part or place but what he had the right and power to go, and being closely related to some of the wealthy families of the lower Klamath, and among the rest to a family of one of the Talths which lived at Wah-tec village, close to where the White Deerskin Dance is held. When it came time for this dance, he took with him a great many of his most valuable articles to use in the dance. He went up to Reck-woy, the mouth of the Klamath, and on up to Wah-tec to visit with his relatives and take part in the dance by putting his valuables in. Everything went along merrily to his satisfaction until the dance was finished at Wah-tec village.

The day all was in readiness to move down to the place where they all make a stop, and only those that have a high birth are allowed to travel on the lower trail and go to the place that is held sacred ground. And here, when he was told not to go, he said, "Why, I am richer than any one here. I can go anyplace." Then when some of his relatives told him to stay back, that he could go on the upper trail with the others that were rich, he protested strongly and still persisted in going, but was told plainly that his riches counted for nothing at this time and place: that with all his riches, he was of low birth, that his mother and father were married in the low marriage, and that he was of the He-na tribe; and that he could give his riches to one that was born right, to take there for him if he wished to do so, or he could take his riches with him on the upper road, to be used on up the hill and at the finishing place. At this he cowered down like a child and wept, leaving all of his wealth, and started back into the mountains, back to the very highest mountains where the bear, panther and wolves were plentiful. All alone he went to where there is a large rock which we call Hah-i-o-claw, and he remained there for three days singing and praying. Then with nothing to eat, he wandered on through the wild timber and brushy country, back to Crescent City (Caw-pay), and proclaimed himself a doctor, and always was known afterward as Caw-pay or Crescent City Doctor, and lived to be old; and all of the old-time white inhabitants of Crescent City well remember this Indian that went by the name of Crescent City or Caw-pay Doctor.

He was an oddity, and many are the jokes that the old-time white men, and some of the white women, played on him. I am related to him and knew him well, and the place where he claimed he went to the large rock, and I will say that it is a wild country, in which there are plenty of wild animals. I have been on this mountain often and seen the landmarks that were left there by the white race on going north.

238

Chapter XXVIII
The Slaves

Among the Klamath Indians there were many slaves, which we called Ki-elth when the white man first came to our country. These slaves came about in many ways. Some were mixed-blood of Klamath and Hoopas, some were all Hoopas, and some were mixed-blood of the Klamath and Smith Rivers and consisted of both men and women; but most of them were Klamaths themselves. Slavery was brought about by wars, famines, and contagious diseases. In case of a famine there would be a shortage of acorns, and no run of salmon in the river for two or three years, and sometimes longer when the winters were long and cold, or dry, with but little rainfall.

All the land and fishing places belonged to the wealthy families, who would gather it all for themselves, leaving little or none for the poor families, which would leave whole families hungry and starving. They would go to some rich man's house and offer themselves as slaves, and these offers were usually accepted. In other cases there would be sickness started in a well-to-do family, and often be a death or doctor bills to pay, and no chance to gather acorns or fish or hunt until they would be reduced to poverty and become hungry and offer themselves as slaves to some rich family or some big doctor, which was most of the time accepted. (This is something like what the white doctor is doing today among his own people.) Sometimes in war or fighting they would take them and let them be slaves in other ways.

Now these wealthy families would have very large and commodious houses, and a house would be full to overflowing in numbers, and all would be mixed up in conversation; and at the time of eating the slaves were first waited on, while their own children sat back or helped to attend to their wants, and they were served with as good as their own family had, and were treated in a way that made them feel at perfect ease in every way. Oftentimes when the houses would become too crowded, they would build another house and let them move into it, as these wealthy families kept close touch with their relations or kindred so as not to marry those that were their own kindred. Sometimes there were families that had slaves that were not good to them, fed them poorly and refused to doctor them. These are not hard to select, as one will hear it mentioned at all times.

I have seen and known many of them that were slaves and were born of slave parents, and some of these slaves were so

well treated by their masters that they at this time claim
kindred with the children of the masters; and the families of
the masters as so tender in speaking to them of it that they do
not let them know, unless they become too familiar or make
the claim too bold, when a few, very few words will halt them
in their claim for all time. These slave children are the kind
that are mostly the Indians that are left today, and trying to
make themselves and the white man believe that they know
the true legends of the Klamath Indians, when in truth they do
not know, and what they do know, such as not being allowed in
certain places, and their birth and so on, they deny to the
whites so as to hide their once low standing.

These slaves were married off, and any and all were allowed
to redeem themselves, to buy their freedom. Many in war
times for bravery and daring deeds gained their liberty, and
after gaining it would be successful, become rich and buy back
their brothers and sisters, or a part of them that they liked
best; and after a long time, by good marriage, they could get
their family back to a good standing among the people; but
they are kept close track of through the generations and can
never get to where one of them can become a Talth and go
through the secrets of the lodge or order. They must be of free-
born parentage for all time before they are admitted to be a
Talth. By this the reader can understand that only the learned
ones are competent to give the true legends of their people, just
as it is with the whites or other people.

Brush Dance (top) at the mouth of the Klamath River, and Jump Dance (bottom) at Pec-wan at the mouth of Pec-wan Creek. Both were held in old houses with their roofs removed. Photos by Ruth K. Roberts. *(Courtesy Humboldt State University)*

Chapter XXIX
The Wild Indian of Mo-reck

This happened many years ago at the village of Mo-reck, which is situated on the north bank of the Klamath River, just below where we put in the fish dam. Up to within a few years ago there lived in this village a family named Plats who had three boys, one of which became sick and died, and in burying him they followed out the old and ancient custom.

The house in which the family resided was very old, and the name of the house was Plats-ah-chene. The boys were called Plats-ots-ene, and the family was very rich. When the rich bury their dead they often put more less valuables in and on the grave, and they did in this case. The sand is put over the grave and kept dry by a board, so they can at any time by looking at the grave see if any one has been meddling with it, or robbing the grave of the valuables, which has been done many times. So the other two brothers of the dead boy noticed one day that things did not look just right, and on a close examination they discovered that it had been robbed; and after fixing the grave, they kept watch for the person or persons that done it, as there was left a part of the valuables in and on the grave. So early one night as they were sitting close to the grave, they heard a noise and kept very still. Soon they saw a man moving along like a shadow in the dark. This wild Indian seemed to feel the presence of the watchers and kept moving stealthily around, but was afraid to come up to the grave. So finally the wild Indian (Oh-ma-ha) left and went down to the river and swam across to the other side, landing just below the Cap-pell village.

One of the brothers cautiously followed behind, telling the other brother to go up the river on the north and keep on the old trail, and keep a close watch and see if the wild Indian tried to swim back somewhere above Cap-pell, while he took a boat, crossed the river and kept close to the Indian, who went up the river and swam back to the north side just below the village of Wah-say. So the brother on the north side went too far up the river and missed the Indian. So when he arrived at the village of Ma-reep and took a boat and crossed over to the south side just below Ma-reep, and remained there on the south side by a large, hollow fir tree, which is called Ta-po, and close to the trail, thus the two brothers were both on the south side. The Indian on the north side became afraid and worked his way up the river until he came nearly opposite Ca-neck, and then swam across to the south side again. As he was dodging from tree to tree, as was the way of these wild Indians, he came up to the large fir tree. The brother that was in the hollow of the tree made a quick grab and caught him with a firm hold, and as he was wrestling with him the other brother came to his assistance and together they held and tied him fast to the fir tree.

This Indian was painted all black with some kind of a mixture of pitch and other ingredients. He begged to be let loose and offered to give them half he had, also if they had any enemies to tell him and he would cause them to become sick and die. This Indian had the ac-gure sack, which he carried under his arm, but refused to give it to them, telling them that they would soon die as they did not know how to handle it, and he would sooner die himself than tell them how to handle it. So the two brothers left him tied to the tree after trying to persuade him to give them the sack, and in the morning they went home, thinking that their folk might become alarmed at their long absence. Upon their arrival they told what they had done, and after eating they went back to the Indian and began another bargain with him. At this he agreed to give them all the wealth he had if they would let him go, but he still refused to give up the ac-gure sack, as it contained poison, and a charm which they could never use unless he told them how, and this he would never do. So they finally agreed to take his wealth and let him go; so he led them to his home, which was west and south to a place on Redwood Creek, where there was a cave in a clump of large rocks, some twenty-five miles from their home. When they went into this cave-house, they found that he had great wealth stored there, and they took it all home, leaving him there with his ac-gure to gather up more wealth with, and he was never seen again.

The Klamath Indians never kill these wild Indians, but in many cases where they had caught them, they most always found that they were rich by robbing graves of wealthy people, and that they always had the ac-gure. The wealth that these two Mo-reck Indians received from this wild Indian made the Mo-reck village so rich that it never afterwards had to ask help from anyone to carry their part through any of the great festivals. These wild Indians are evidently a former part of our own cast-off people, and of late years have entirely disappeared; and the Indians are wondering what has become of them. Some think they have gone back into the tribe in other places, or went out and mixed with the present white people so as not to be known by them.

"Hupa Woman," a portrait by Edward S. Curtis, copyrighted 1923.

Chapter XXX
How a Cor-tep Girl
Had Her Wish Granted

About sixty years ago there lived a girl in the Cor-tep village by the name of Metch-cher-us-ah-may, and her parents urged her to marry a young man who lived farther up the river at the village of Mo-reck. (I have forgotten his name.) The girl did not like the man, yet her parents kept urging her to marry him against her will. There was two of her girl friends that was going down the river to Reck-woy, so she got into the boat or Indian canoe with them and started down the river. As they glided along Metch-cher-us-ah-may kept wishing that some wild animal would take her, kill her and eat her. When they got to a place called Hay-way-gaw, they all camped out on the bank of the river, back some twenty yards or more from the water's edge. The canoe was pulled up on the sloping sand so as to make it safe for the night; then they made a fire, cooked their evening meal and then talked until it was time to go to bed. All this time Metch-cher-us-ah-may was wishing some harm would come to her. The three girls made their bed for the night so that all three could sleep together, and when they went to bed Metch-cher-us-ah-may slept in the center so all went to sleep. In the morning she was missing; she got her wish. She had been taken from between the other two girls, and on examination they could see very plainly where a wild animal had dragged her over the dry sand, down to the edge of the water, into the river, and disappeared with her; and she was never seen again. They thought an animal of the leopard species took her, as some of the animals have been seen a number of times on the lower Klamath, and the Indians are very much afraid of them. This happened when I was a little girl.

Chapter XXXI
Our Tobacco

The white race of people that the Klamath Indians found in this land had a weed they called tobacco, which we call Hah-koom, and [the white race] taught them to use it by smoking it in the pipe and to cultivate it by selecting a proper place, pile brush over the ground and then burn it, which would leave the ground with a loose layer of wood ashes. Over this, while the ashes were yet dry and loose, they would sow the seed and protect the crop by putting around it a brush fence. From year to year they would select from the best stalks seed for the next year, and at times to hold the seed for a number of years if necessary, for if kept properly it will grow after being kept for a long time. The only thing that will bother or destroy the crop of tobacco is the deer, and they often jump over the brush fence and eat every part of the crop, even to the roots.

When an Indian takes his pipe to smoke, he inhales the smoke and keeps it in his lungs for ten or fifteen seconds and then blows it out through his nose mostly, some through the mouth; and then he gives a slow grunt, saying a few words in a plain audible tone. These words are to the Wa-gas, the white people we loved so well, wishing that the Wa-gas would give them good luck, long life, that they could see them come back, or that they themselves could go to see them and be with them, and many other kinds of wishes for the Wa-gas. The old women doctors use tobacco very freely and have pipes that hold a handful of tobacco at a single smoking, and they ask the Wa-gas to give them good luck in curing a sick person. The doctors are about the only ones of the women that smoke. The Indians have the most complete control over themselves, and can smoke one, two or three times a day, or quit for a week or longer without a murmur.

Chapter XXXII
Our Mermaids

The Klamath Indians tell of the Mermaid that they said could be seen at night come and sit on a rock out in the middle of the river, at a place called Ca-neck. This rock is in a rocky and rough place in the river, some thirty miles up the river from its mouth, and some nine miles above where the White Deerskin Dance is held. This rock is in the middle of the river and the water in the summertime, at the low stage, just covers the top of it. On each side are whirls and eddies which the Indians have used for fishing with dip nets for many generations. There was never more than two of these Mermaids seen at a time, but they have been seen many times in the generations gone. They had very long hair, and were half fish and half women, but it is not known whether they were male or female. They looked like women, and would sit there combing their long hair for hours at a time, and as they went away one could see their long hair floating in the water. The Indians say that for the past twenty years or more, they have not seen them and think they have been washed away, or that the river has been filled by the gravel and debris from the mines, which have destroyed them. They also say that they never had any fear of the Mermaids, but looked upon them as a freak of nature. They could see them plainly in the summer months while fishing, when the moon was full, and sometimes they would be only a few yards away from them. These Mermaids we call Squerth-tucks.

The open landscape in this and other photos was typical of the time, maintained by the Indian practice of burning the meadowland to keep it free of brush, thus improving its value as hunting ground and increasing the yield of edible seeds and roots. Photo by A.W. Ericson.

Chapter XXXIII
Fairy Tales
The Woman of Sin

Hundreds of years ago a young man and his wife resided at what is called Tu-rep village, which is located on the south side of the Klamath River about six miles from its mouth. The Tu-rep Bar on the river is very large, consisting of fifty or a hundred acres of rich and productive soil. This man's wife before her marriage belonged at the Si-alth village, across the river from Tu-rep on the north side. They lived very happy together for a number of years, he being very kind to her in every way and never spoke in a cross manner at any time. As the years went by he began to drift away from her and their home, neglecting her more and more. It seemed that a soul affinity had come into his life: a woman at the Reck-woy village, at the mouth of the river, was enticing him away from his wife and home. He found a resistless charm in her serpent-like arms, and as the days went by he would tarry longer in her company, and he would be loath to part with her at all. At last his wife was being left alone so much and neglected that she became suspicious that another woman had robbed her of his love. She found her suspicion to be true, as her husband was now giving all of his attention to the woman at Reck-woy. The wife became very sad and broken-hearted over her husband's actions and unfaithfulness, and went about her work in a dispirited manner; and her attitude and appearance became one of profound sadness. In company she always seemed downhearted, as the same sad look was always upon her face, making her appear to the visitors as wretched and lonely.

As the miserable wife spent the lonely days at Tu-rep village, the people decided to give a large entertainment; a host of guests gathered to make merry. Among the crowd was a man from the Ur-ner village, which is nine or ten miles up the river at the mouth of Blue Creek. During the entertainment the Ur-ner man was attracted to the lonely Tu-rep wife, who appeared to him to be very sad and lonely in the midst of such gaiety. He came over to where she was seated and began a conversation by exchanging a few remarks. He thought he might be wrong in addressing her so boldly, and started to walk away, but something stirred his inner emotions strangely, so much so that he could not resist the temptation to return to her. This time, after a few remarks he summoned up courage to inquire into her troubled life, as he said she seemed very lonely. Deeply impressed by his winning manner and kind words, her confidence was easily won, and she readily related to him her unhappy marriage and how unfaithful her husband had grown. He at once became more interested, and listened patiently to her story of sorrow; and with his sympathetic words of comfort, strange emotions that had long been dead within her breast thrilled into life once more. She had become a victim of his beguiling words of comfort, as he drew her into his arms of passionate love. Alone and together, they planned a secret meeting place that her husband and the village folks might not know of their clandestine meetings.

When the Tu-rep husband would go down the river to Reck-

Several generations of women, the oldest with chin tattoos, the youngest looking out to a new world, yet held together by family traditions and loyalties.

woy to bask in the love of the woman of his affections, his wife would wait until darkness of night had cast its gloom over the village, when she would creep carefully forth from her dwelling and meet her lover. She had a long way to go up the Tu-rep Bar from her house, and each step she would take, she would cover her footprints with stones. In this manner she would cover her tracks over for a distance of at least one mile along the river bar, and when she reached the upper end of the bar she would step out into the water; and as before she covered over her tracks with stones until she stepped into her lover's boat.

The Ur-ner Indian would come across the river from the opposite bank and take her into his canoe and paddle back to what is known as Stah-win Bar. This is also a large bar, covered with huge redwoods. Together, they would wander into the inky blackness of the huge redwoods, where they would enjoy each other's company until a late hour at night, when the Ur-ner man would again take his soul affinity into his canoe and return her to the upper end of Tu-rep Bar, where she would leave him and proceed down the bar to her home, as before covering over her footprints with stones. She held these clandestine meetings with the Ur-ner Indian in that manner everytime her husband would leave her and go to Reck-woy. After a while her husband became suspicious of her action, as when he returned home at night he never found her at home, yet he was very kind to her. He made every attempt to trace her footsteps, but they were always lost upon the bar, and all his efforts were futile. At last, in desperation he made up his mind to try other plans to detect her mysterious whereabouts. He would start down the river on a pretense of going to Reck-woy, but would hide where he could see his wife's movements around the house. This was kept up for sometime, but he could not find out which way she had gone. But in his earnest endeavors to discover her whereabouts, one night he saw her covering over her footprints with stones as she went to meet her lover. Her shame and sin was at last discovered in spite of all her efforts and precaution to hide her disgrace from human knowledge. This covering of footprints with stones is called in our language, "Way-nah-mah way-lap-po-lah hah-elth-werm-chelth," which means covering the tracks of sin and shame with stones. To this day there can be seen at Tu-rep Bar, in the summer months when the waters of the river is low, the rows of stones that this sinful woman used to cover up her footprints of shame, and they stand out in strange relief along the water's edge where they were supposed to have been placed centuries ago by the woman of sin. The Indians point to these stones as a warning to all married women that no matter how secretly they sin against the marriage vows, they will be discovered sooner or later, and their sins will be reflected upon them throughout their lives.

The moral of this story is to keep women from sinning, and when they are tempted into sin, that they are forever burdened with the heavy stones of disgrace that points to their sins, and time cannot efface it.

What Happened to Two Ma-reep Girls

A number of generations back, there lived in Ma-reep village a man and his wife with their three girls. The oldest of them was a good, dutiful child, helped her mother in every way she could, while the other two were naughty, idle, cross and pouty. When it came time for their meals, the oldest would eat and act like a perfect lady, but the other two girls always kept up their naughty ways. They would go away in a corner and pout for more of this or that thing, and their mother kept telling them that if they did not stop being naughty, and act in a better manner and eat their meals properly, that a big owl would come and carry them off. They kept on until one night, sure enough, a large owl came and took them and carried them about a mile down the river and placed them on a large, high rock, where they could not get down. They sat there and turned to stone, and are sitting there to this day, and look like two little girls sitting up there. This rock we call Hoaks-or-reck, and Klamath Indian mothers have been pointing to these two little stone girls, telling them this fairy tale to keep them from being naughty and to have them conduct themselves in a good, mannerly way. This rock is close to the river on the north bank at the lower end of Ma-reep Rapids.

The Adventures of a Coyote

Long ages ago, a Coyote with his family resided at He-melth, which is a place on the Klamath River that is famous in Indian lore. One lovely day in early spring, Mr. and Mrs. Coyote with all their children journeyed over the hills of the Klamath from He-melth to a place on the mountainside known as On-a-gap. This was a place where they went annually to gather green grasses, upon which they would feast during the spring months. The family was camping out and having a good time. They kept on moving toward the mountaintop when there suddenly came quite an unexpected snowstorm. The weather turned freezing cold, and Mr. and Mrs. Coyote did everything possible to save the lives of their children, but of no avail. One by one they perished in the cold snow, as it kept snowing and falling very fast. The fond parents were left desolate and grief-stricken in the gloom of the storm, as they never could call back their loved ones. (The Coyote we call Say-gap.)

As they laid the little bodies in their graves of snow, Mr. Coyote grew desperate over his great loss, and determined to seek revenge against the Sun. The Sun, he argued, heartlessly murdered his children, because it had refused to shine and give them warmth, so he started out at once upon one of the longest journeys ever made by any living animal. He chased the Sun over mountains, hills, through canyons, across vast plains and valleys, and past rivers and lakes, until he at last came to the ocean. Here he lost it, for it sank into the waves with a mocking laugh and left him standing alone upon the shores of darkness. Darkness closed around him with its mighty arms, and he stood there on the shores of the restless ocean for several minutes in utter despair. Weary in body and limbs, and sad at heart for his great loss, the truth flashed upon him that he could never in this world get his revenge, as the being of his wrath was swift in its flight through space. Thus on the shore he stood, when he suddenly turned his back on the west with a kick of contempt in that direction, where the Sun (his great enemy) had sank.

In silence he gazed towards the east and then away towards the northern horizon, and there in the far north he saw a more pleasing scene where he buried his great burden of sorrow. While he still stood there gazing, he saw the seven stars, winking down through the heavens at him, and they kept winking for him to join them. Suddenly he felt himself rising from the earth as if he had been transformed into an Angel with wings, and he rose far away to the Kingdom of Heaven. Up he soared, ever up, until he was at last flying among the seven stars, and when he reached them, he began to dance and sing, as they were all girls and also sisters. They asked him not to keep on singing, as they said he did not know how to sing properly and said they would teach him how to sing so he could join them in some of their songs. So he became flattered to think that the sisters were taking so much interest in him and he became very vain at once, as some narrow-minded people do when they become associated with a superior circle.

He was rather enthusiastic now, to think what a good escape he had made from the cruel earth to a beautiful abode in Heaven. He flattered himself so much in his wild enthusiasm that he thought himself very wise, and he would display some of his talent before the sisters. As they offered to teach him, he replied to them, "I can sing beautifully; I used to sing for my wife and children down on the earth; they always said my voice was good, and I believe I know a good deal about singing, and do not need any training. So never mind, girls, about teaching me, for my voice is just splendid and I can sing perfectly." The sisters looked at each other and felt very disappointed to think that the Coyote persisted in knowing all about the fine arts, when he practically did not know the first step. After some persuasion they decided they would never be able to teach him any of the fine arts of singing, for the stars of Heaven were much different from those on earth. They reasoned, too, that perhaps he was out of his natural mind, after traveling so many millions of miles through space. The sisters replied as good-naturedly as they could: "Very well, kind sir, we are deeply grieved to find that by our billion of years of experience and knowledge, we are not able to teach you anything, and you may proceed as you like."

The Coyote began to dance and sing again among his friends until he grew very tired, and when he could no longer sing and dance, he began to talk to them in a broken tone. His head grew dizzy as his mind wandered from the songs and drifted into thought about himself. He kept repeating the words as he danced until he lost his pipe, tobacco pouch, belt and deerskin trousers, which caused the sisters to smile and wink among themselves. They tried to persuade him not to talk so much, but he kept right on and would not heed them. They became very weary and bored over this stupid nonsense, and the elder sister said they would join him in his revelry. One on each side of him took his hand in theirs, formed one large circle, and began to dance and sing around him. They dragged him faster and faster until they whirled him as fast as they could go. His poor head was in a dizzy whirl, and he began to fear for his safety, not knowing when they would let him rest, as it seemed they had been whirling him for centuries. They might go on whirling him for a thousand years, and he felt so famished and weak that he could not endure this treatment much longer. "Ouch!" he exclaimed in a terrible voice, "I say, girls, I cannot glide your fast whirls any longer, I am afraid I will fall down in a heap and die, or else my bones fly to pieces." "So you shall fall in a heap, Mr. Coyote," exclaimed the girls in a loud chorus, "down with you to the earth from whence you came, as you are not a bright pupil here in Heaven. Up here you must be very brilliant, and you have always been stupid enough to think that you knew it all. We are weary of your revelry, so farewell. We wish you many happy days down on the earth, and again we say farewell," and they pushed him down from his place in Heaven.

He fell so rapidly through space that he found it impossible to keep himself together, and the bones of his body fell to pieces and went flying and whizzing in each direction, but somehow they managed to fall in a heap at Ca-neck, which is a very ancient village and the most famous among my people for stories, as so many wonderful tales begin there. The Coyote's bones laid bleaching in the sun for a short time near this village when a heavy rainstorm caused the river to overflow its banks. The rising waters of the river took the Coyote's bones and carried them down to the mouth of the river at Reck-woy, where they were washed upon the sand beach. After being planted there in the sand for several days, a slender shoot sprang up and unfurled its green foliage above the sand. In time this slender shoot grew into a tall alder tree, and the Coyote and his bones were now transformed into a tree.

One day an old woman with her wood basket on her back and a stone hatchet in her hand came along the beach looking for some wood. She took a great fancy to this alder tree, as she thought it would make good wood for the fire; it was just the kind of a tree she had been looking for, for sometime, and was pleased upon finding it. So she began to chop it, and to her great surprise the tree sprang from the earth and vanished in a flash, and then took up the shape of a Coyote which stood before her. "Ouch!" he yelled in a loud voice, "Go away, old woman. How dare you cut me to pieces like that?" The old woman became more frightened than ever, as she dropped her hatchet and ran for her life back to the village. She could not find any reason for such a strange encounter, and came to the conclusion that it was some of the Indian devils trying to frighten her. The Coyote, to his great relief, was once more in his own natural body, and he set out to travel upon the earth again. He ventured to the rabbits, as he had a desire to visit them. Upon reaching the rabbits' home, he found Mrs. Rabbit away and only her small children there. Upon entering the house he asked the children to give him something to eat, as he was very hungry, not having had anything to eat for a long time. The children were too young to understand what he was saying, and all of them became frightened and ran out of the house. When they were all safely outside, they set fire to the house in hopes of burning the Coyote to death, and he was busy inside, going through the shelves looking for something to eat. But as fortune favored him this time, he heard the flames crackling in time to make his escape from a dreadful death.

After his narrow escape he decided to go and stay with his grandmother at Weitchpec, and he journeyed slowly up the river until he reached her home. As soon as he arrived there he had a long story to tell her. He said he was almost dead from hunger, as he had been on a long journey without any food, and asked her to cook the best she could afford as he needed it to build up his strength again; and he also informed her that many of his cousins were coming to visit her. He explained to her that he had left them a few miles down the river to camp for the night, and they had sent him ahead to tell her they were coming, and for his grandmother to prepare a feast and be ready for them. She told him there was nothing to eat except tur-perks, which are blighted acorns that fall to the ground and are worm-eaten, that she was sorry for her guests but it was the best she could do. She at once set about cooking great basketfulls of the tur-perks, as she never doubted but what her grandson was telling the truth. When these were cooked she placed the baskets on the table before the Coyote, never doubting but what he would leave plenty for his cousins to eat. She never dreamed that one small being could eat so much at one time, and was greatly disappointed and humiliated when she found that he had eaten all the acorns, even licking the baskets clean and dry. As he finished this large meal he heaved a sigh of relief, as it was the first meal he had eaten for over a hundred years; just how long ago he first left the earth to go to Heaven he could not remember. His cousins were not coming he just wished to deceive his grandmother, that she might cook a great quantity so he could feast by himself.

He deceived her for the first time very cleverly, as she did not doubt the story of his cousins coming. After this meal the Coyote called to her and said, "I am going to fish tonight, and if my luck is good our baskets will be filled by daybreak. Now my dear, you may cook tonight another large quantity of tur-perks, and tomorrow I will help you prepare the fish for cooking, as I think my cousins will arrive at sunset." His grandmother still believed his story to be true, but she was very tired, and after he had gone to fish she decided to go to bed, thinking she would have plenty of time on the morrow to cook the tur-perks for the cousins, as they were not coming until evening of the next day. When the Coyote reached the bank of the river he did not even pretend to fish but jumped from boulder to boulder and bruised his head and face as much as he could. Sometime in the night he returned and repeated to her a pitiful tale of how someone had attacked him and given him a severe beating—of how some of the other people would not allow him to fish, etc. She listened patiently to his tale of woe and realized for the first time that he was telling her falsehoods. After he had finished his story, she became very angry and gave him a severe scolding for being so deceitful. The Coyote did not stay with her very long, as he wearied and annoyed her so much she planned to get rid of him.

One day she hired a young man to take him across the river to the village of Pec-toolth, where she instructed him to camp for the night. That night after dark, the young man asked the Coyote to sleep at his feet, which the Coyote gladly did, as he was somewhat tired from tramping through the woods that day, and he was soon fast asleep. Then the young man quietly left the bed and rolled a log in the place he had been lying in. He did this to deceive the Coyote when he awoke, as he would most likely see the log and think he was still sleeping there; then he hurried away and left him asleep and alone at Pecktoolth. The Coyote woke up during the night and looked about him, and soon discovered the log and that the young man had left him alone. He jumped to his feet hastily and ran down to the banks of the river, and when he arrived there he saw the young man standing on a high rock on the opposite side of the river. He yelled until he was hoarse for him to come over in his canoe and take him across to his grandmother's. The young man refused to help him, which made him very angry, and he called him all the names he could think of and begged him in a pleading manner, but of no avail. At length the Coyote became so enraged that he yelled at the top of his voice that he would murder him if he ever reached him, and he seized a sharp stone and ran up and down the river for a long time, swearing as fast as he could utter his words. The man stood still on the rock with a mocking smile on his face and watched the frantic efforts of the Coyote. When he thought he was getting pretty tired, the young man called out to him to swim across the river; he dared him and said it was easy to swim across.

The Coyote at once took up the dare, and plunged into the river and began to swim with all his might, as he was compelled to swim against the current. He was almost successful in getting across when the young man shouted to him to look back across the river, as there was something coming down the bank. The Coyote was foolish enough to look back over his shoulder, and as he did so the strong current swept him back on the same side he started from. He immediately made another desperate attempt to swim the river. He swam and swam, fighting against the strong current until he became exhausted and it was impossible for him to swim any longer. Realizing he would soon drown, he called again and again to the young man to rescue him in a boat, but the other stood immovable on the rock and calmly replied, "I cannot help you, for your last day on earth has ended." The Coyote, crying the mournful wail of death, sank into the waters of the river to rise no more.

A Bear Story

Many years ago the Indians were warring among themselves at the village of Hop-paw, near the mouth of the river. A portion of them whipped the others, and those who were defeated in the battle moved away from there and went back in the mountains to live, while the victorious warriors also left the village for a few day's stay at a place known as Si-alth.

While the Indians were all away, a bear strayed into the village and went into one of the Indian houses, where he discovered a very large basket filled with beautiful Indian

White Deerskin Dance at Hoopa. Like all ceremonies, this dance was conceived by the Spirit Beings, the Wa-gas—and passed along to humans. It was part of the World Renewal Ceremonies, the most significant of all northwestern California rituals, held to restore balance, bring peace and "fix the world." Photo by A.W. Ericson about 1894.

A symbol of endurance. Born in 1810 and close to 100 years old when this photo was taken, Mrs. Childs still works at making a traditional open-weave storage basket. Photo by A.W. Ericson.

dresses and strings of Indian money and other Indian ornaments. He was very happy when he discovered this basket and began to take the things out and look them over carefully. As he came to the dresses he would try each one on and then dance, but he could not seem to find one that suited his idea of fashion. He kept on throwing the dresses aside as he pulled them off. He wanted one that rattled as he danced. At last he found the one he wanted, for when he put it on and danced, the shells began to rattle, as there were a great many on the dress. As he danced, to his great delight, the shells rang like music in his ears, and well satisfied with the dress, he pulled it off and put it back in the basket with all the other articles. After he had finished storing them away in the basket he began to tear up the earthen floor and scatter things all over the house. After doing all the damage he could, he shouldered the large basket and started for the woods, and traveled some distance to a large, hollow redwood tree. He decided to stop here and put on the dress with many shells and put it on, and began to dance and sing, having a glorious time all by himself, as he had no comrades to join him in the fun. This is the song he sang while he danced; "Ho-wen-ah-a, ho-wen-ah-a, nah-hay, nah-hay." After he had danced for some time, he became so tired that he could no longer sing. The dress began to weigh so heavily upon him that he became exhausted, but he managed to keep on dancing; he loved to hear the music of the shells as he danced about.

After visiting for several days at Si-alth, the Indians returned to their homes at Hop-paw. When they reached the village they discovered that everything had been turned topsy-turvy in one of the houses, and that the large basket of Indian dresses was missing. They at once suggested that some of their enemies had returned while they were away and stolen the things, and they all followed in hot pursuit to recover the stolen articles. But they could find no trace of them, and in despair gave up the chase. Some of them made a closer inspection of the house, and this time they were sure they saw bear tracks in the soft ground. The Indians now followed the bear tracks closely, which led them to the large redwood tree, and as they approached it they could see that it was hollow and had a large roomy place inside; and glancing in, they saw the bear dancing, dressed in one of the dresses. One of the smaller boys became tired watching the bear and asked if he might go up near the tree, and the older Indians decided to let him go and asked him to try to get the dresses away from the bear. The boy agreed, and went up until he was afraid to go nearer. The bear's attention was now attracted to the boy, and he saw at once that the Indians had discovered his hiding place, and stopped dancing and left the tree, carrying with him the Indian dresses, determined to take them to his own home, which was in a treetop near by.

This tree was hollow up its trunk and in the top of this hollow the bear made his home. He tugged with all his might at the huge basket, but it was so large he could not pull it through the hollow to his nest, and when he saw that he could not pull it through, it made him mad and he tried to dig the tree up by the roots. He dug so rapidly that he soon found he had dug a cave under the tree, and being fatigued from his strenuous efforts, he seized the basket and pulled it after him into the cave. Once in there he thought himself secure from the Indians. As the bear disappeared into the cave with the basket, all the Indians ventured up near the tree; they began talking as to what they would do, being very anxious to recover the things, as it meant a great loss of riches if they could not recover them again. They finally agreed they would kindle a fire at the mouth of the cave and smoke the bear out of his den, so they gathered up a large pile of wood and dry branches and made a fire. The Indians lined up ready for him when he came out. The owner of the articles was an old man, and he took his place near the cave, with his bow drawn, ready to shoot the bear; but his arrow did not wound the bear fatally, and the bear seized him and crushed him to death. The enraged bear then turned upon the other Indians, but at last he sank to the ground riddled with arrows. They recovered the basket of dresses and returned home in a mournful procession, for one of their members had departed to the spirit land. The bear in his wild revelry had also lost his life.

The Wooing of Robin Red-breast

Long centuries ago, before the world was inhabited by very many people, Robin Red-breast lived as a handsome young man by himself in a magnificent mansion on the Klamath River. This skeptical young man always laughed mockingly at the suggestion of matrimony, as he was very rich and kept many servants about. In fact, he kept a servant for each room of his splendid mansion.

He would often go by himself on moonlight strolls by the river or walk in the sunrise in early morning through the woods. The young maidens would catch a glimpse of him as he passed their windows, or as they peeked from out the bushes at him, admiring all the charms of his physical manhood. But proud young Red-breast would walk haughtily by them whenever he chanced to meet them, and positively refused to accept any of their attentions that they were so eager to bestow upon him. Every maiden that chanced to catch a glimpse of him imagined herself in love with him, and her lonely heart would invariably yearn for his love that he might make her happy.

The laws of olden-times were very different from the laws of today. It was the rule then that when a young maid fell in love with a youth, it was her place to go and call on him first at his home, also to propose matrimony, unless the young man preferred to do so himself; then it was proper that he should. This was true in the case of Red-breast. As in the days of yore, when a young man returned a woman's affections, he would accept her love and make her his wife. And if he did not return her affections, he would refuse to consider her proposal of marriage.

Many young ladies called each day at Red-breast's home, seeking the loving devotion that he might bestow upon them. He always kept a door usher to announce the arrival of any young lady that would call to seek his acquaintance and desire to unite her fortune with his. The latter was usually her purpose in wishing a private interview. Red-breast gave strict orders to the usher not to admit any young lady that might call inside the door of his mansion, and besides he could never show her into his presence without consulting him first. When the usher would announce to Red-breast that a young lady was at the door wishing to interview him, Red-breast would always ask the kind and color of her dress. If the usher replied that she wore a suit of teach-ah-me-tah, he was told to send her away, as he did not wish to see her.

One by one, the girls came to the mansion in hopes of securing an interview, but to their great disappointment they were all turned away from the door. One can imagine how many poor broken hearts followed each other as they had been dismissed from the door of love to go forth into the lonely world to weep. Some of these girls were foolish enough to shut themselves in dark cells, that they might never be seen by the man who ruined their hopes of a happy wedded life. Other compassionate souls threw themselves into the sea, that their early sorrows and disappointments might be ended forever. Poor deluded girls. If they had only known how little Red-breast cared for their miseries, and how he mocked them in his mansion, they would never even have considered him as worthy of notice. However, many of the girls were not so foolish as to destroy all their future happiness, but forgot the mocking Red-breast and sought other lovers whom they married and were very happy.

It had now come to pass that all the girls in the world had called at the mansion of Red-breast for the purpose of wooing him for a husband, except one. All these girls had agreed among themselves that each take their turn in calling upon Red-breast until he selected one of them for his wife. Now all the girls in the world had called with exception of one, and all the other girls were restless and wondering what her fate would be. She was a sweet young thing with cheeks as red as cherries, eyes that sparkled like dew-drops, and hair that hung in ringlets. It was an ideal autumn morning when this maid called at Red-breast's mansion. The madrone berries were ripe and hung in crimson clusters from the branches of the tree, filling the atmosphere with a dewy scent of sweetness. Heaven and earth seemed blending together and then fading away into the melancholy shadows of autumn. Such was the appearance of the surrounding world when this shy, sweet maiden came tripping lightly up the long, wooded avenues to the door of Red-breast's mansion with her heart all aflutter.

The usher greeted her with a pleasant "Good morning," as her appearance was very stunning, and he bade her wait at the door until he returned with his message from his master. Upon announcing her arrival, the haughty Red-breast said, "Ah! I don't care the snap of my fingers for the prettiest and sweetest maiden that ever walked the earth. It is not for her love and companionship that I care, but for what she might wear; her beautiful gown if it is made of the right material is all I want. I say again that they are all foolish young things to seek my love, for I have none to waste upon them; it is all concentrated upon myself, and no one else." Then he asked the usher the same question, as to what kind of dress she wore. For the first time the usher replied that she did not wear a dress of the teach-ah-me-tah like all the other girls had worn, but she wore a gown of pretty red, bedewed with clustering ornaments of its same gorgeous hues. "My!" exclaimed Red-breast, "You can show her in at once," and he jumped to his feet in delight, his eyes sparkling with false pride. "Go tell her quick that she is the only girl that ever had the honor to be admitted into my presence. Now I will woo her with all my heart and flatter her very soul away for the purpose, but not for my wife, you know. You know what I am, so mind you don't put her wise. Poor little girl, poor little foolish girl, it is a shame to treat her so cruel, but I cannot help it when she wears such a tempting gown of red—red at last, my favorite color, and that color I am going to have."

A minute later a sweet, shy maid of scarce three seasons-old was ushered into his halls and the magnificent apartments in which she stood before Red-breast. Her heart had ceased to beat for a few moments as he rose and greeted her in an elegant manner. He was far handsomer than she ever dreamed a man could be, and for the first time in her life she fancied that she was deeply in love. Breathlessly, she recollected the stories of the other girls that had been before her, and now she could hardly blame them for their mad actions of self-destruction over such a striking personality. Red-breast received the maiden with a hearty welcome of flattery as he dismissed the usher from the apartment, that they might be alone to plan out the future. Gallantly, he knelt at the fair maiden's feet and poured out to her full measures of his love. In his elegant and commanding language, he pictured in her mind how he had turned away so many other girls from his door who had come to seek him as their lover, how he had done [so] because he could never love [them,] and knew that someday he would find his only true love, which he believed to be her, as he had never felt the emotion of love until he first gazed into her bright eyes.

His sweet voice sounded in her ears so soft, and the touch of his fingers was as magical as Heaven itself. Her cheeks blushed redder than ever as she listened to his tender words of devotion. She shyly whispered "Yes" as he rose and pressed her against his breast, and they planned together for the marriage vows. They both agreed they would exchange the wedding vows on the following morning. Then he held her by the hand and showed her into a nice room where he said she could spend the night in peaceful dreams, and then he took his leave, leaving her alone in her room; and he told her that this room would always be her own private room, where she could retreat and find solace in being alone. Once alone, she sat still for a long time, dreaming of the blissful future she would enjoy with a husband that so many had tried to woo but could never win because he loved her only.

Night came with its shadows, and she found herself very tired, as her poor brain had been kept in a constant whirl since meeting Red-breast. Wearily she took off her beautiful gown and laid it carefully on a chair beside her bed, and then hid her face under the silken covers. Soon in slumberland, she did not waken until morning, and the sun was already high in the sky. The gown she wore was the beautiful spangles of the madrone berries that blushed in their tint of the deepest vermilion red. While the maiden was sleeping, Red-breast stole softly into the room and devoured the beautiful gown, and all that night he feasted upon the berries and ornaments of the gown. As he gulped down the last berry, he crept softly to the side of the sleeping beauty and gazed a farewell look upon her innocent face. He then changed his mansion into a dreary isle of autumn dampness and flew away as a bird. Henceforth Red-breast never again appeared on earth as a man, but has ever since been on earth as a bird.

Sad was the maiden that woke up that morning to find only a terrible disappointment awaiting her. She found in her heart no solace, but grief, bitter grief that had no compassion upon her bitter soul. Looking about her in her loneliness, she saw that Red-breast had deceived her, and that he had selfishly eaten her pretty gown; all that she could find of it was the ugly strips that had held the ornaments in their place, and lo, this maiden so young and fair, and once so beautiful, fled down the damp aisles weeping, for the chill of winter was upon her and had left her desolate, without her clothing.

The moral of this story is that young women should have a care in pursuing handsome young men, lest they be deceived and left in desolation.

Dr. Bear and Mrs. Skunk

Once upon a time a father and mother skunk (wah-chelth) were rearing a family of two children, and there was no food for them to eat. The old folks were in great distress about what to do, as they were all starving. The mother was very anxious for her family, and one day she happened to think of a good plan to secure something to eat. So she announced to her family that she would play sick and have the bear (chee-ur-ra) come and doctor her. Her husband and children were delighted with her plan, and Mrs. Skunk warned her children to keep very quiet when Mr. Bear came to doctor her. So she went to bed, feigning to be very ill, while Mr. Skunk went after Dr. Bear and found him at home. The Doctor accompanied Mr. Skunk at once to the bedside of his wife and, walking into the room, began asking Mrs. Skunk about her illness, and she replied in a very weak voice, pretending to feel very miserable, and asked her children to go to one side of the room and be very quiet, as she wanted Dr. Bear to examine her. The children went to one side of the room at once, as they had been cautioned by their mother to keep very still, as she was going to throw musk in the Bear's face and blind him. The Bear began to get things ready to doctor Mrs. Skunk, and as he was about ready to examine her, the children became very anxious and restless, and began whispering to each other and indulging in a big tete-a-tete, about what a large dinner they were going to have when their mother killed the Bear. They kept whispering so much that the Bear became suspicious of their actions and listened closely, and his sharp ears caught a few words of their conversation about what their mother was going to do. He began moving towards the door to make his exit, when the mother Skunk saw that he was about ready to get away and threw the musk with all her might at the Bear's face, but it missed his eyes and he escaped safely. Mrs. Skunk became very angry with her children, who had spoiled her plans by being overanxious and whispering too much. Instead of getting the bear meat as they had anticipated, they both received a good sound thrashing from their mother which taught them a lesson for the future.

How The Animals Conquered The Moon

Many years ago there was a total eclipse of the moon which lasted for several days and nights. The night continued so dark that the people and animals were not able to see to go about, so all the animals of the animal kingdom held a council and decided to devour the moon, as it had become a useless planet and would not give them light at night. The animals journeyed from the earth up to the moon and began a fierce battle to conquer and devour it, and after a long struggle the moon lost its balance in the heavens and fell earthward. It struck the earth at Ca-neck on the Klamath River, where the waters whirl and rush into fearful rapids. At the lower terminations of these rapids where there is a large round depression in the land, on the south and west side of the river, is the place where the moon is supposed to have struck the earth when the animals threw it down from the heavens. While the animals and snakes were wrestling with the moon at Ca-neck, it was then the frog stepped forth and objected, saying that they should not devour the moon completely, as they would need it to light the world at night in the future. Listening to the frog's wise council, they all agreed to allow him to restore the moon to its proper place. So the frog began at once to gather all the blood of the moon and fuse it together with its other remnants, and when he had completed the task, all the reptiles and animals rendered their assistance in trying to throw the moon back into the heavens so it would shine again. The great multitude of animals became exhausted in their mighty efforts, as they could not even move it from its resting place on earth. They were all so tired that they were about ready to give it up in despair, when the little ant (hah-pooth) came forward and suggested that he was able to do it. The multitude roared with laughter at the ant and taunted him with jeers, saying: "You little hah-pooth, what can a little insignificant thing like you do with the great big moon?" However, the little ant saw the opportunity to show his power of great strength, even if he was little, and rushed in among the crowd and made his way right under the moon. The moon began at once to raise from the earth, and with one mighty effort the little hah-pooth threw the moon back into the heavens where it has ever since remained.

The Klamath Indians always remark when the moon is full, that the dark place on its face (known to the white man as the "man in the moon") is the frog in the moon. Whenever there is an eclipse of the moon, it is said that a huge frog is trying to swallow the moon.

The Acorn

Many years ago several families were out camping in the fall, in the last part of October or November, gathering acorns for food. (When the families get all fixed up in their acorn camps, all go forth to pick the acorns each day as they drop from the tree, using the large baskets to put them in and carry to camp. In the evening when all have gathered at the camp-house and the evening meal is over, all the family—men, women and children— take their places and commence taking the hulls off so as to get the meat or kernel out. This is done by the teeth, and it is wonderful how expert we become at it; and it is seldom a kernel is mashed or bruised. These kernels are nearly always in halves, sometimes in three pieces, and once in a great while there will be four pieces; and to find one that is divided into four pieces just as it grew in the shell is not a common occurrence. There is on the inside of the outer shell a very thin skin that covers the kernel, or meat of the acorn.)

There was a young Indian girl out with her basket picking acorns, and as she went along with her basket picking up acorns she would, as often as she could, place some in her mouth and crack the hull and take the kernel out and put it in the basket with the ones that were not hulled. As she was going along, she happened to open one where the kernel was in four parts, which at once became very amusing to her. So she set her basket down, and on taking a look at it she took the outer hull off and made a neat little cradle out of it; then she took the inner skin part and made a nice set of baby clothes. After she did this she took the whole of the kernel and covered it with the clothes and placed it in the cradle that she had made of the hull. After all was finished she looked at it and then put it in the hollow of an oak tree and went on picking her acorns until time to go back to the camphouse. When it came time for them all to return to their homes, she had forgotten what she had done. One day while she was preparing some acorn flour she heard a noise behind her, some one saying "Mother, mother," and on looking behind her she beheld a little boy; and as soon as she saw him she knew that he was formed from the acorn that she had fixed and left in the hollow oak tree. She raised the Sa-quan, or pestle, in her hand and tried to catch the boy, but he ran from her, and she followed after him; and the race kept up until the boy got to the edge of the ocean, where there was a man in a boat. So the boy jumped into the boat. The man pushed the boat off and together they started out to sea, and had got well out when the girl arrived at the sea shore. She hurled the stone pestle at them and it fell into the sea, and the top of it stuck up and is there to this day.

Any Indian will tell his white brother this story as a true part to their religion, as calmly and seriously as if it was the truth, and perhaps some of the lower class really believe it. Yet it is only a fairy tale.

This is the rock that sits out in the ocean some eight or ten miles from the land, at the present time, from Orick or the mouth of Redwood Creek. This rock the white man calls Redding Rock; the Klamath Indians call it Sa-quan-ow. The true facts concerning this rock are told in a preceding chapter.

The Blue Jay

There was an old mother deer making mush for her family's breakfast one morning; and while she was cooking it she broke her leg, and she then allowed the marrow from the bone to run into the mush as she stirred it. This made the mush very palatable and oily. The Blue Jay who happened along at the time watched the deer cooking the mush and saw her break her leg and mix the marrow fat with the mush, and when the mush was cooked the Blue Jay tasted it and found it very delicious. That day when the Blue Jay went home, she decided she would make her acorn mush in the same way, so after fixing her mush she broke her leg to get the marrow which she stirred into the mush, but to her great disappointment the substance she took from her leg was not oil but blood, and when she saw how bloody it made her mush, and which spoiled it, she became very mad for being so simple, so she at once turned upon herself and plucked out all her tail-feathers and stuck them in the top of her head; and ever after the Blue Jay has worn a topknot of feathers on the head.

The Mournful Coo of the Dove

The Dove (Ah-rah-way), since the deluge of the world, has been considered by the Klamath Indians as the sacred bird. They carry the symbol of the dove in their ceremonial worship in the Sacred Lodge, and worship the bird as divine. Around this little bird is woven a pathetic tale of why he coos so much and always seems so sorrowful.

Long ago a family of doves made their home and nesting place on a level bench of land about half a mile up from the

Pec-wan village, on the northeast side. On this bench-like piece of land on the hillside stood a very large live oak tree and close by the vicinity of this tree is a small spring of water which gushes forth, the rest of the flat being covered with grasses. In a little sheltered cove of this flat, the doves would make their nests and rear their families. When the baby doves grew strong and large enough to fly, they would all fly up into the live oak tree. There they would hide among the branches when danger was near, and all the families would roost among the branches of the trees every night. At this time there was a handsome young male dove who announced his intentions of taking a trip up the river to Weitchpec, and while visiting among friends went with shiftless companions who taught him how to play Indian cards, which are made of small sticks and called pair-cauk, and the game wah-choo. The game became so fascinating that he spent the remainder of his time gambling, and did not realize that he had left a sick grandmother at home, and that she wished him to come back home at once. He was so deeply interested in the game that he did not take any heed of the message, and continued to play cards. Later he received a message that his grandmother was dead; but in the revelry of the game it seemed to him but folly, and he played on, not heeding the words of the messenger, who kept repeating the words that his grandmother was dead until he succeeded in diverting the attention of the youthful gambler. The young gambler looked up sadly from his cards and said, "I will now shuffle the cards again and again, yes, shuffle them again and again. My grandmother is dead, and to let the world know that I mourn her loss deeply, I will coo among the lonesome bushes the mournful coo of a broken heart, the piteous coo of a grief that knows no ending while I live."

The beautiful moral of this story is to teach and impress upon the minds of the children that they should not drift into shiftless ways, neglecting to respect and cherish their grand-mothers and to love them as dearly as their own mothers, and even more in respect to old age. Indian mothers repeat the story to their children and mourn as the doves, by repeating the words: "Wee-poo-poo, wee-poo-poo-poo-poo, whee-whee-whee-poo-poo," thus illustrating that they might become very sad and mournful by not being kind and thoughtful to the aged and making their sunset years bright and cheerful.

I could give enough of these fairy stories to make a book. All classes of my people can, on meeting his white brother, sit down and tell him these fairy tales as a part of our religion, with a twinkle in his eye, and let him pass on. Some of our fairy stories are partly founded on truth and then carried off into an imaginary sense, so as to make them long.

THE END

Index